DINOSAURUS

THE COMPLETE GUIDE TO DINOSAURS

DINOSAURUS

THE COMPLETE GUIDE TO DINOSAURS

STEVE PARKER

Published by Firefly Books Ltd. 2016

First printing

Publisher Cataloging-in-Publication Data (U.S.)

Names: Parker, Steve, 1952-, author.
Title: Dinosaurus : the complete guide to dinosaurs / Steve Parker.
Description: Second edition. | Richmond Hill, Ontario, Canada : Firefly Books,
    2016. | Includes index. | Summary: The second edition covers discoveries
    made in the 13 years since the first edition was published. It covers traits and
    behaviors and includes many illustrations.
Identifiers: ISBN 978-1-77085-776-6 (paperback)
Subjects: LCSH: Dinosaurs.
Classification: LCC QE861.4P375 |DDC 567.9 – dc23

Library and Archives Canada Cataloguing in Publication

CIP data for this title is available from Library and Archives Canada

Published in the United States by
Firefly Books (U.S.) Inc.
P.O. Box 1338, Ellicott Station
Buffalo, New York 14205

Published in Canada by
Firefly Books Ltd.
50 Staples Avenue, Unit 1
Richmond Hill, Ontario L4B 0A7

ISBN 978-1-77085-776-6
QTT.SAUR3

This book was conceived, designed and
produced by:
Quintet Publishing Limited
Ovest House
58 West Street
Brighton, East Sussex
BN3 1DD
United Kingdom

Design and Editorial Content: Tall Tree Ltd.
Art Director: Michael Charles
Editorial Director: Emma Bastow
Publisher: Mark Searle

10 9 8 7 6 5 4 3 2 1

Printed in China by C & C Offset Printing Co Ltd.

FOREWORD

Almost everyone is interested in dinosaurs at some point in his or her life – be it at the age of five or 95. Even the great fact and fiction writer Arthur C. Clarke traces his early interest in science to dinosaurs, recalling that his first exposure to these "saurians" as a boy in rural England was a series of cards his father gave him.

Why the great interest in this long-gone group? What is it about dinosaurs that has drawn our attention so intensely for so long? Maybe it has been simply because some dinosaurs are big, and nasty and, more importantly – extinct! Perhaps this ongoing infatuation is that there are so many different kinds of dinosaur.

Most of the well-known dinosaurs are from either North America, typically the west (Wyoming, Montana and Alberta), or Eurasia, for example Mongolia. More recent finds in South America, Australia, Antarctica and Alaska are not so widely known, but it will not be long before younger generations are picking their way through such new discoveries for themselves.

The latest finds of bigger and smaller dinosaurs in places like Argentina, and of a range of small but varied polar dinosaurs have combined with studies showing that many dinosaurs were anything but big, slow moving and dim-witted, to change common perceptions of this very successful group. We now know that some dinosaurs had feathers and were at least gliding if not flying. Furthermore the discovery of a variety of tough little critters that lived near the North and South Poles, suggests that some of these dinosaurs must have been warm-blooded to deal with such severe conditions.

What has made dinosaurs even more interesting in recent years are the many studies that have centered on the companions of these creatures and the environments in which they lived during the Mesozoic Era. Current research focuses on why so many of these otherwise successful animals were nearly wiped out 65 million years ago and on how they evolved from reptilian ancestors in the first place. The result, as shown here, is an extensive resource on the world in which dinosaurs prospered – and died – with as much detail on the ancient habitats as on the inhabitants themselves.

Dinosaurus cannot hope to include every known dinosaur – we would need a small library for that – but it certainly offers excellent coverage of many of the creatures that existed, their environment and contemporaries. Many of the newest dinosaurs get a mention too, giving enthusiasts a much broader understanding of the dinosaur system as a whole.

Professor Patricia Vickers Rich
Chair in Palaeontology,
Monash University

Founding Director,
Monash Science Centre,
Melbourne, Victoria
Australia

Dr Thomas H. Rich
Curator,
Vertebrate Palaeontology
Museum Victoria
Melbourne, Victoria
Australia

CONTENTS

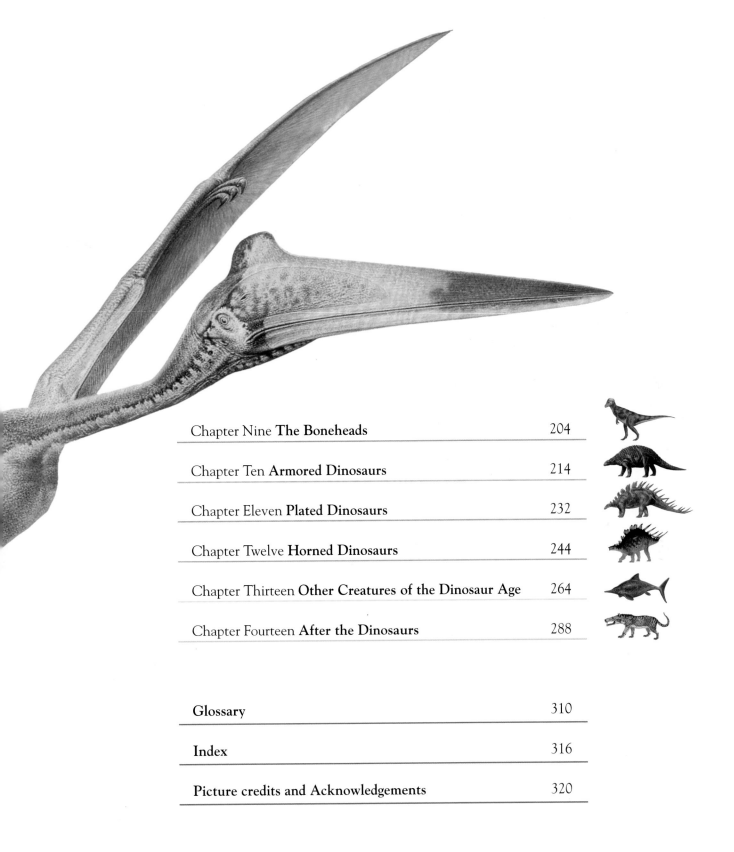

INTRODUCTION

DINOSAURS ARE THE MOST FAMOUS INHABITANTS OF EARTH'S REMOTE GEOLOGICAL PAST. EVER SINCE 1841, WHEN RICHARD OWEN FIRST RECOGNIZED THE DINOSAURS AS A DISTINCT GROUP OF ANCIENT REPTILES, THEY HAVE TAKEN CENTER STAGE IN POPULAR IMAGINATION ABOUT PAST LIFE. IMAGES OF THESE ANCIENT AND EXTINCT ANIMALS, SOME OF WHICH WERE TRULY MONSTROUS MEAT-EATING PREDATORS DISPLACED THE DRAGONS OF EARLIER MYTH AND LEGEND. THE DINOSAURS WERE A REMARKABLE GROUP OF ANIMALS AND MANY OF THEM WERE EXTRAORDINARY CREATURES, QUITE UNLIKE ANYTHING ALIVE TODAY. THEY VARIED FROM CHICKEN-SIZED, FEATHERED DINOSAURS, WHICH WERE THE ANCESTORS OF TODAY'S BIRDS, TO IMMENSE ANIMALS WHOSE SIZE AND WEIGHT HAS ONLY BEEN MATCHED BY BIGGEST OF THE MAMMALIAN WHALES. FOR SOME 150 MILLION YEARS, THE DINOSAURS DOMINATED LIFE ON LAND EVEN THOUGH THE TOTAL NUMBER OF KNOWN DINOSAUR SPECIES (AROUND 1000) IS CONSIDERABLY LESS THAN THAT OF THEIR REPTILIAN RELATIVES, THE LIVING LIZARDS (AROUND 5000 SPECIES), OR THE LIVING MAMMALS (AROUND 4600 SPECIES).

LONG BEFORE THE DINOSAURS

The history of the dinosaurs and how they fit into the evolution of life is just part of a story of epic dimensions, which is still only partly known. Over 200 years of scientific investigation has transformed our knowledge and understanding of the development of life from its microbial beginnings in the depths of Precambrian time over three billion years ago. The story that has been revealed is a surprising one that has had to be constantly rewritten as new discoveries have overthrown older ideas and expectations.

We now know that far from having a smooth progression from simple to more complex organisms, life has evolved in fits and starts. From its Precambrian beginnings there was a long period of development confined to the oceans with simple and mostly

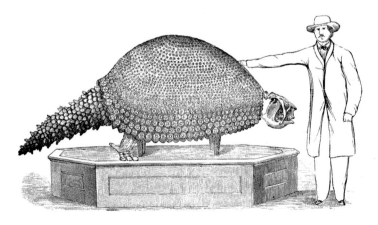

ABOVE Fossils of the "giant armadillo" Glyptodon, some just a few thousand years old, litter certain regions of South America.

LEFT Staring death in the face: this fossil of *Tyrannosaurus* teeth, jaws and skull shows how detailed preservation can be.

microscopic unicellular and then multicellular life. This microbial development lasted around three billion years before the larger and more complex but largely soft-bodied organisms first appeared around 580 million years ago in late Precambrian (Ediacaran Period) times. The fossil record of the Ediacaran biota has only been discovered in recent decades. It was a precursor to the bulk of the fossil record, which began in Cambrian times around 541 million years ago, and is comprised of the protective spines, shells, and carapaces of familiar kinds of marine creatures, such as sponges and molluscs and less familiar groups such as the brachiopods and trilobites.

The story of how life evolved from these beginnings to occupy the land, freshwaters, and the airways has only been detailed over the last 150 years. We now know that life was confined to the oceans from its deep Precambrian beginnings until Ordovician times around 450 million years ago, when the first primitive plants invaded the land. Meanwhile in the sea, animals with backbones, the first vertebrate ancestors of all four-limbed animals from dinosaurs to humans, had evolved as fish.

Eventually, some fish groups were able to invade the freshwaters of the Devonian continents. Around 395 million years ago, some of them had their paired fins adapted as muscular limbs with toe-like digits, which we recognize as the first tetrapods. Fossil remains of the first well-adapted landliving tetrapods do not appear until Early Carboniferous times, around 345 million years ago. But even then, it still took nearly another hundred million years for their descendants to produce the first dinosaurs in Late Triassic times, around 230 million years ago.

Geological timeline

Over the last 200 years earth scientists have discovered that Earth's rock record has a dynamic history, but it was not until the 1950s that reliable numerical ages could be obtained for any of these rocks. When first available those dates confirmed what geologists had long suspected – that Earth has an antiquity of some 4.55 billion years. But there is another story of how the history of geological time was first investigated and subdivided into periods and other intervals with names, which are familiar to us today. Geological mapping and analysis of the rock record has revealed a complex and often dramatic and ever changing history of Earth environments and their inhabitants.

From the end of the 18th century, pioneer geologists such as James Hutton were able to demonstrate that close examination of rock strata exposed at Earth's surface revealed a long history of repeated cycles of erosion, deposition and uplift that could not be confined within the old Bible derived timescale of a few thousand millennia.

Throughout the first decades of the 19th century, successions of strata exposed at the surface was described along with their fossil content. Geologists such as William Smith in Britain and Georges Cuvier and Adolphe Brongniart in France recognised that successive strata had unique and characteristic fossil forms. From this, it was evident that fossils

LEFT Fossilized shells of bottom-dwelling marine invertebrates called trilobites.

ABOVE The *Dicynodon* was an early ancestor of modern-day mammals.

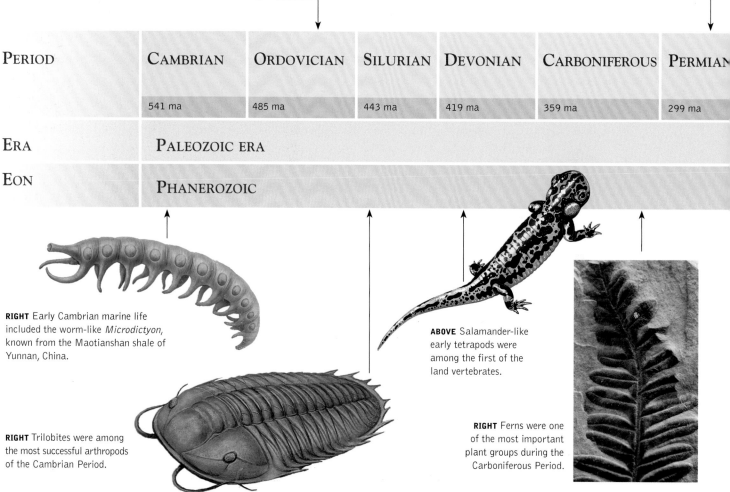

PERIOD	CAMBRIAN	ORDOVICIAN	SILURIAN	DEVONIAN	CARBONIFEROUS	PERMIAN
	541 ma	485 ma	443 ma	419 ma	359 ma	299 ma
ERA	PALEOZOIC ERA					
EON	PHANEROZOIC					

RIGHT Early Cambrian marine life included the worm-like *Microdictyon*, known from the Maotianshan shale of Yunnan, China.

ABOVE Salamander-like early tetrapods were among the first of the land vertebrates.

RIGHT Trilobites were among the most successful arthropods of the Cambrian Period.

RIGHT Ferns were one of the most important plant groups during the Carboniferous Period.

could be used to identify the sequence of strata and correlate similar aged strata across continents. Slowly a history of the deposition of successive strata (stratigraphic record) was built up, which revealed dramatic changes in depositional environments, sea levels, geological events and phenomena.

The late 19th century discovery of radioactivity, locked up in naturally occurring minerals within some rocks, changed the way that Earth history could be chronicled and subdivided. It became possible to measure the length of time that has elapsed since certain naturally occurring minerals, containing radioactive elements, such as uranium and rubidium, were first formed. After a hundred years of investigation a large number of radiometric dates have been tied to the stratigraphic column. We now have accurate dates for many of the boundaries between geological periods, their epochs and stages. The dates are constantly being refined as better data becomes available but the general numerical chronology of geological history as seen in the rock record of strata is now well established.

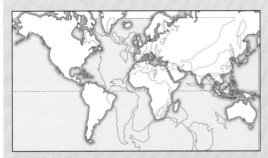

Each Factfile shows a map to indicate the location of fossil discoveries of each animal. The solid map indicates the modern world, while the red outline shows the land mass formation during the animal's existence: for example, Devonian, Triassic, Cretaceous periods. Period maps are detailed on page 12.

ABOVE Marine reptiles, such as elasmosaurs, became widespread during the Mesozoic Era.

RIGHT The Mesozoic Era ended in a mass extinction, probably caused by an asteroid striking the Gulf of Mexico.

LEFT Mammal species evolved, such as this *Mesopithecus* monkey.

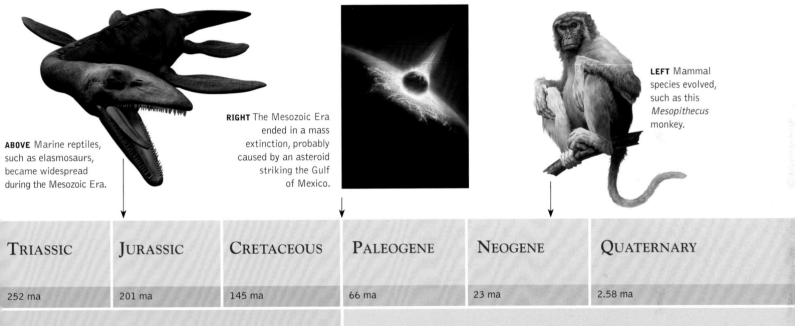

TRIASSIC	JURASSIC	CRETACEOUS	PALEOGENE	NEOGENE	QUATERNARY
252 ma	201 ma	145 ma	66 ma	23 ma	2.58 ma

MESOZOIC ERA	CENOZOIC ERA

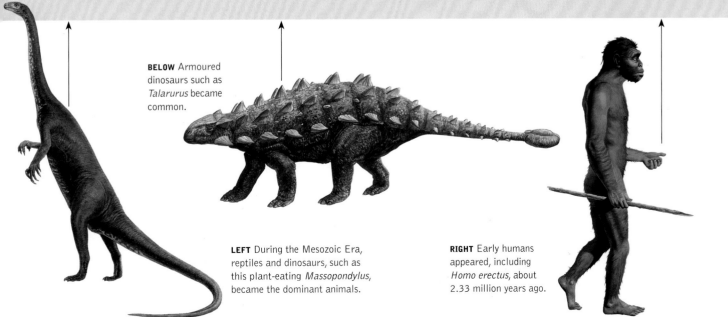

BELOW Armoured dinosaurs such as *Talarurus* became common.

LEFT During the Mesozoic Era, reptiles and dinosaurs, such as this plant-eating *Massopondylus*, became the dominant animals.

RIGHT Early humans appeared, including *Homo erectus*, about 2.33 million years ago.

1.CAMBRIAN 541–485 mya
Paleozoic Era

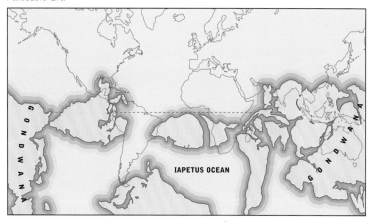

2.DEVONIAN 419–359 mya
Paleozoic Era

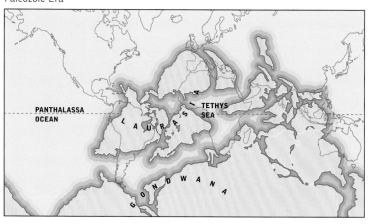

3. CARBONIFEROUS 359–299 mya
Paleozoic Era

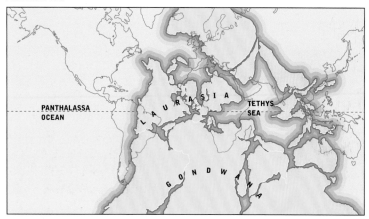

4.TRIASSIC 252–201 mya
Mesozoic Era

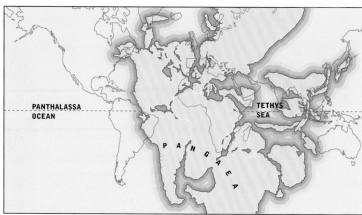

5.JURASSIC 201–145 mya
Mesozoic Era

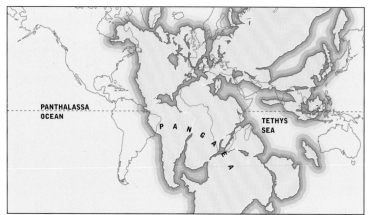

6.CRETACEOUS 145–66 mya
Mesozoic Era

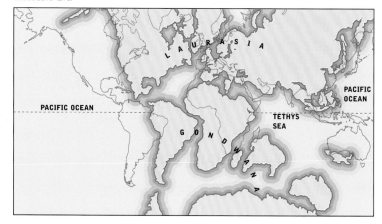

7. PALEOGENE–NEOGENE 66–2.58 mya
Cenozoic Era

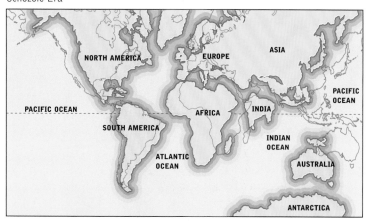

8. QUATERNARY 2.58 mya–Present
Cenozoic Era

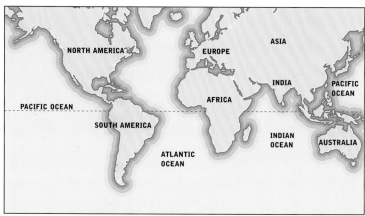

CHANGING WORLD

THE BIGGEST REVOLUTION IN EARTH SCIENCE OCCURRED IN RECENT DECADES WITH THE DISCOVERY THAT EARTH'S OUTERMOST ROCK LAYER, KNOWN AS THE CRUST OR LITHOSPHERE, IS BROKEN INTO JUST A FEW (EIGHT) CONTINENT-SIZED RIGID PLATES AND A NUMBER OF SMALLER PLATES (AROUND TWO DOZEN). FURTHERMORE, THESE PLATES ARE IN CONSTANT MOTION RELATIVE TO ONE ANOTHER – A PROCESS KNOWN AS PLATE TECTONIC MOTION, WHICH MOVES AT RATES OF JUST A FEW CENTIMETERS A YEAR. AS A RESULT, THE ARRANGEMENT OF OCEANS AND CONTINENTS HAS CONSTANTLY CHANGED IN THE MOST DRAMATIC WAY OVER THE VAST SPAN OF GEOLOGICAL TIME. SOME CRUSTAL PLATES HAVE SPLIT APART TO FORM NEW OCEANS, OTHERS HAVE COLLIDED TO FORM MOUNTAIN RANGES AND YET OTHERS HAVE SLID PAST ONE ANOTHER, GENERATING CATASTROPHIC EARTHQUAKES. OVER TIME, OCEANS HAVE OPENED AND CLOSED AND CONTINENTS HAVE MOVED HUGE DISTANCES FROM ONE HEMISPHERE INTO THE OTHER.

For instance, the history of the formation of Britain and Ireland is quite extraordinary. Although now part of the Eurasian plate, the British Isles are formed from two quite separate small plate fragments. Most of England, Wales and southern Ireland were originally attached to North Africa. And, Scotland and Northern Ireland were part of North America, when both of these continents lay in the southern hemisphere during the early part of the Palaeozoic Era, around 450 million years ago. The plate fragments were first joined together in late Devonian times when the region that is Ireland and Britain today became a small part of a vast supercontinent called Laurussia. This landmass straddled the equator with North America joined to Europe and Russia with Britain and Ireland in the middle. This equatorial landmass was colonised by the first extensive land communities with forests, lakes and rivers, in which lived the newly evolving tetrapod vertebrates.

The supercontinent became even bigger in Permian and Triassic times when Laurussia and the southern supercontinent of Gondwana joined together to form one vast landmass, called Pangea. It stretched from pole to pole and was surrounded by a single global ocean, called Panthalassia, which covered two-thirds of Earth's surface. Pangea was home to the rapidly evolving reptiles, including the first dinosaurs by Late Triassic times.

No sooner had Pangea formed than it began to break up with the North American and African plates rifting apart as the Central Atlantic Ocean formed in early Jurassic times. The rift spread southwards to form the South Atlantic, as South America and Africa moved apart. It then opened northwards, separating North America and Western Europe, to form the North Atlantic. The northern rift opened to the west of Ireland in Early Cenozoic times, around 55 million years ago. As a result, Ireland and Britain became part of Europe, whilst Greenland became an extension of the North American plate. The modern geography of continents and oceans gradually emerged with Europe and North America moving into higher and cooler latitudes.

There was a similarly dramatic history for the great southern continents of South America, Africa, Antarctica, India and Australia, which had all joined together as the supercontinent of Gondwana in early Palaeozoic times. Following the Triassic mergence of Gondwana with Laurussia to form Pangea and its subsequent breakup, the southern continents gradually moved into their current positions. Most extraordinary of all was the passage of the Indian continent from the southern hemisphere around 25 million years ago across the equator to collide with the southern margin of Asia. The unstoppable energy of the collision resulted in the formation of the Himalayan mountain belt and the uplift of the Tibetan plateau, a motion that continues today.

Quite apart from the enormous dynamic forces involved with plate motion, which have constantly changed the face of Earth over geological time, the plate tectonic processes have had a dramatic impact upon the history of life and climate.

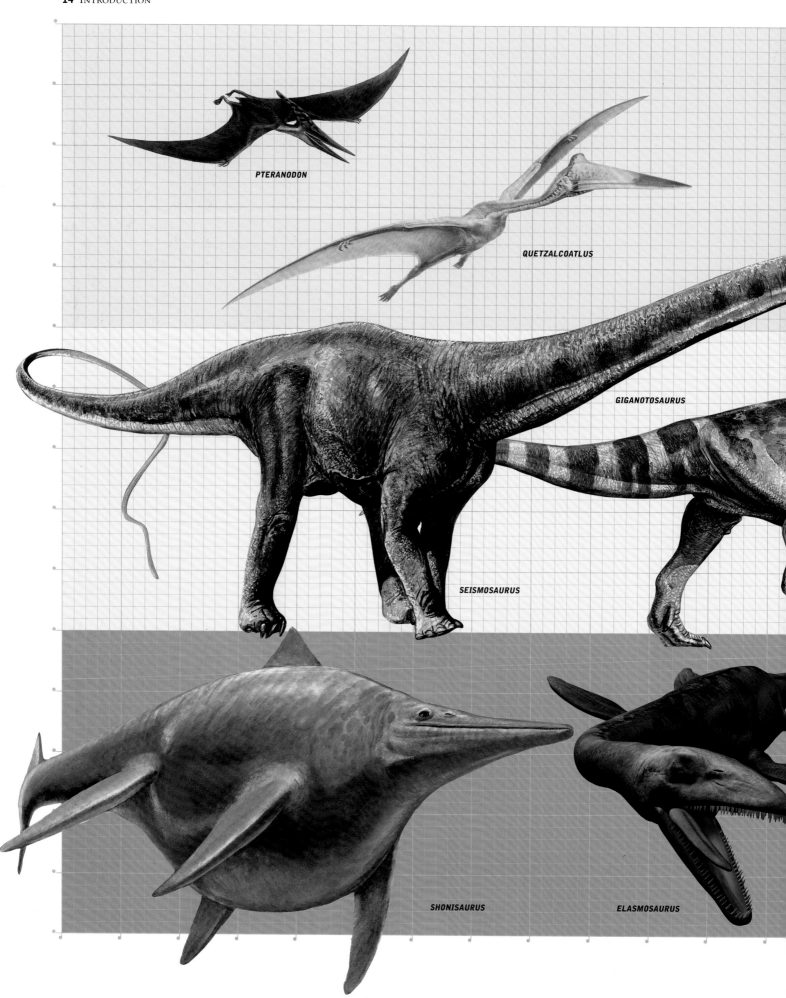

PTERANODON

QUETZALCOATLUS

GIGANOTOSAURUS

SEISMOSAURUS

SHONISAURUS

ELASMOSAURUS

Prehistoric life to scale

ALTHOUGH MANY DINOSAURS AND OTHER PREHISTORIC ANIMALS WERE INDEED HUGE, SOME WERE MUCH SMALLER THAN WE LIKE TO IMAGINE. IN THIS DIAGRAM THE SIZE OF THE ANIMALS IS COMPARED WITH THAT OF A 1.83-METER (6-FOOT) MAN.

Seismosaurus was a very long dinosaur at up to 52 meters (197 feet); the heaviest is thought to have been *Argentinosaurus* at 70–80 metric tons (77–88 tons). *Giganotosaurus* was the largest predator at 14 meters (46 feet) tall, bigger than *Tyrannosaurus rex* which had been thought, until 1994, to be the largest. *Anchiceratops* measured 4–5 meters (13–16 feet), but other ceratopsians, such as *Protoceratops*, were no bigger than a pig. *Sinosauropteryx* was one of the smaller dinosaurs, reaching a maximum length of only 1 meter (3 feet). *Quetzalcoatlus* was one of the largest flying creatures ever, with a wingspan of 10–11 meters (33–36 feet). *Ophthalmosaurus*, while not especially large, holds the record for the largest eyeballs of any vertebrate, almost 10 centimeters (3 inches) across.

Each Animal Factfile has an indicator bar which compares the size of the animal to that of a 1.8-meter (6-foot) man. If the man equals 1 and the colored bar extends to 3 for a certain animal, that animal is three times larger than man. The scale alters between chapters to allow for a range of comparative sizes. For example, the largest animal in one chapter may be about 3 times the size of the man, but in another chapter nearly 30 times the size of the man.

6 FEET

1 METER

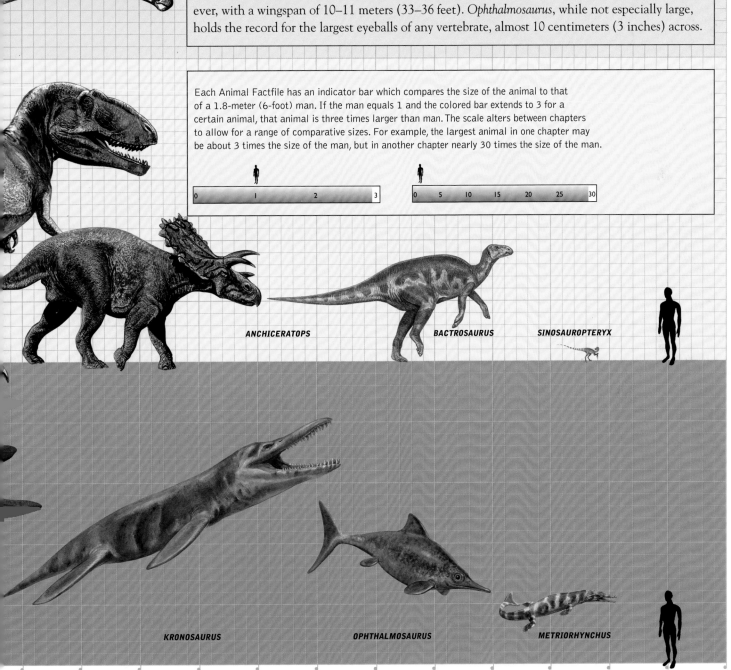

ANCHICERATOPS

BACTROSAURUS

SINOSAUROPTERYX

KRONOSAURUS

OPHTHALMOSAURUS

METRIORHYNCHUS

STRONG SKELETONS The bony skeleton of vertebrate animals has evolved to serve a number of essential functions. The articulated bones of the skeleton provide a robust protection and internal flexible support for the weight of the body tissues and sites of attachment for the muscles. As a result, the body is not only held together but can be moved through water, on land or in the air by the movement of muscle powered fins or limbs which articulate with the body.

SUPERSIZED ANIMALS The bony vertebrate skeleton is strong enough to support the evolution of the largest animals known, the land living sauropod dinosaurs and the marine whales. Growing to some 30 meters (98 feet) long and weighing up to 90 tonnes (99 tons) in the case of the dinosaurs and about twice that weight in the whales, these animals are at the upper size limits for life on Earth. The only other organism that outgrows them are giant redwood trees.

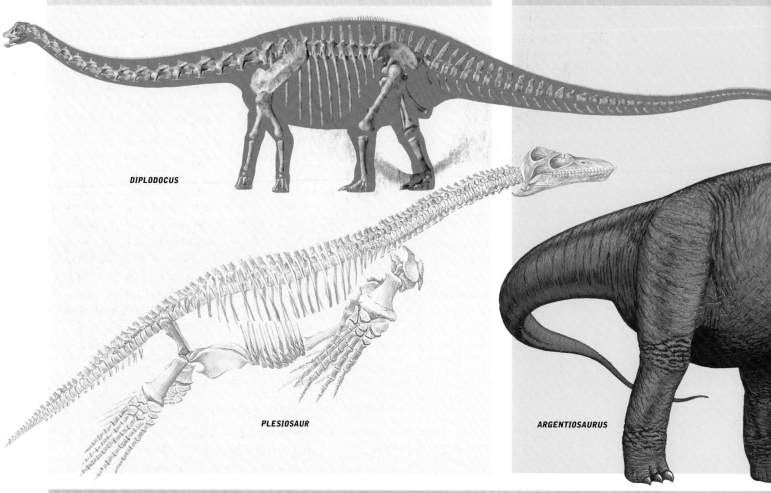

DIPLODOCUS

PLESIOSAUR

ARGENTIOSAURUS

TYPES OF VERTEBRATES Vertebrates include all those animals which evolved with backbones. They range from fish through the various tetrapods, whose limbs have allowed them to conquer the land and airways – the amphibians, reptiles, birds and mammals and all their extinct relatives.

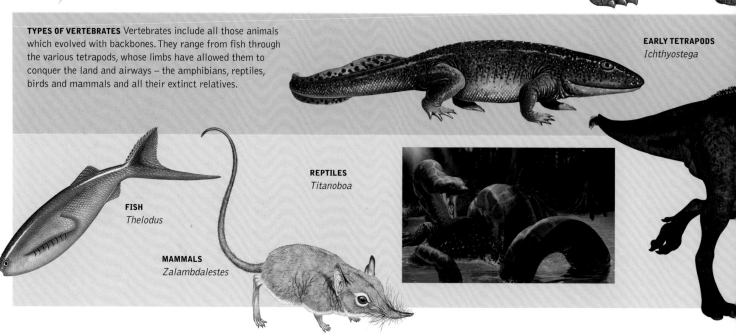

EARLY TETRAPODS
Ichthyostega

FISH
Thelodus

REPTILES
Titanoboa

MAMMALS
Zalambdalestes

ANIMALS WITH BACKBONES

FOR ANY ANIMAL TO LIVE ON LAND AND GROW TO ANY GREAT SIZE REQUIRES AN INTERNAL SUPPORTIVE SKELETON, WHICH CAN HOLD THE BODY TOGETHER AND ALLOW IT TO MOVE AGAINST THE FORCES OF GRAVITY.

The evolution of the vertebrate skeleton first occurred in Cambrian times when all life was still confined to the sea. From these primitive aquatic ancestors the vertebrates have evolved and diversified to include a large variety of fish and animals with four limbs – the tetrapods. We now know that the first tetrapods were still aquatic animals that evolved in Devonian times from a particular group of fish, which had two pairs of stout muscular fins with an internal supporting skeleton and a connection with the backbone through shoulder and pelvic girdles.

The paired muscular limbs of the first tetrapods then became adapted for a whole range of vertebrate animals, which today include the amphibians, reptiles, birds and mammals, including humans. In some of these groups the forelimbs became further adapted as arms (dinosaurs and primates) or wings (pterosaurs, birds and bats) and in some, the limbs have been reduced or lost altogether (caecilian amphibians, snakes and cetaceans).

Altogether, there are some 65,000 species of living vertebrates and a much greater but unknown number, which have become extinct. They include some major groups, such as the non-avian dinosaurs, the flying pterosaur reptiles and several groups of marine reptiles, such as the ichthyosaurs, plesiosaurs and mosasaurs.

The vertebrate skeleton with its elongate and flexible backbone made of numerous articulating vertebrae is a highly adaptable structure, which along with its surrounding muscles both strengthens a body and allows it to bend. The basic sideways flexing has been used for movement by fish and snakes. Invasion of the land, where the forces of gravity have more impact than in the water, has adapted the tetrapod skeleton. The limbs and girdle connections to the backbone allow the body to be lifted off the ground with a reduction of friction allowing more for rapid movement using the limbs and feet.

The backbone has to support the weight of the head and body and muscle attachments to the girdles and the backbone are strengthened and modified for movement of the limbs. Additionally, the ribs, which are connected to the backbone, are strengthened to form a supportive and protective cage for the lungs and other internal organs. Movement on land by the early tetrapod vertebrates was still initially through sideways flexure of the backbone and articulation with limbs that sprawl sideways from the body, a method still seen in the reptilian lizards and snakes. However, this kind of movement puts considerable stress on the skeleton and is of limited efficiency for rapid locomotion and increase in body size. The largest and fastest moving land animals today are the mammals whose vertebrate skeletons have been adapted to allow for a basic up and down flexure of the backbone with the limbs brought under the body as both supportive and mobile struts. However it was not just the mammals and their ancestors that adapted this more advanced arrangement of the skeleton with erect limbs.

One group of early tetrapods, the archosaurs, which means "ruling reptiles", are today represented by the crocodiles and birds, also evolved this arrangement of the limbs in Early Triassic times following the end Permian extinction. The first of the archosaurs were the pseudosuchians, many of which were somewhat crocodile-like and eventually gave rise to the true crocodilians in Late Triassic times. The other main group of archosaurs, which also adopted the advanced skeleton, are variously known as the ornithosuchians or, more recently, the avemetatarsalians. They include the pterosaurs, all the dinosaurs and their bird descendants. The earliest of avemetatarsalians, whose name means "bird foot" and is derived from the bird-like structure of the foot, were small dinosaur-like animals such as *Asilisaurus* from Middle Triassic age strata in Tanzania. True dinosaurs, such as the carnivorous theropods *Staurikosaurus* and *Herrerasaurus*, first appear in Late Triassic times.

ARCHOSAURS
Alioramus

THE MESOZOIC ERA

THE MESOZOIC ERA, OFTEN REFERRED TO AS THE "AGE OF REPTILES", BEGAN WITH A MASS EXTINCTION EVENT AND ENDED WITH ANOTHER ONE SOME 186 MILLION YEARS LATER. ALTHOUGH THE ERA IS MOST FAMOUS FOR ITS DINOSAURS, THERE WAS AN OVERALL CHANGE IN THE GLOBAL BIOTA OF PLANTS AND ANIMALS FROM THAT OF THE PREVIOUS PALAEOZOIC ERA. APART FROM THE DINOSAURS, LIFE ON LAND AND IN THE SEAS SAW THE RISE OF MANY OTHER REPTILE GROUPS. PLANT LIFE CAME TO BE DOMINATED BY FERNS, CYCADS, GINKGOPHYTES, BENNETTITALEANS AND OTHER UNUSUAL FORMS. THE ERA ALSO SAW THE EVOLUTION OF MANY GROUPS THAT TODAY DOMINATE OUR MODERN BIOTA, INCLUDING THE MODERN CONIFERS, FLOWERING PLANTS (ANGIOSPERMS) AND MANY OF THEIR POLLINATING INSECTS, ALONG WITH THE MAMMALS AND BIRDS AND THE BONY FISH (TELEOSTS) IN BOTH MARINE AND FRESHWATERS.

LEFT This scene depicts the shores of a lake reconstructed from fossils found in Australia dating from the Triassic Period. On the left are lycopod trees (*Pleuromeia longicaulis*). At top right is the seed fern *Dicroidium* and at lower right, the herbivore *Dicynodon*. At the upper left is a fly closely-related to the *Limoniidae* (small crane flies) and to the lower left is the insect *Clatrotitan andersoni* on a gymnosperm. A female scorpionfly is at the upper right.

The beginning of the Mesozoic Era saw the Triassic recovery from the most catastrophic mass extinction in the history of life, the end Permian extinction, which marked the end of the earlier Palaeozoic Era. The main cause was probably climate change following the eruption of huge volumes of lava in Siberia and the release of climate changing gases into the atmosphere. An estimated 90 per cent or more of all marine species and around 70 per cent of all land-living organisms died out.

The Triassic Period saw global geography dominated by the supercontinent of Pangea, which stretched from pole to pole. The immense size of the continental landmass had a drastic effect on global climate with no polar ice, extensive aridity and the development of vast deserts in its interior. Cold-blooded reptiles, which reproduced by laying eggs, were more tolerant of such conditions than many of the earlier tetrapods, which were more dependent upon water. Likewise, plants, which reproduced by means of seeds (gymnosperms) rather than spores, also flourished.

The breakup of Pangea from Early Jurassic times saw the rifting of Gondwana away from Eurasia with the Tethys Ocean extending westwards. The Central Atlantic also began to open as a rift extended northwards to separate North America from Eurasia. The southern Gondwanan supercontinent also broke up with Africa, India, Australia and Antarctica moved apart towards their modern positions. As Antarctica moved southwards it continued to have extensive forests inhabited by a Gondwanan fauna, which included some dinosaurs.

All these plate motions reconfigured the circulation of ocean waters and were accompanied by rising sea levels along with new seaways, which flooded into the continental landmasses. The movement of the separate continents carried them across climate zones along with their resident plants and animals. Climates became more humid with much greater marine influences and new weather patterns, all of which impacted upon environments and the life they supported.

Life in the oceans and on land diversified enormously in Jurassic times. Marine life included an extraordinary variety of reptiles from plesiosaurs and ichthyosaurs to crocodiles and turtles. On land the archosaur reptiles dominated, especially with the evolution of many different kinds of dinosaurs. It was during this period that the first of the bird-like dinosaurs evolved along with the primitive "live-bearing" (therian) mammals.

The Cretaceous Period was first characterized by the European outcrops of the soft white limestone, known as Chalk (the Latin for chalk is *creta*, from which the name Cretaceous is derived). Global warming with a greenhouse climate produced high sea levels and warm ocean waters with low oxygen levels and the widespread deposition of carbonate mud deposits. Newly evolving flowering plants, birds and small mammals, along with the bony fish in the sea were all increasing in diversity.

The end of the Cretaceous Period and the whole Mesozoic Era was marked by an extinction event associated with an asteroid impact. Sixty-six million years ago, an 11 kilometers (7 miles) wide asteroid crashed into the Gulf of Mexico causing devastation throughout Central America. Dust, aerosols and acid rain from the impact enhanced global climate change, which had already been instigated by the vast volcanic eruption of the Deccan lavas of India. Plant and animal communities collapsed with the loss of the top predators and large herbivores.

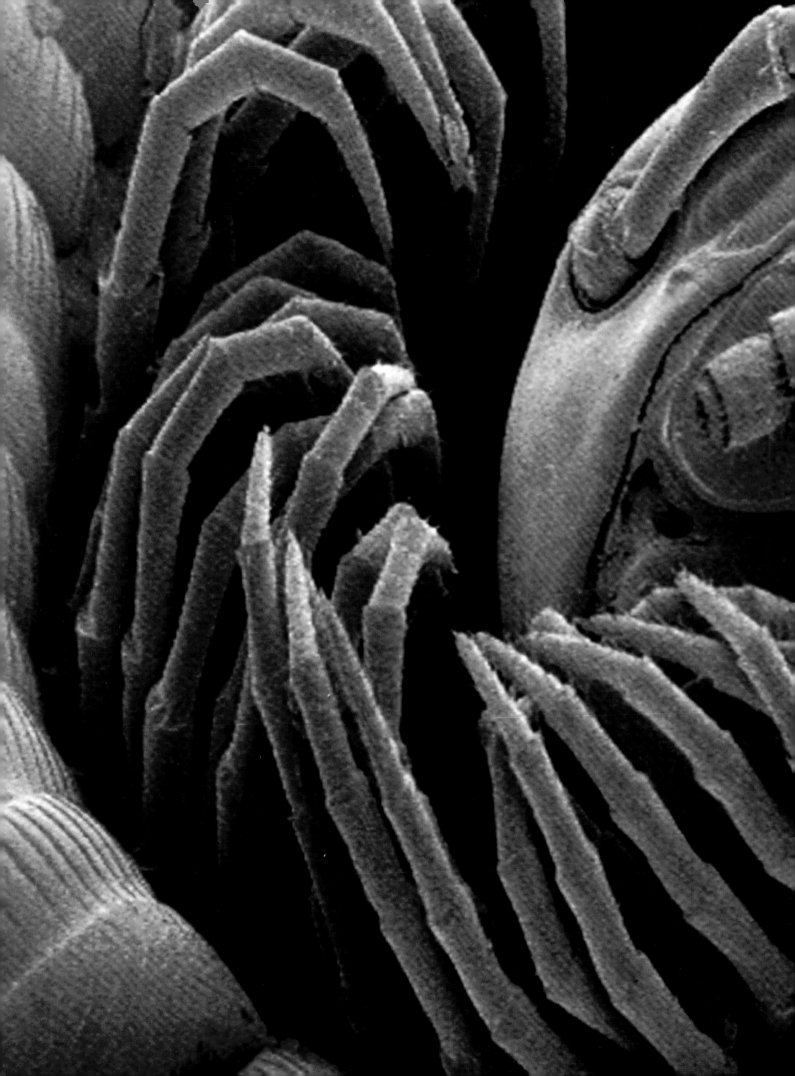

CHAPTER ONE

CONQUERORS OF THE LAND

FROM THE DEVONIAN PERIOD, SOME 400 MILLION YEARS AGO, ANIMALS BEGAN TO WRIGGLE FROM THE WATER TO CRAWL THROUGH THE MARSHES AND THEN WALK ON DRY LAND — AND BY THE PERMIAN PERIOD, 230 MILLION YEARS AGO, THE STAGE WAS SET FOR THE RISE OF THE DINOSAURS.

OUT OF THE WATER

MANY POPULAR ACCOUNTS OF PREHISTORY BEGIN WITH DINOSAURS, WHICH PERHAPS GIVES THE
IMPRESSION THAT THEY WERE THE FIRST LAND ANIMALS, OR EVEN THE EARLIEST CREATURES.
HOWEVER, VERTEBRATES – ANIMALS WITH BACKBONES – TOOK TO LIVING ON LAND WELL OVER 100
MILLION YEARS BEFORE THE FIRST DINOSAURS APPEARED. LONG BEFORE EVEN THIS TIME,
INVERTEBRATES (ANIMALS WITHOUT BACKBONES), SUCH AS MITES, MILLIPEDES, SCORPIONS AND
INSECTS, WERE CRAWLING ACROSS THE GROUND OR CLIMBING UP PREHISTORIC PLANTS. THE MOVE OF
VERTEBRATES FROM WATER TO LAND WAS A MAJOR STEP, HOWEVER, BOTH LITERALLY AND FOR
EVOLUTION. IT OPENED UP WHOLE NEW HABITATS, WHERE LARGER LAND-DWELLING ANIMALS COULD
ADAPT – WITH LITTLE COMPETITION – TO NEW FOOD SOURCES AND ENVIRONMENTAL CONDITIONS.

FIN TO LIMB

A key event was "fin to limb" – the change from
a fish's fin to a leg suitable for walking. This began
in certain sarcopterygian or "lobe-fin" fish, a group
that persists today in the coelacanths and lungfish.
Each fin had a fleshy base with bones and muscles
inside, used for controlling the shape and
movement of the main fin surface. In some lobe-
fins, however, the base gradually became larger
while the fin part shrank, as the appendage was
used to push against surfaces harder and more
resistant than water. The bones became longer,
and the muscle more powerful, until the fin had
disappeared and the lobe became a leg.

TETRAPODS

The number of limbs in the first land vertebrates
derived from the standard fish pattern of two sets
of paired fins, the pectoral fins and the pelvic fins.
The resulting four-limbed animals are known as
tetrapods (which simply means "four feet"). Some
of the earliest examples, from the Late Devonian
period more than 360 million years ago, are shown
on the following pages. At one time, these were
thought to have been fully capable land-walkers,
since the evolutionary impetus for the change from
fin to limb change was the need to crawl between
pools as they dried out. However, newer studies
have suggested that tetrapods may well have
evolved in water. At first, their limbs were not legs
for walking, but paddles for swimming or pushing
through water plants. Only later did tetrapods
venture away from their aquatic environment onto
dry ground, as the paddles became legs.

LAND-DWELLING

The walking limb was only one of a whole range of
features needed by tetrapods to conquer dry land.
Others included lungs to obtain oxygen
by breathing air, rather than gills, which filtered
oxygen from water. Lungs were not especially new
– several groups of fish had already evolved them,
perhaps to aid breathing in warm, still pools with
low-oxygen water. (Various kinds of air-gulping
fish still do this today, for example the group
known colloquially as "bony-tongues", which
includes the world's larges freshwater fish, the
arapaima.) Another need was for skin that could
prevent moisture and body fluids being lost too fast
in open air – in water, this was not a problem.
Most of the early tetrapods are what might be
called "amphibians," although in newer
classification schemes "amphibian" is a loose and
descriptive term for a variety of groups. One
change that these "amphibians" probably did not
achieve was to break free of water when breeding.
Their young stages, or larvae, led an aquatic
life. Full independence of the watery
environment came later with the appearance
of the shelled amniote egg, and with it, the
beginning of the reptiles.

PREVIOUS PAGE A colored scanning electron micrograph of
a coiled garden millipede magnified about 15 times. Its major
group, the arthropods, were the first creatures to live on land.

LEFT The pioneering tetrapods (four-legged backboned
animals) *Ichthyostega* rest on a bank among giant tree-ferns
and similar ancient plants, in the warm, dank Devonian forests
of what is today cold Greenland.

ICHTHYOSTEGA AND ACANTHOSTEGA

ANIMAL FACTFILE

Ichthyostega

Meaning: Fish plate

Pronunciation: Ick-thee-owe-stay-gah

Period: Late Devonian

Main group: Tetrapoda

Length: 1 meter (39 inches)

Diet: Animals

Fossil sites: Greenland

Among the first tetrapods (four-legged back-boned animals) were *Acanthostega* and *Ichthyostega*. In earlier classification schemes they were formerly both included in the group called labyrinthodonts, which were the first types of amphibians (as shown on page 22). *Labyrinthodont*, meaning "labyrinth teeth," refers to the folded pattern of very hard enamel on the teeth of these animals. Their teeth are one of the features that link them to the fish that were probably their ancestors – the lobe-fin fish known as osteolepiforms, a group that included *Eusthenopteron* and *Panderichthys*.

Acanthostega approached 1 meter (39 inches) in length and outwardly resembled a large, big-mouthed newt or salamander. Its limbs were probably not strong enough to support it for easy walking on land but were used as swimming paddles or for pushing through swamps. Its wide mouth had jaws studded with small sharp teeth, and its tail

had low but long fins on the upper side and underside. It had gills but it could almost certainly also breathe air.

Ichthyostega was slightly longer and bulkier than *Acanthostega*, and also dwelled in fresh water. It lived around the same time, during the Late Devonian period some 360 million years ago, and in the same region, present-day Greenland. It was more heavily built and had more powerful limbs, especially the front pair. For many years it was regarded as the main ancestor of modern tetrapods, but because of the details of its skeletal structure it is now generally seen as being on a "side branch" of the tetrapods' family tree. It had seven toes on each back foot, compared to *Acanthostega*'s eight on the front feet. Even earlier tetrapods include the recently re-studied *Elginerpeton* from fossils preserved in Scotland from almost 370 million years ago.

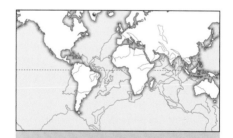

ANIMAL FACTFILE

Acanthostega

Meaning: Spine or thorn plate

Pronunciation: Ak-anne-thoe-stay-gah

Period: Late Devonian

Main group: Tetrapoda

Length: 1 meter (39 inches)

Diet: Animals

Fossil sites: Greenland

ABOVE The numbers of toes of early amphibian-type animals like *Ichthyostega* have been much disputed, ranging from four to eight per foot.

EOGYRINUS

The amphibious four-legged vertebrates known as anthracosaurs persisted for more than 100 million years – almost the same time span as the Age of Dinosaurs. Many types came and went, among them the massive *Eogyrinus*. It was one of the longest of all amphibian-type animals and one of the largest of all the creatures of its time. *Eogyrinus*, like Seymouria (on the following page), belonged to the subgroup that arose in the Late Carboniferous period, more than 300 million years ago, but had died out by the end of the next period, the Permian.

At nearly 5 meters (16 1/2 feet), *Eogyrinus* would rival most crocodiles today in overall length. Its body shape also was similar to a crocodile's, although generally slimmer, as was its skull, with long, powerful jaws equipped with sharp teeth. Its limbs were relatively small and weak, however, and on land *Eogyrinus* may have moved by a combination of wriggling, slithering and pushing with its feet. Its tail was extremely long, resembling a modern eel's, with a long dorsal fin on the upper side. This suggests that it lived mainly in water, and swam by lashing the tail from side to side, again like a crocodile. *Eogyrinus* lived at a time of warm, humid conditions when much of the land was covered by thick forests of giant ferns and other swamp-loving "coal forest" plants. It probably preyed on victims such as fish and smaller tetrapods.

ANIMAL FACTFILE
Eogyrinus
Meaning: Dawn ring or circle
Pronunciation: Ee-owe-jiy-rin-uss
Period: Late Carboniferous
Main group: Tetrapoda (Anthracosauria)
Length: 4.6 meters (15 feet)
Diet: Medium-sized prey
Fossil sites: Europe

| 0 | 1 | 2 | 3 | 4 | 5 | 6 |

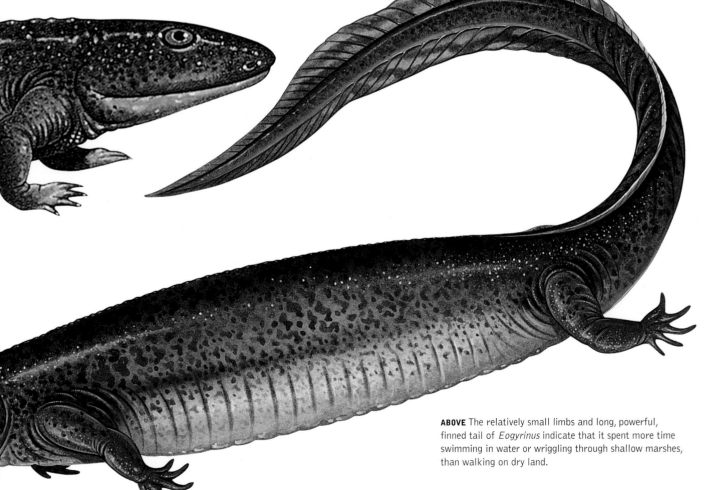

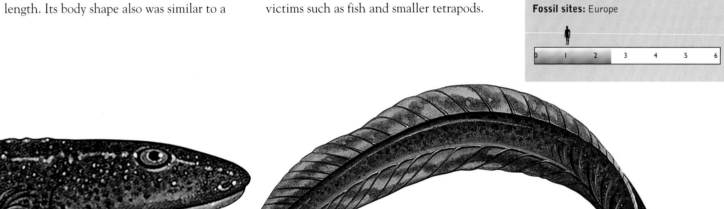

ABOVE The relatively small limbs and long, powerful, finned tail of *Eogyrinus* indicate that it spent more time swimming in water or wriggling through shallow marshes, than walking on dry land.

SEYMOURIA

Many excellently preserved fossils of this 60-centimeter (2-foot) predator have been found in rocks in Texas known as the Red Beds. The rocks, which date back to the Permian period, have also yielded remains of many other impressive creatures, such as the "sailback" *Dimetrodon* (described later in this chapter). *Seymouria* was named after the town of Seymour, Texas, where some of its fossils were uncovered. It resembled a large lizard or even a crocodile, with a wide mouth and sharp teeth for grabbing prey. *Seymouria* was a member of the amphibious group called the tetrapods, like other creatures shown so far in this chapter. Within this main group, it is placed in the anthracosaur subgroup, like *Eogyrinus* (on the previous page). Fossils of other animals and also plants found with those of *Seymouria* show that the habitat of the time was fairly dry upland, here and there dotted with rivers and lakes. Although

Seymouria was able to live on both land and in water, it probably dwelled mostly on land.

The scientists who first studied the remains of *Seymouria* thought that it might be a reptile. It had reptilian features, including the structure of its shoulder bones and hipbones, and the joints between the skull and the cervical vertebrae (neck backbones). However, there were small details that were not reptilian, such as the presence of lines on the skulls of young specimens. These usually accommodated the lateral line sense that detects waterborne vibrations, clearly seen as a line along each side of the body in fish. Several types of *Seymouria* are known from most of the Permian period.

RIGHT A fine specimen of *Seymouria* from Texas showing the sturdy or robust construction of the skeleton, with thick-set bones for carrying considerable weight on land.

BELOW *Seymouria* was a tough, reptilian-looking tetrapod well adapted to dry land. But it retained amphibious features such as the lateral line, seen as a stripe along length of the upper body, which detects ripples and vibrations when submerged in water.

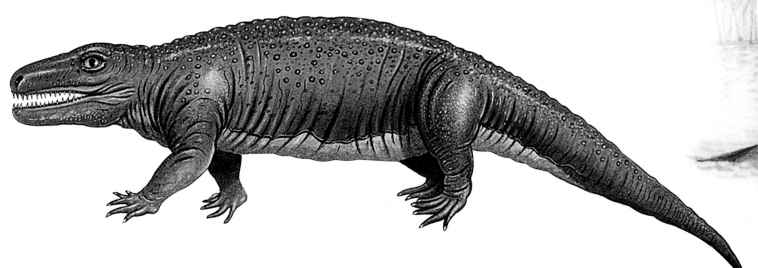

DIADECTES

The four-legged land vertebrates known generally as "amphibians" were all meat-eaters, or perhaps scavengers, until the appearance of creatures such as *Diadectes* in the Early Permian period. Its front teeth were spoon-shaped and stuck out slightly from the jaw at a forward angle, while its back teeth were broad and suited to crushing. This arrangement seems to indicate that it gathered plant matter and chewed it at length, although an alternative suggestion is that it picked up shellfish with the probing front teeth and crunched them with the rear teeth. However, the wide, bulky body of *Diadectes* also indicates a slow herbivore rather than a fast-moving predator. Indeed, it was one of the largest land-dwellers of its time, at 3 meters (10 feet) in length. Its shoulder bones and hipbones were very large, to anchor the powerful muscles that moved its four sturdy limbs. It may have used its large,

strong feet, with their five blunt-clawed digits, to dig up plant matter. Its tail was relatively short and thin.

Diadectes had several reptilian features in its bones, especially in its skull. It had a partly developed secondary bony palate (the "shelf" that separates the mouth cavity from the nose chamber), allowing more convenient breathing through the nasal airways while the mouth was full of food. This feature is found in certain more advanced reptiles. At one stage, *Diadectes* was suggested as an ancestor for the herbivorous reptiles, but plant-eating was being taken up already, at around the same time as *Diadectes* lived, by reptiles, or reptile-like creatures, such as *Edaphosaurus*.

ANIMAL FACTFILE
Diadectes
Meaning: Biter-through, penetrating bite
Pronunciation: Dye-ah-deck-teez
Period: Early Permian
Main group: Tetrapoda (Diadectomorpha)
Length: 3 meters (10 feet)
Weight: Up to 100 kilograms (220 pounds)
Diet: Plants
Fossil sites: North America

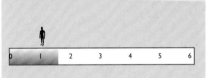

LEFT *Diadectes* was one of the first amphibian-like tetrapods to take up plant-eating, at least, if the suggestion is correct that its teeth were adapted to raking in and chewing plant material.

ERYOPS

Many of the large, four-legged, amphibian-type creatures which lived in Carboniferous and Permian times belonged to the very successful and long-lasting temnospondyl group. Another of its members was *Eryops*. Its name, which means "long eye," was coined in 1887 by Edward Drinker Cope, an American fossil-hunter, as he hurried to name dozens of dinosaurs and many other creatures. *Eryops* certainly had a broad, long-snouted head, with powerful jaws that bore many small, spiky teeth. The entire build of the creature was sturdy and strong, with a bulky wide body, short but well-built legs, and a medium-length, tapering, finless tail. It was probably a semi-aquatic hunter. It could have lurked in swamps, with just its eyes and nostrils (on the top of its head) showing above the water, or it might have prowled riverbanks and lakeshores for any likely prey.

Fossils of *Eryops* have been found at various sites in Oklahoma, Texas, New Mexico, and other parts of North America. Its kind survived for several million years, into the Permian period, when they faced competition from newly evolving large predators of the mammal-like reptile group. The temnospondyls, which appeared in the Early Carboniferous period, 350 million years ago, persisted for 150 million years. They became extinct by the Early Jurassic when larger meat-eating dinosaurs known as therapods began to dominate the land. However, during their long time span, some temnospondyls may have given rise to the ancestors of today's amphibians, the frogs and toads, known as lissamphibians.

RIGHT The enormous mouth of *Eryops* would be difficult to open on land, because of the weight of the head and lower jaw, the position of the jaw joint, and the need to lift the head clear of the ground. So *Eryops* probably hunted in water, grabbing prey like fish in its massive gape.

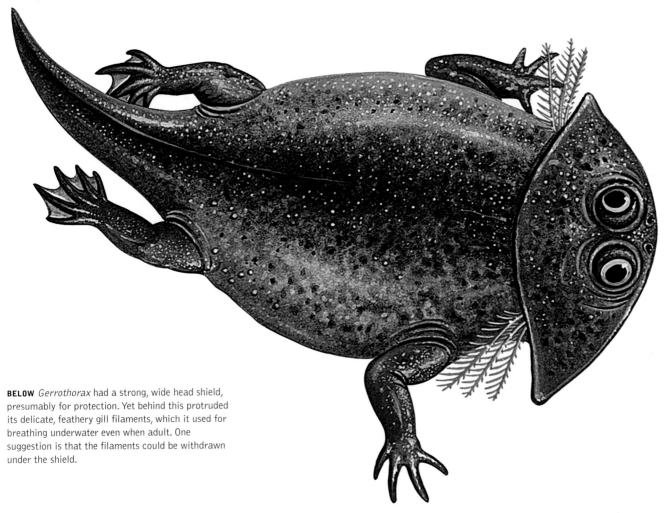

BELOW *Gerrothorax* had a strong, wide head shield, presumably for protection. Yet behind this protruded its delicate, feathery gill filaments, which it used for breathing underwater even when adult. One suggestion is that the filaments could be withdrawn under the shield.

GERROTHORAX

Amphibian animals such as frogs and toads begin life as aquatic young – as larvae or tadpoles – that breathe in water by means of gills. A few of today's amphibians – for example, the axolotl – keep their gills and continue to live underwater even when adult. The same is true for *Gerrothorax*, a 1-meter (39-inch) predator which lived during Late Triassic times, when the dinosaurs were beginning to spread and take over the land. *Gerrothorax* is regarded as a member of the temnospondyl group, along with *Eryops* (see opposite). Its fossils have been recovered from several sites in Sweden, southern Germany, and other parts of Europe.

Gerrothorax looked like a tubby tadpole growing four small, weak limbs. Three pairs of feathery gills protruded from the sides of the head, just behind the animal's most distinctive feature – its strange-shaped skull. This was extraordinarily wide, and extended

into pointed "wings" on either side. Both the head and body were flattened and armored with tough "plates." Perhaps *Gerrothorax*'s most remarkable feature, its very large, close-set eyes were situated on the top of the skull, meaning that it could look only upward. It has been suggested that this ambush-predator lay in wait for prey on the bed of a swamp or lake, perhaps camouflaged by its coloring and unusual outline. It would then suddenly lunge upward to swallow its victims in its gaping mouth.

Gerrothorax showed a combination of immature or larval-type (tadpole) features in what was presumably a sexually mature body, able to reproduce. Several kinds of modern amphibians like the axolotl mentioned above also retain juvenile features in the sexually mature state. This condition is known as neoteny.

ANIMAL FACTFILE
Gerrothorax
Meaning: Chest carrier
Pronunciation: Jeh-row-thore-acks
Period: Middle to Late Triassic
Main group: Temnospondyli
Length: 1 meter (39 inches)
Weight: 20–25 kilograms (44–55 pounds)
Diet: Smaller animals
Fossil sites: Europe, Greenland

DIPLOCAULUS

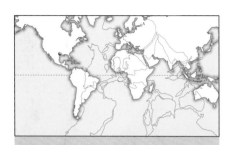

Although its name means "double stalk," *Diplocaulus* is informally known as "boomerang head." This was yet another amphibian-type freshwater creature that is known from fossils in the Permian rocks of Texas. It is placed in the group called the lepospondyls, which were common during the Carboniferous and Permian periods, but did not make it into the Triassic period, at the start of the Age of Dinosaurs. Nevertheless, they may have given rise to the modern amphibians, such as frogs and newts.

Some lepospondyls were shaped like newts or salamanders, and are known as nectrideans. *Diplocaulus* was a nectridean too, but it was unusual in many ways. *Diplocaulus* was very flat, with a low skull, a wide, pancake-like body, and a short tail with small fins running along the upper side and underside. Its limbs were small and flat, and stuck out sideways from the body. The large eyes on the upper side of the almost horizontal face could see upward as well as sideways. All this suggests a bottom-dweller, watching the waters above for food and danger. *Diplocaulus* also had backswept "wings" on its head, formed from an extended bone at the rear of each side of the skull, which tapered to a point. There are many ideas about the functions of these extensions. They may have made the head so wide that even the larger predators of the time could not fit *Diplocaulus* into their mouths. On the other hand, since their shape, more curved on the upper surface than the lower, is reminiscent of an airplane wing, it has been suggested that they may have been "water wings," with water flowing past lifting the head, perhaps as *Diplocaulus* swam from one resting place to another.

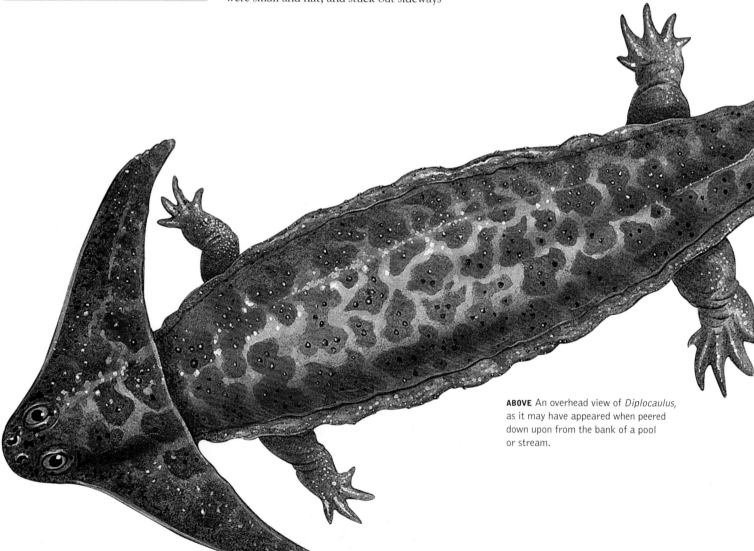

ABOVE An overhead view of *Diplocaulus,* as it may have appeared when peered down upon from the bank of a pool or stream.

RIGHT *Karaurus* would be difficult to distinguish from salamanders today, such as the tiger salamander of North America and the fire salamander of Eurasia. It probably lived a similar lifestyle, as a voracious predator in damp forests.

ANIMAL FACTFILE
Karaurus
Meaning: Head-tail
Pronunciation: Karra-urr-uss
Period: Late Jurassic
Main group: Amphibia (Batrachia)
Length: 20 centimeters (8 inches)
Diet: Small animals
Fossil sites: Central Asia

TRIADOBATRACHUS AND KARAURUS

From the many and hugely varied amphibian-type creatures of prehistory, only three main groups survive today. These are frogs and toads (anurans or salientians); salamanders and newts (caudatans or urodelans); and the caecilians or apodans (gymnophiones), which are less familiar and worm-shaped. Together the three groups are called lissamphibians.

The earliest frog-like creature in the fossil record is a single specimen known from rocks in Madagascar and dated to the Early Triassic period, around 240 million years ago – before the dinosaurs evolved. This creature, *Triadobatrachus*, was just 10 centimeters (4 inches) long, including its very short tail, a feature which nearly all modern frogs lack. Its back legs were longer and more powerful than the front ones, but not greatly so.

This is another feature which suggests that *Triadobatrachus* was intermediate between

modern frogs and their probable ancestors, a subgroup of the lepospondyls (see *Diplocaulus*, opposite). In many other respects, *Triadobatrachus* looked like a modern frog and probably behaved like one.

Karaurus was one of the earliest known tailed amphibians, or salamanders. It dated from Late Jurassic times and was very similar to salamanders of today, despite the intervening time span of 150 million years. It had a broad head, four strong legs and a total length of 20 centimeters (8 inches).

Karaurus was probably a small but fierce predator, preying on even smaller animals, such as insects, worms and grubs. It could most likely move about on land as well as in water in the moist Jurassic forests, keeping out of the way of the giant sauropod dinosaurs of that time. Fossils of *Karaurus* have been found in Kazakhstan, Central Asia.

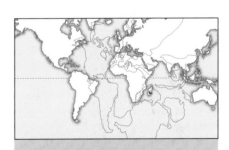

ANIMAL FACTFILE
Triadobatrachus
Meaning: Triassic frog
Pronunciation: Try-add-owe-bat-rack-uss
Period: Triassic
Main group: Amphibia (Anura)
Length: 10 centimeters (4 inches)
Diet: Insects and other small creatures
Fossil sites: Madagascar

Mesosaurus

ANIMAL FACTFILE

Mesosaurus

Meaning: Middle reptile

Pronunciation: Mezz-owe-sore-uss

Period: Early Permian

Main group: Mesosauria

Length: 70–100 centimeters
(28–39 inches)

Diet: Small food items

Fossil sites: Brazil, southern Africa

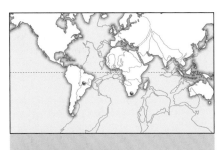

It may seem strange that, after reptiles had spent millions of years of evolution becoming free of the water, some returned to an aquatic life. *Mesosaurus* was one of the first reptiles known to have done this. It had features that make it seem like a combination of modern lizards, crocodiles and salamanders, although it was only distantly related to any of these creatures. It had a very long tail, extensively finned both on the upper and lower midlines; large limbs with big webbed feet, the rear pair being even larger than the front pair; and a long, slim body. Its skull was likewise slim and elongated, and the narrow jaws were full of long, needle-like teeth. The total length of *Mesosaurus* was up to 1 meter (39 inches), but, being so slim, it was a relatively small predator. It probably pursued small fish, shrimps and other prey of the same relative size. Its plentiful, spiky teeth were used as grabbing tools or stabbing weapons or perhaps *Mesosaurus* gaped its mouth wide and closed it around small prey so that its teeth trapped them like the bars of a cage.

Mesosaurus has given its name to a group of freshwater reptiles, the mesosaurs, that appeared during the Permian period, more than 250 million years ago, but did not survive its end. Their relationship to other reptiles is unclear, although they are usually viewed as a companion group to pareiasaurs and other early reptiles. Fossils of *Mesosaurus* have been found in both South America and Africa. Several other fossil reptiles and other creatures show a similar distribution between these two continents. This is taken as further evidence – in addition to geological similarities, and the close "fit" between their coastlines – that these two great land masses were joined during the Permian period, and drifted apart as the Atlantic Ocean was formed at a later time.

BELOW *Mesosaurus* swam mainly with its large webbed rear feet and long-finned tail. Its ribs were thickened to resist water pressure, and with the sturdy limb girdles (shoulders and hips), provided firm anchorage for the swimming muscles.

PROGANOCHELYS

The turtles and tortoises form a specialized group of reptiles known as chelonians. Their characteristic feature is, of course, their shell, which is made of two parts, the upper forming a domed carapace over the back and the flatter plastron covering the underside. Each part has two layers, an inner one of bony plates and an outer one of horny plates, and each layer is made of many of these plates joined at the edges, like a jigsaw puzzle. The first chelonians, known from the fossil record of the Triassic period, were strikingly similar to their modern relatives, despite a gap of more than 200 million years.

Proganochelys lived at around the same time as the early dinosaurs. It had a fully formed shell of some 60 plates, as all-over protection against land predators: it was a terrestrial chelonian, or tortoise, rather than a water-dwelling turtle. It also had a spiky tail, perhaps tipped with a lump of bone. Unlike many modern chelonians, *Proganochelys* could not pull its head or legs into its shell for even better protection. However, it had the typical chelonian skeletal structure – shoulder bones and hipbones within the rib cage rather than outside it, and wide, flat ribs attached to the inside of the shell along with the vertebrae (backbones). *Proganochelys* also possessed the typical chelonian jaws, which lack teeth but have sharp bony edges for chopping through plant food. Fossils of *Proganochelys* come from rocks in southern Germany and possibly also Thailand. Similar creatures, also land-dwellers, are known from slightly later fossils found on other continents, including Africa, Asia and North America. (See also Archelon, page 36.) They and *Proganochelys* had bony lumps or knobs on the head and neck to help protect these parts, and hard lumps on the palate inside the mouth, to help mash food which the sharp-rimmed jaws had cropped.

ANIMAL FACTFILE
Proganochelys

Meaning: Before lustrous chelonian

Pronunciation: Pro-gan-owe-kell-iss

Period: Late Triassic

Main group: Reptilia (Testudinata)

Length: Shell 60 centimeters (2 feet)

Diet: Plants

Fossil sites: Germany, also possibly Thailand

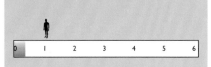

HYLONOMUS

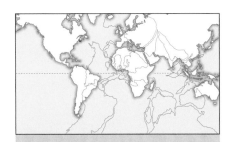

ANIMAL FACTFILE

Hylonomus

Meaning: Forest mouse

Pronunciation: High-low-nom-uss

Period: Late Carboniferous

Main group: Reptilia (Romeriida)

Length: Head to tail 20 centimeters (8 inches)

Diet: Small animals

Fossil sites: Canada (Nova Scotia)

Hylonomus is generally regarded, if not as the first known reptile, then as one of the very earliest. It was fully adapted for life on land, with no gills or skeletal features in common with the many amphibian-type animals described on previous pages. *Hylonomus* fossils are known from rocks of the Late Carboniferous period, some 300 million years ago, at the Joggins site in Nova Scotia (eastern Canada). The total length of *Hylonomus* was 20 centimeters (8 inches), including its long, flexible tail. Its strong skull and sturdy jaws had small, cone-shaped, sharp-pointed teeth, so *Hylonomus* was probably a predator of insects, worms and similar small creatures. In general appearance, it resembled a modern lizard, but it lived long before this type of reptile appeared, and had different skeletal features. *Hylonomus* is pictured here perhaps about to become trapped as described below.

Many specimens of Hylonomus have been found beautifully preserved inside the old, rotten stumps of giant club mosses, known as Sigillaria, that grew as large as some modern trees. Perhaps *Hylonomus* was hibernating, sheltering from adverse conditions such as a drought or cooler spell. However, other creatures such as insects and millipedes also populated these sites. More probably, the club moss forest was flooded, perhaps by salty water, causing the plants to die and topple, and leaving the lower stumps in the ground. These gradually rotted from within to leave bucket-like holes. Small creatures could have fallen into these, as perhaps did *Hylonomus*; or it may have climbed in to eat them, become trapped, and eventually died. The stump interiors would then have been filled with mud during the next flood, and the long process of fossilization could begin.

BELOW This illustration shows *Hylonomus* approximately life-sized. It was slim, long-legged, big-footed and whippy-tailed, suggesting a fast, darting mover like a modern lizard. However the lizard group would not evolve for another 50-plus million years.

LEFT One of the first very large reptiles, the pareiasaur *Scutosaurus* foreshadowed the big, armored, plant-eating dinosaurs which would evolve more than 100 million years later.

SCUTOSAURUS

This massive beast was as big as a modern rhinoceros, and had a protective covering of bony plates, spikes and knobs. It therefore looks similar to some of the armored or plated dinosaurs, such as *Ankylosaurus*. It was an entirely different type of reptile, however, and not a dinosaur at all. It belonged among the pareiasaurs, which were in turn part of a larger group of very early reptiles called the parareptiles. (In some older classification schemes, pareiasaurs are included in an alternative group, the captorhinids or cotylosaurs.)

Pareiasaurs were among the first really large reptiles. They were squat, heavy plant-eaters that used the serrated (saw-toothed) edges of the leaf-like teeth in their jaws, and also on their palates, to nip off and shred large quantities of plants, such as horsetails and ferns. Their strong, pillar-like legs were angled slightly diagonally from the body, and then

downward at the joints, rather than supporting the body directly from straight underneath, as in dinosaurs.

Scutosaurus had a very short tail, five blunt curved claws on each of its broad feet, irregular conical lumps over its back, and a skull extended at the cheeks as a type of neck shield.

There were many lumps, bumps and warty growths on its head – in particular, a downward-facing spike grew from the rear of each side of the lower jaw, and small groups of lumps were set on the snout. These structures seem to have first appeared in juveniles and thereafter enlarged with age.

As in the dinosaurs later, these spikes and lumps of *Scutosaurus* may have been merely for display – signs of physical maturity and readiness to breed – or they may have been actual weapons used against rivals at breeding time, or against enemies.

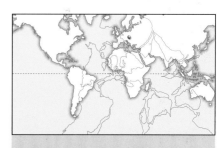

ANIMAL FACTFILE
Scutosaurus
Meaning: Shield reptile

Pronunciation: Skoot-owe-sore-uss

Period: Late Permian

Main group: Reptilia (Parareptilia)

Length: 3 meters (9½ feet)

Diet: Plants

Fossil sites: Russia

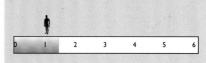

RIGHT The huge front flippers of *Archelon* were each well over one meter (39 inches) long, and flapped up and down with a "flying underwater" motion, rather than rowing forward and backward.

ARCHELON

Following their first appearance in the Triassic period, the chelonians – the turtles and tortoises – spread widely and soon evolved into a variety of sizes, although their overall shape was less varied. The largest chelonian that ever lived, as far as known from the fossil record, was the massive *Archelon* of the Late Cretaceous period. Its shell was 3.7 meters (12½ feet) long, which is twice the length of the shell of the biggest chelonian today, the leatherback turtle. The span between the tips of *Archelon*'s outstretched front limbs, or flippers, was around the same. All four limbs were greatly modified for swimming, with enormously powerful shoulder and hip muscles, and the five digits on each of its huge feet were enclosed in a large paddle-like web or "mitten." The front limbs provided most of the propulsion, flapping up and down with a motion like that of a bird's wings.

Archelon roamed the seas toward the end of the dinosaur age. Its jaws, though weak and toothless, were sharply rimmed and scissor-like, so that as in some of today's marine turtles (including the leatherback) *Archelon* fed by chopping up jellyfish and similar soft-bodied sea animals. Also like the leatherback, *Archelon* had a shell that was not a solid dome of bony plates, as in other chelonians, but comprised of bony struts with wide spaces between. In life, this scaffolding-like structure was probably covered and filled in by tough, thick, rubbery skin – hence the name of its modern relative, the leatherback. This greatly reduced the amount of bone and consequently the weight of the turtle, although its mass was usually buoyed up by water. Still, *Archelon* probably came ashore to lay its eggs, like all reptiles today. The need to move briefly on land may have limited its size.

ANIMAL FACTFILE

Archelon

Meaning: Ruling chelonian, ruling turtle

Pronunciation: Ark-eh-lon

Period: Late Cretaceous

Main group: Testudinata

Length: 4-plus meters (12-plus feet)

Diet: Probably soft-bodied sea creatures

Fossil sites: USA (Kansas, South Dakota)

YOUNGINA

Over half of all the species of reptiles in the world today are lizards – there are more than 4,500 different types. Their evolutionary origins are unclear and much debated. Part of the problem is that, from the outside, many prehistoric reptiles looked extremely similar to lizards, although further study of the details of their skulls and skeletons has shown that there were different types of reptiles. At one time, *Youngina* was suggested as the ancestor of the lizard group, mainly because of similarities in the rear parts of the skull. Now, however, this long, slim reptile is regarded as a member of the group known as neodiapsids, named from the two openings or "windows" in each side of the skull, one of them just behind the eye socket. Most neodiapsids lived during the Permian and Early Triassic periods. Their parent group, the diapsids, is one of the major reptile groups. The neodiapsids – but not *Youngina* itself – probably gave rise to two

of the greatest reptile groups of all: the squamates, including lizards and snakes; and the archosaurs, including crocodiles and dinosaurs and also the pterosaurs.

Youngina was so long and slim, with small legs and a strong skull bearing a long, low, pointed snout, that it resembled the burrowing lizards of today. Fossil specimens of several juvenile *Youngina* were found preserved in a burrow, where it appears they gathered for shelter, perhaps to escape extreme temperatures outside. *Youngina*'s sharp teeth indicate that it was a predator of worms, grubs, insects and other small creatures. But its teeth were unusual in that they grew on the inside of the mouth – on the palate – as well as along the rims of the jaws. *Youngina* was named in 1914 by Robert Broom and includes genera formerly known as Youngoides and Youngopsis.

ANIMAL FACTFILE
Youngina
Meaning: Of Young
Pronunciation: Yung-in-ah
Period: Late Permian
Main group: Diapsida
Length: Up to 50 centimeters (20 inches) head to tail
Diet: Small creatures
Fossil sites: South Africa

RIGHT The sharp claws of *Youngina* were suited to scratching in loose soil for small animal prey and perhaps to digging burrows for shelter.

Coelurosauravus and Icarosaurus

So-called "flying lizards" evolved at various times through prehistory and also live today in the forests of Southeast Asia. In fact, none of them has ever really been able to fly – they have all been gliders – and by no means were all of them lizards. *Coelurosauravus* was a member of a different reptile group, the weigeltisaurs, named for *Weigeltisaurus*, a similar glider from the Late Permian period, whose fossils have been found in Germany and England. Weigeltisaurs were diapsid reptiles, like Youngina (see previous page). *Coelurosauravus* had a lizard-like shape and small, sharp teeth, but its most distinctive features were its two large "wings." Each consisted of long, thin rods of bone supporting a skin-like gliding membrane. The "wings" could be extended like fans for gliding or folded along the body when not in use. *Coelurosauravus* had long toes with sharp claws to grip bark as it scampered, jumped at

take off and then landed among the trees. The wings could be tilted or changed in shape slightly by muscles at the rod bases.

The thin bony struts of the wings of *Coelurosauravus* were not connected to other parts of the skeleton. In the modern flying lizard Draco, they are connected. The gliding membranes of this true lizard are held out by long, thin extensions of the ribs. Draco glides mainly to escape enemies or to move to new feeding places. *Icarosaurus* was a similar creature from the Late Triassic period. Its fossils were found in New Jersey. Another glider of the same time and type was *Kuehneosaurus*, which lived in what is now western England. These creatures were close cousins of early lizards. Their wings were longer and slimmer than those of today, but were held out in the same way on very long, slim, extended ribs.

ANIMAL FACTFILE
Coelurosauravus
Meaning: Coelurosaur grandfather
Pronunciation: Seel-yur-owe-sore-av-uss
Period: Late Permian
Main group: Reptilia (Weigeltisauridae)
Length: Head to tail 60 centimeters (2 feet)
Diet: Insects and similar small creatures
Fossil sites: Europe, Madagascar

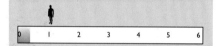

| 0 | 1 | 2 | 3 | 4 | 5 | 6 |

BELOW About 22 slim, slightly curved, rod-like lengths of bone support each wing of *Coelurosauravus*. The reason for the curious spike-edged crest around the rear of the skull is not known.

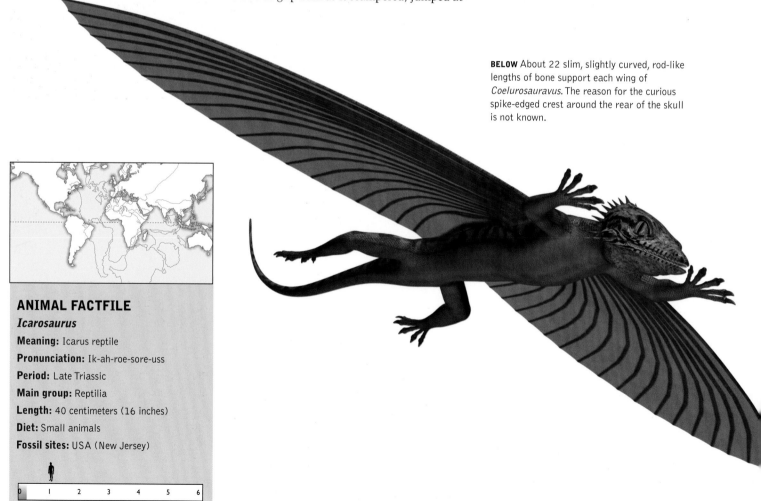

ANIMAL FACTFILE
Icarosaurus
Meaning: Icarus reptile
Pronunciation: Ik-ah-roe-sore-uss
Period: Late Triassic
Main group: Reptilia
Length: 40 centimeters (16 inches)
Diet: Small animals
Fossil sites: USA (New Jersey)

| 0 | 1 | 2 | 3 | 4 | 5 | 6 |

DINILYSIA

The snakes, with almost 3,000 living species, make up the second-largest group of living reptiles. They have their own subgroup, Serpentes, but are included with the lizards, Lacertilia, in the larger group known as the squamates. Some experts propose that snakes evolved from lizards, some time during the Early to mid-Cretaceous period, more than 100 million years ago. Perhaps some lizards took to a burrowing way of life and lost their limbs completely. Then some of these newly evolved snakes, in turn, gave up tunneling and lived again on the surface, up in trees or even in water. After all, a few lizards today, such as the slow worm, are limbless. Another proposal is that snakes evolved from the same reptiles that gave rise to the ferocious sea reptiles known as mosasaurs (see page 283).

The most ancient types of modern snakes are the pythons and boas, which kill their prey by suffocation – coiling around and squeezing, or constricting, the breath out of them. *Dinilysia* was perhaps a very early snake of this kind. It lived in Patagonia, in the southeastern corner of South America, during the Late Cretaceous period, when the Age of Dinosaurs was coming to an end. It was about 1.8 meters (6 feet) long and had the typical snake skeleton: a skull of loosely connected, strut-like bones; sharp teeth in its jaws; and a long body made up chiefly of dozens of vertebrae (backbones), each with a pair of ribs. *Dinilysia* had small, vestigial limb bones. Some of today's pythons and boas still retain tiny vestiges of their rear limb bones, but not the front ones, which have completely disappeared. The hip parts are encased within the muscle and flesh of the rear lower body, and what is left of the leg is just visible on the surface as a small claw or spur.

ANIMAL FACTFILE
Dinilysia
Meaning: Two lilies or flowers
Pronunciation: Die-nill-iz-ee-ah
Period: Late Cretaceous
Main group: Reptilia (Squamata)
Length: 1.8 meters (6 feet)
Diet: Smaller animals
Fossil sites: South America

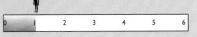

SCAPHONYX

ANIMAL FACTFILE

Scaphonyx

Meaning: Canoe claw

Pronunciation: Ska-fonn-icks

Period: Late Triassic

Main group: Reptilia (Rhynchosauria)

Length: Head and body 1.8 meters (6 feet)

Weight: 40 kilograms (88 pounds)

Diet: Plants

Fossil sites: Scotland, North America, South America, and India

Rhynchosaurs such as *Scaphonyx* are sometimes referred to as the "sheep of the Triassic." Being reptiles and not mammals, they had scales rather than wool, but they were very numerous plant-eaters, around the same size as modern sheep, and can be imagined dotted over the landscape, munching on low-growing plants such as ferns. (There were no flowers, herbs or grasses at the time.) Also, like some sheep today, rhynchosaurs were probably occasional victims of large predators – in their case, early dinosaurs such as *Herrerasaurus* and the mainly land-dwelling crocodiles of the time.

Rhynchosaurs were related to the major archosaur group of reptiles, which included crocodiles and dinosaurs. *Scaphonyx* was typical, with its bulky pig-like body, squat but sturdy limbs, thick tail, and upper jaw that curved down at its pointed tip like a bird's beak. (The name rhynchosaur means "beak

reptile.") Some rhynchosaurs had skulls that widened in the cheek region to form small neck frills or shields. The beak probably hooked and gathered vegetation, and the many broad-topped chewing teeth were arranged in long rows in the cheek region. The lower jaws were narrow-edged and fitted into grooves in the upper jaws, so that the teeth came together with a combined chopping, shearing and crushing action.

Rhynchosaurs were very abundant, but only for a relatively short time. In some areas which are rich and varied in fossil remains, those of rhynchosaurs make up more than half of all the preserved larger plant-eating animals. They faded away at the end of the Triassic period, perhaps in the face of competition for food as herbivorous dinosaurs spread across the land.

RIGHT The narrow, hooked, parrot-like beak of herbivorous *Scaphonyx* was a recurrent plant-cropping design in prehistoric times. Several types of dinosaurs evolved very similar features, including the horned dinosaurs or ceratopsians such as *Triceratops*.

DEINOSUCHUS (PHOBOSUCHUS)

For decades, *Deinosuchus* has enjoyed fame as the largest crocodile that ever lived. But it now has a rival, discovered in 1970, in *Sarcosuchus* (see page 275). This is partly because specimens of *Sarcosuchus* discovered in Africa show that it grew bigger than was believed from its remains found earlier in South America. It is also because recent studies of the fossil skull of *Deinosuchus*, which is the only part discovered, have resulted in reduced estimates of the animal's total length, from more than 15 meters (16½ yards) to nearer 10 meters (11 yards). Even at this reduced estimate, *Deinosuchus* was larger still than the biggest crocodile and biggest reptile today, the saltwater crocodile of southern and Southeast Asia and Australia. *Deinosuchus* lived a few tens of millions of years later than *Sarcosuchus*, and on a different continent, North America.

The skull of *Deinosuchus* measures more than 2 meters (2 yards) from front to back and has a broad rather than narrow snout. Its proportions are similar to the skull of today's Nile crocodile, which specializes in hunting large prey like antelope and zebra. *Deinosuchus* probably lurked in rivers or swamps, waiting for prey to come and drink from the water's edge. It would grab the victim in its massive jaws, studded with long but not especially sharp teeth, and then drag it into the water to drown, or perhaps spin around lengthwise like a top, to tear off chunks of flesh. Its prey probably included dinosaurs and, perhaps, large fish or swimming reptiles.

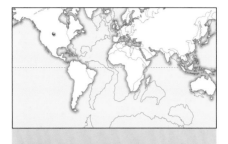

ANIMAL FACTFILE
Deinosuchus

Meaning: Terrible crocodile

Pronunciation: Day-no-sook-uss

Period: Late Cretaceous

Main group: Crocodylomorpha

Length: 10 meters (11 yards) some estimates up to 15 meters (16½ yards)

Weight: 2–3 metric tons (2–3 tons)

Diet: Large animals

Fossil sites: USA

0	1	2	3	4	5	6

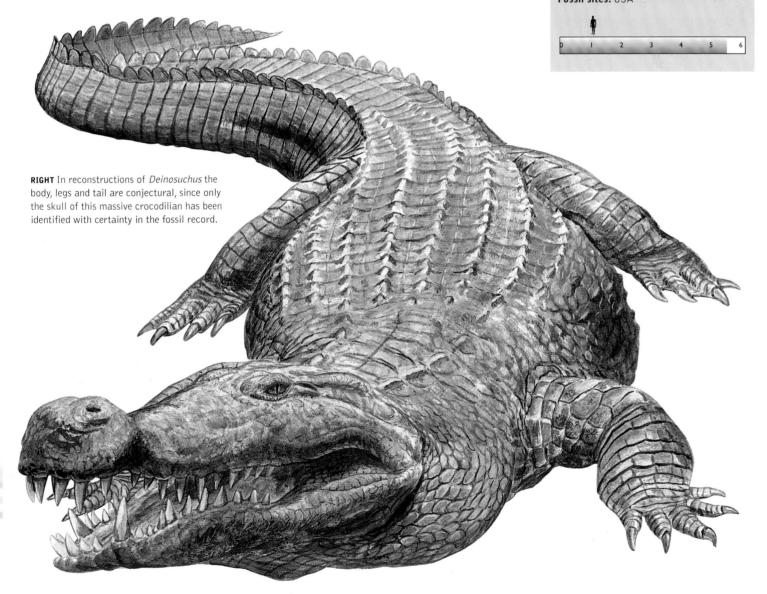

RIGHT In reconstructions of *Deinosuchus* the body, legs and tail are conjectural, since only the skull of this massive crocodilian has been identified with certainty in the fossil record.

RIGHT Paleoecological evidence from fossils preserved with *Dimetrodon*, of other animals and also plants, shows that it lived in a dry, scrubby landscape dotted with winding brooks and small pools but also subject to long droughts.

DIMETRODON

ANIMAL FACTFILE
Dimetrodon
Meaning: Two-form teeth, two types of teeth
Pronunciation: Die-met-roe-don
Period: Early Permian
Main group: Synapsida (Pelycosauria)
Length: Up to 4 meters (13 feet)
Diet: Larger animals
Fossil sites: North America, Europe

One of the prehistoric animals most likely to be called a dinosaur, even though it was not, is *Dimetrodon*. It often appears in illustrations and reconstructions of the ancient world, sporting a large back "sail" and fearsomely long, sharp fangs. Yet *Dimetrodon* appeared, and died out before the dinosaurs, and in some modern classification systems it is not even regarded as a true reptile. Instead, it is placed in a group known as synapsids, which are defined by a certain opening in each side of the skull. Synapsids are also known informally and confusingly by yet another name: the "mammal-like reptiles." (See also the following pages of this chapter.) Within the synapsid group, Dimetrodon belonged to the pelycosaur subgroup, alongside its plant-eating cousin, and probable victim, *Edaphosaurus* (opposite).

Dimetrodon grew to 3.5 meters (11½ feet) in length and was one of the greatest land hunters of the Early Permian period, some 280 million years ago. It is a common find in the fossil-rich rocks of Texas and Oklahoma, as well as in some parts of Europe. It had a large head, a squat but long body, sprawling limbs at the sides, and a slim, tapering tail. Its teeth were varied in size and shape, which was unusual for reptile-like creatures of its time. They were smaller but sharp at the front of the jaw, for gripping; large and canine-like slightly farther back, for stabbing and tearing; and lower but more substantial at the rear of the jaws, for slicing and chewing. The "sail" or "fin" on *Dimetrodon*'s back was a thin layer of skin and flesh held up by spine-like extensions of the vertebrae (backbones), up to 1 meter (39 inches) tall.

RIGHT The back sail or fin of *Edaphosaurus* was slightly more leaf- or shell-shaped than the crescent-like curve of *Dimetrodon's* (opposite). Also there were small cross-pieces of bone along the length of each stiff spine holding up the sail, which *Dimetrodon* lacked.

EDAPHOSAURUS

Like the flesh-eating *Dimetrodon* (opposite), Edaphosaurus was a member of the pelycosaur subgroup of early synapsids. Pelycosaurs appeared during the Late Carboniferous period. By the Early Permian, when *Edaphosaurus* and *Dimetrodon* lived, their fossils at certain sites – which were in scrubby uplands at the time – outnumber the fossils of all other backboned animals. Although pelycosaurs and other synapsids are sometimes called "mammal-like reptiles," *Edaphosaurus* was not very mammal-like and, despite its superficial resemblance to *Dimetrodon*, it was not a predator. It was probably a plant-eater, with peg-shaped teeth for gathering and chewing plant food. This partly mashed vegetation would be swallowed into the large, roomy guts in the tubby, short-legged body, where it could be fermented and digested to release its nutrients.

Like *Dimetrodon*, *Edaphosaurus* had a tall "fin" or "sail" on its back, held up by neural spines, long vertical extensions of the vertebrae (backbones). This sail- or fin-like arrangement has occurred in several different groups of prehistoric animals, including dinosaurs (see also page 174). The most common theory about the sail's function is that it helped with temperature regulation. The large area of the sail, when positioned at a right angle to the rising sun, would absorb warmth and pass it, via the blood flowing through it, into the animal's body. This would quickly raise the animal's body temperature to allow more and faster activity after the cool night. Alternatively, standing in the shade and at a right angle to a breeze would cool the body. In addition, the sail may have been brightly colored to aid in recognition, for example, by breeding partners.

ANIMAL FACTFILE
Edaphosaurus
Meaning: Pavement reptile
Pronunciation: Ed-aff-owe-sore-uss
Period: Late Carboniferous to Early Permian
Main group: Synapsida (Edaphosauridae)
Length: Up to 3 meters (10 feet)
Diet: Plants
Fossil sites: North America, Europe

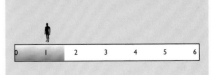

MOSCHOPS

Moschops was a synapsid or "mammal-like reptile" (like the animals on the previous two pages, and those in the following pages of this chapter). Its fossils have been unearthed from the Karroo Beds (rock layers) of South Africa. It was a massive, heavily built beast, with a body about the size of an average rhinoceros and a short, slightly tapering tail. The rear limbs were smaller and directly under the body, while the front pair were powerful and sprawled at an angle, sideways and then downward. The general shape and posture of *Moschops* have led some to compare it to the sumo wrestlers of Japan.

Moschops had foreshortened jaws equipped with teeth shaped like chisels, which it used for cutting and chopping plants. Its most unusual feature was on its forehead and the top of its head, where the skull bone was greatly thickened. This suggests that *Moschops* had head-to-head battles, pushing

or butting, probably with others of its kind – perhaps to defeat rivals for partners at breeding time, or to establish a senior position in the group. (See also pachycephalosaur dinosaurs, page 204.)

Moschops belonged to the synapsid subgroup known as therapsids. These evolved during the Permian period and in many areas they took over from the previously more common rival subgroup of synapsids, the pelycosaurs, such as *Dimetrodon* and *Edaphosaurus*. Because of its thickened skull dome, *Moschops* is classified with the dinocephalian ("terrible-headed") therapsids, although it lacked the lumps, horns, bumps and spikes that grew on the heads of other types – some of which were even bigger.

ABOVE The heavily-muscled forequarters, squat posture and thickened forehead bone all suggest that *Moschops* engaged in pushing or head-butting contests, perhaps with rivals at breeding time.

LYSTROSAURUS

The creatures in the last portion of this chapter were all "mammal-like reptiles," although in newer classification schemes they are regarded as neither mammals nor reptiles, but as members of a distinct group, the synapsids. The earlier synapsids, such as *Dimetrodon* and the other pelycosaurs, were followed by the early therapsids, including *Moschops* (opposite). In the Early Permian period came another group of therapsids, the dicynodonts. *Lystrosaurus* and *Dicynodon* were two examples. *Lystrosaurus* was a later and fairly small type from the Early Triassic period. It was about the size of a pig but with stouter limbs, the front two being more splayed than the rear pair. Fossils of *Lystrosaurus* have been found over a huge range, including sites in eastern Europe, western Asia, China and India, southern Africa and Antarctica. This supports the view that these landmasses were joined together at the time.

The name dicynodont means "two dog teeth." Most types had two long teeth growing from near the front of the upper jaw, and usually pointing downward and being visible outside the mouth as tusks. The front of the upper jaw was also unusual, being shaped like a modern bird of prey's downwardly hooked beak. This feature was common in many plant-eating dinosaurs and also the reptiles known as the rhynchosaurs, which lived at the same time as the dicynodonts (see *Scaphonyx*, page 40). The dicynodonts were even more unusual in that most had very few teeth other than the tusks, or none at all. They cropped vegetation with their "beaks," and presumably mashed it up mainly in the guts. The possible uses of their tusks are discussed on the next page.

BELOW Long bodies and short tails, as shown by *Lystrosaurus*, were a feature of many herbivorous synapsids from the Late Permian and Early Triassic periods.

ANIMAL FACTFILE
Lystrosaurus
Meaning: Shovel reptile
Pronunciation: List-row-sore-uss
Period: Late Permian to Early Triassic
Main group: Synapsida (Dicynodontia)
Length: Head and body 1 meter (39 inches)
Diet: Plants
Fossil sites: Southern Africa, India, China, Russia, Antarctica

Dicynodon

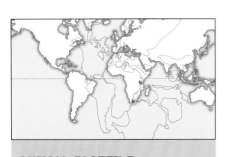

ANIMAL FACTFILE
Dicynodon

Meaning: Two dog-teeth
Pronunciation: Die-sigh-no-don
Period: Late Permian
Main group: Synapsida (Dicynodontia)
Length: Head and body 1.2 meters (4 feet)
Diet: Plants
Fossil sites: Africa

This stocky plant-eater has given its name to the dicynodont group of synapsids (explained on the previous page). It was one of the earlier types, from the Late Permian period some 260–250 million years ago, and its fossils have been uncovered in Tanzania (East Africa) and also in South Africa. Like many other earlier dicynodonts, it was pig-sized, around 1 meter (39 inches) or slightly more in length, with a short tail, and was low-slung on short limbs. Later members of the group reached much greater sizes, up to 3 meters (9½ feet) long and perhaps 1 metric ton (1 ton) in weight – as big as a medium-sized hippopotamus today. There are other similarities to modern hippopotamuses too, in the wide, barrel-like body and stocky limbs. At one time, dicynodonts were regarded as semi-aquatic, living in swamps and lakes. However, other fossils found with their remains show that many kinds lived in fairly dry, scrubland-type landscapes.

Why did *Dicynodon* and its cousins have just two main tusk-like teeth? One suggestion is that they were used for digging, to reach ground-level or underground plant matter such as roots and runners.

Another idea is that they were used for defense against predators, since there were several types of larger meat-eaters at the time, including dry-land members of the crocodile family and other hunting reptiles. A third proposal is that the tusks were used for intimidating or jabbing rivals during the mating season, or, if not for actual battle, then in visual displays of strength and maturity.

The last dicynodonts lived at the end of the Triassic period. Like many other medium-sized plant-eaters, especially reptiles and reptile-like ones, they probably suffered from the rapid spread of the dinosaurs, including predation by the meat-eating types and competition for plant food by the herbivorous dinosaurs.

BELOW *Lycaenops* had the build of a strong, persistent runner and would use its speed to hunt down *Dicynodons*..

LYCAENOPS

As time passed, the "mammal-like reptiles" shown over these pages gradually became less like reptiles and more like mammals, although they probably belonged to neither of these groups, being synapsids (see page 44). *Lycaenops* was a Late Permian type, and in its body posture and proportions it showed many changes from the usual reptile pattern. It probably stood tall on its four longish legs, which were positioned directly below the body as in dinosaurs and mammals, rather than splayed out to the sides as in most reptiles. *Lycaenops* also had a long, blunt snout with a high tip. This was partly to accommodate the roots of the canines – two long, fang-like teeth that grew from the upper jaw. These teeth are most familiar in mammal carnivores such as dogs and cats, and reached tremendous size in the saber-toothed cats, such as *Smilodon* (see page 309å). The other teeth in the jaws of *Lycaenops* were smaller and more typical of reptilian flesh-eaters.

Remains of *Lycaenops* are known from the fossil-rich Late Permian rocks of South Africa, specifically the area known as the Karoo Basin, Great Karoo and Karoo Desert in the south-west of the country. The remains show that it was slim and lightly built, probably able to run faster and for longer distances than most of the other squat, heavily-built reptiles of its day. Perhaps it hunted in packs, like modern wolves, running down and slashing at big, slow herbivores. *Lycaenops* is placed in the subgroup called gorgonopsians within the larger therapsid group. Gorgonopsians may have evolved from the much more reptile-like pelycosaurs (shown on previous pages), such as *Dimetrodon*, but they became extinct toward the very end of the Permian period.

ANIMAL FACTFILE
Lycaenops
Meaning: Wolf face
Pronunciation: Lie-seen-ops
Period: Mid to Late Permian
Main group: Synapsida (Therapsida)
Length: Head and body up to 1 meter (39 inches)
Weight: 10–15 kilograms (22–33 pounds)
Diet: Prey animals, such as small reptiles
Fossil sites: South Africa

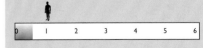

Cynognathus

Cynognathus, "dog jaw," was not a dog, although at a quick glance it might be mistaken for some strange kind of dog-like mammal. As it is usually reconstructed, it had a body covered with fur, ear flaps, crouching legs beneath its body and three types of teeth in its jaws, including an upper pair of long, sharp, dog-like canines. In fact, *Cynognathus* was a member of the subgroup known as the cynodonts, within the larger therapsid group, which was in turn part of the larger synapsid group. Synapsids are often known as "mammal-like reptiles," although they were neither mammal nor reptile. The cynodonts were the synapsids that resembled mammals the most. Indeed, they are regarded as the ancestors of the mammal group. (See also *Thrinaxodon*, opposite.)

Cynognathus was slightly smaller than a modern wolf, but much more heavily and powerfully built, with thicker limbs, a wider head and a more substantial, less pointed snout. Its jaws and teeth showed very mammal-like features. For example, the lower jaw was composed mostly of just one bone, the dentary, while in most reptiles the dentary was just one of up to six or seven bones making up the lower jaw. Also, in most reptiles all the teeth in the jaws were much the same, but the teeth of *Cynognathus* and other cynodonts were of three types. There were small incisors at the front for nipping or cutting, then large spear-like canines for stabbing, and, behind them, in the cheek region, smaller teeth for slicing or shearing. The earbones were also mammal-like rather than reptile-like: fossils show signs of three ear bones (malleus, incus and stapes) in a row or sequence to conduct sounds, much like our own ears, while reptiles have just one longer bone, the columella. These tiny ear bones help to distinguish mammals from reptiles.

BELOW *Cynognathus* was perhaps the closest that the "mammal-like reptiles" came to truly mammalian predators such as wolves. Its teeth showed increasing specialization, with the typical carnivore's enlarged, sharp canine or "fang." This fossil is from the Karoo region of South Africa.

THRINAXODON

This small but well-equipped hunter was a cynodont or "dog-tooth" (as explained opposite). The synapsids, the main group to which it belonged, are sometimes called "mammal-like reptiles," but *Thrinaxodon* was very much toward the mammal end of the range, and only a few features separated it from the true mammals that would appear later in the Triassic period. *Thrinaxodon* was about the size of a modern pet cat, but it had shorter, slightly more flexed or crouching legs – especially the front pair – and a short, tapered tail. Its build and slim body suggest that it may have lived like a stoat, in a burrow.

Thrinaxodon had three types of teeth, like *Cynognathus*, all suited to catching, impaling and slicing up animal prey like worms, grubs and small reptiles. Its skull shows tiny pits or holes toward the tip of the snout area. These are seen in many mammal skulls. They house the nerves that supply the roots of the

whiskers, long, thick hairs that probably evolved after the basic covering of fur. It follows that *Thrinaxodon* and other cynodonts may well have been hairy or furry too. This suggests, in turn, that they could have been warm-blooded, with the fur for insulation. Inside the skull was a secondary bony palate, which separated the air passages between the nose and throat from the mouth chamber. This allowed breathing while eating – another mammalian feature. *Thrinaxodon*'s brain was relatively large compared to its body size. All of these traits, plus those described for *Cynognathus* opposite, made the cynodonts the most mammal-like of creatures, without actually being mammals.

ABOVE *Thrinaxodon* showed many mammal- rather than reptile-like features, such as a distinct heel bone on each foot, and a lower jaw made mostly of one bone rather than two or three.

ANIMAL FACTFILE
Thrinaxodon

Meaning: Three-pronged tooth, trident tooth
Pronunciation: Thrin-axe-owe-don
Period: Late Permian to Early Triassic
Main group: Synapsida (Cynodontia)
Length: 50 centimeters (19½ inches) including tail
Weight: 1–2 kilograms (2–4½ pounds)
Diet: Small animals
Fossil sites: Southern Africa, Antarctica

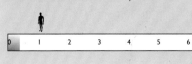

CHAPTER TWO

THE FIRST DINOSAURS

THE LATE TRIASSIC PERIOD SAW THE RISE OF REPTILES THAT WOULD
DOMINATE LIFE ON LAND FOR MORE THAN 160 MILLION YEARS – LONGER
THAN ANY OTHER GROUP OF CREATURES.

WHAT ARE DINOSAURS?

WHAT EXACTLY WAS A DINOSAUR? WAS IT A FIERCE CREATURE WITH GREEN SKIN, A TERRIBLE ROAR AND A MOUTH DRIPPING WITH BLOOD? PERHAPS, BUT NOTHING HAS BEEN FOUND AMONG THE FOSSILS TO SUPPORT THIS PICTURE. DINOSAURS ARE DEFINED FROM CERTAIN FEATURES OF THEIR FOSSILS, MAINLY BONES, TEETH, CLAWS AND HORNS. CERTAIN BONES OF THE SKULL AND SKELETON ARE IMPORTANT – THE UPPER SKULL, THE UPPER BONE IN THE LIMB (HUMERUS), THE FRONT DIGITS ("FINGERS"), THE HIPBONE (PELVIS), THE SHINBONE (TIBIA) AND THE ANKLEBONES (TARSALS).

DINOSAUR DETAILS

Some of these fossil features may seem small and insignificant. For example, the hipbone (pelvis) has a bowl-shaped socket called the acetabulum, into which fits the ball-shaped head (or upper end) of the thighbone (femur). This general structure of the hip joint is found in all vertebrates, but dinosaurs' hip joints are distinguished from those of other reptiles in three different ways. First, the pelvic socket had a ridge or rim that was thicker on the upper (higher) part than the lower. This acetabular ridge rested on the ball-shaped end of the thighbone. Second, the thighbone's head projected from its main length or shaft at a right angle. Third, the acetabulum socket was not a complete bowl of bone, but was "open," with a hole or window in the deepest part. Around ten other details of the skeleton, inconspicuous to the casual observer, add up to the suite of characteristics or traits that define a dinosaur, but the importance of finding a hipbone in a fossil cannot be underestimated.

STANDING TALL

The above details add up to a hip joint that, among reptiles, is unique to dinosaurs. On the animal's outside, it shows in the position of the leg relative to the main body. Dinosaurs had an "upright stance": when standing, the leg was directly below the main body, with the knee joint straight. This supported body weight efficiently, and in a naturally balanced way. In contrast, most other reptiles have had a "sprawling stance," as seen in today's lizards – the leg joins to the body at an angle, with its upper portion directed sideways and its lower part down. This structure needs more muscle power and is less energy efficient in movement. The upright stance may be one of the reasons why dinosaurs became so successful.

WHERE DINOSAURS BEGAN

Remains from South America, and especially Argentina, are among the earliest dinosaur fossils known to science. They date to almost 230 million years ago. As shown on the next few pages, most of these dinosaurs were from the theropod group – predators that habitually moved on their two larger rear limbs (bipedally), with smaller front "arms," and long, sharp teeth that they used to bite their prey. Likely ancestors for these types of dinosaurs are discussed in the previous chapter. The picture has been complicated by recent discoveries of fossils from different types of early dinosaurs, the prosauropods, in Madagascar. This may push the origins of the dinosaurs farther back, into the Middle Triassic. Almost as soon as the dinosaurs appeared, they began to spread and evolve into many shapes and sizes, with devastating effects on the creatures of the time.

PREVIOUS PAGE Three-toed dinosaur footprints, each larger than a dinner plate, are revealed in a curiously geometric mud-cracked slab of rock about 150 million years old, from Utah. These are footprints of a large theropod or meat-eating dinosaur, the group to which the huge and terrifying *Allosaurus* belonged.

LEFT Slight and slim, with alert and darting bird-like behavior, the carnivorous *Coelophysis* is one of the best-known early dinosaurs from 225 million years ago. *Coelophysis* relied on its speed and agility to hunt animals such as small reptiles.

EORAPTOR

Among the earliest dinosaur remains yet discovered, the fossils of *Eoraptor* have been dated to around 228 million years ago. They were unearthed in the Andean foothills of Argentina in 1991 by teams from the local area and the University of Chicago, and named two years later by Paul Sereno, of the university, and his colleagues. Layers of volcanic ash associated with the discovery allowed relatively accurate age assessment.

Eoraptor was a small theropod – a member of the meat-eating group of dinosaurs. In its proportions, it resembled many of the later predatory types, with a long slim head and neck, long and tapering tail, short forelimbs and long, powerful rear limbs for bipedal walking and running. However, the teeth at the front of the jaw were, unusually, leaf-shaped, rather than the sharp, blade-edged daggers or spear-like points typical of carnivorous dinosaurs.

Eoraptor can be viewed as a small, early, primitive theropod, exactly what might be expected as one of the first "twigs" on the predator branch of the dinosaurs' evolutionary tree. It had lightweight, hollow bones, similar to those of the slightly later and much better-known *Coelophysis*. *Eoraptor*, a slim, fast, agile predator, probably hunted various small creatures, including lizards and other little reptiles, and perhaps also large bugs and worms. It had five digits on each forelimb – an early feature, since the number of digits was reduced in later theropods to three or even two. *Eoraptor*'s digits had sharp claws for scrabbling in soil or grabbing victims. A less likely possibility is that *Eoraptor* scavenged on the dead and dying carcasses of larger reptiles, because its teeth were not designed for dealing with tough food. Rather they were small, sharp and back-curved, and so better suited to grabbing and cutting small prey.

DINO FACTFILE
Eoraptor
Meaning: Dawn thief, dawn hunter
Pronunciation: Ee-owe-rap-tore
Period: Late Triassic
Main group: Theropoda
Length: 1 meter (3 feet)
Weight: 3–15 kilograms (7–21 pounds)
Diet: Small animals
Fossils: Argentina

0	1	2	3	4	5	6

ABOVE *Eoraptor* would hunt any small creature that might make a meal. Its total length of about 1 meter (3 feet) is indicated by fossils, but weight estimates vary from 3 kilograms (6 pounds) to more than four times as much.

STAURIKOSAURUS

A much-debated discovery, *Staurikosaurus* is one of the few major fossil dinosaur finds from Brazil, where it was discovered in the far south near Santa Maria, and one of the most hotly debated of all dinosaur finds. In general features, this creature was a smallish theropod or meat-eater, larger than *Eoraptor* but not as bulky as *Herrerasaurus*, both dinosaurs from slightly earlier in the same period and found in neighboring Argentina. The remains of *Staurikosaurus* are relatively incomplete, but they allow estimates of its total length, snout to tail, at about 2 meters (6½ feet) or slightly more. It was a slim, quick predator, with long jaws armed with many small, pointed teeth. Its probable victims included varied small reptiles, and the young, and perhaps the eggs, of the larger reptiles that abounded at the time, such as the crocodile-like rauisuchians and the plant-eating rhynchosaurs.

Like its cousins, *Eoraptor* and *Herrerasaurus*, *Staurikosaurus* had made the advance to an almost fully upright posture. This important feature defines the group that included these dinosaurs and differs from the slightly sprawling posture shown by their ancestors (see page 54). It is the structure of the ball-and-socket hip joint that reveals this change. In a sprawling posture, with the thighbone at an angle to the bowl-like hip socket, the pressure pushes both upward and sideways, into the socket. The socket itself is strengthened to resist these stresses. In an upright posture, with the thighbone almost vertically below the socket, there is more weight-bearing pressure on the upper part of the bowl. *Staurikosaurus* shows an enlarged "lip" around the upper hip socket, to cope with this pressure. However the hipbone is one of only a few of its fossils discovered.

ABOVE Like many of the early meat-eating dinosaurs, *Staurikosaurus* had a slim and flexible neck, so that its long-jawed head could rapidly flick at, poke and peck food items.

DINO FACTFILE
Staurikosaurus

Meaning: Cross reptile (from the Southern Hemisphere constellation known as the Southern Cross)

Pronunciation: Store-ick-owe-sore-uss

Period: Late Triassic

Main group: Theropoda

Length: 2.3 meters (7½ feet)

Weight: 30 kilograms (66 pounds)

Diet: Small animals

Fossils: Southern Brazil

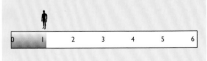

HERRERASAURUS

DINO FACTFILE

Herrerasaurus

Meaning: Herrera's reptile

Pronunciation: He-ray-raar-sore-uss

Period: Late Triassic

Main group: Theropoda

Length: Up to 5 meters (17 feet)

Weight: 270 kilograms (590 pounds)

Diet: Small and medium-sized animals

Fossils: Argentina

One of the best-known early dinosaurs, *Herrerasaurus* was named after the Argentine farmer, Victorino Herrera, who was the first to notice a fossil skeleton of one of these creatures in the rocky outcrops of the Andean foothills near San Juan. In 1988 a team led by Paul Sereno of the University of Chicago excavated this well-preserved and almost complete specimen. Similar remains found in the same general area included bones from the back limbs, the hip and the tail. The possibility that *Herrerasaurus* was a very early type of dinosaur that predated the major division of the group into its two great subgroups, Saurischia and Ornithischia, has been proposed. Otherwise it may be that *Herrerasaurus* was a saurischian or "reptile-hipped" dinosaur, but had not yet evolved features that would place it in the main saurischian subgroup of meat-eaters – the theropods.

What is known, from reconstruction, is that *Herrerasaurus* was a medium-sized, powerfully built predator. It had many sharp, rear-curved teeth in its very long jaws. Its forelimbs were short and had five digits, but the fourth and fifth digits were greatly reduced and also clawless, more like stubby stumps. This dinosaur had strong hind limbs with short thighs, and very long feet and toes – the proportions of a rapid runner. Its tail was long and whippy, and helped *Herrerasaurus* to twist and turn at speed. The hunter ran with its body held horizontal and neck curved upward, so that its head could face forward. Other predators of around 228 million years ago in South America included the bigger and stronger but sprawling-postured, four-limbed, crocodile-like reptiles known as rauisuchians. *Herrerasaurus* and its cousins represent an evolutionary breakthrough among reptilian predators for the next 160 million years.

LEFT *Herrerasaurus* was about the same size as today's largest lizard, the powerful and muscular komodo dragon. However this very early predatory dinosaur could probably move far faster than its distant reptilian cousin of today.

BELOW *Coelophysis* was fast, light and agile, with hollow, bird-like, weight-saving bones.

COELOPHYSIS

Few early dinosaurs are as well known as *Coelophysis*. In the 1940s thousands of fossils were uncovered at a site known as Ghost Ranch in New Mexico. They were the jumbled, broken bones of hundreds of individual *Coelophysis* dinosaurs that had probably endured a mass death of some kind. Perhaps they all perished together in a flash flood, or perhaps they died in more scattered groups and then rushing waters washed their rotting remains into one small area. The fossils date from 220–225 million years ago.

Coelophysis was a predator, but very slim and lightly built. Its overall proportions, with long beak-like jaws, flexible stork-type neck, distinctively shaped pelvis (hipbone) joints, and hollow bones to save weight, are all features shared by early birds. The many small, sharp teeth are better suited to snapping up small creatures, like insects, with pecking movements of the long neck, than to

tearing lumps of flesh from bigger prey. The sharp-clawed fingers could grab small items or scratch in earth for grubs and worms. *Coelophysis* may also have eaten fish, grabbing them with a forward jab of the head, in the manner of herons today. It was doubtless a fast and agile mover, leaping and darting after prey, and also to escape from its enemies.

In 1998, a fossil skull of *Coelophysis* was taken into space in the space shuttle Endeavor. Transferred to the Russian space station Mir, it traveled more than 6 million kilometers (3.7 million miles) around the Earth. So it was that one of North America's earliest dinosaurs became the first "dino-astronaut."

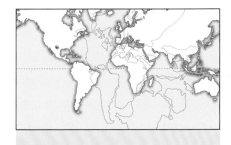

DINO FACTFILE
Coelophysis
Meaning: Hollow form, hollow shape
Pronunciation: See-low-fye-siss
Period: Late Triassic
Main group: Theropoda
Length: 3 meters (10 feet)
Weight: 15–20 kilograms (33–44 pounds)
Diet: Small animals
Fossils: Southwestern USA (New Mexico)

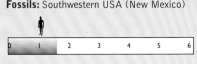

RIGHT The head, jaws and teeth of "Segi reptile" are mainly conjectural, but this early dinosaur was certainly very light-framed and probably caught small creatures by a combination of alert senses and rapid reactions.

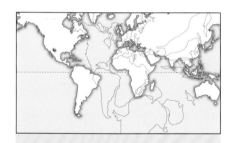

DINO FACTFILE
Segisaurus

Meaning: Segi reptile
(after its discovery site)

Pronunciation: Say-ee-sore-uss

Period: Early Jurassic

Main group: Theropoda

Length: 1 meter (39 inches)

Weight: 5 kilograms (11 pounds)

Diet: Small animals

Fossils: USA (Arizona)

SEGISAURUS

Segisaurus is not as well known as the similar *Coelophysis* (see page 59) because it did not leave plentiful fossil remains. The first specimen of what is now identified as *Segisaurus* was unearthed near Segi Canyon, Arizona, in an area known as Navajo Sandstone, in 1933 and described in 1936. It was incomplete, however, lacking a head with the all-important teeth. The fragmentary remains consisted of parts of the front and rear limbs, bits of the pelvis (hipbone) and a few ribs and vertebrae (backbones). From these parts, *Segisaurus* was reconstructed as a theropod (meat-eater), similar to but smaller than *Coelophysis*, and probably belonging to the theropod sub-group known as the ceratosaurs.

Segisaurus probably sprinted at speed on its long back legs and three-toed feet, holding its shorter forelimbs, with their sharp-clawed digits, near to its chest. The slender proportions of the fossil bones show that this dinosaur was lightly built, able to twist suddenly as it pursued prey, aided by flicking its tail sideways as a combined counterbalance and rudder to jerk the body in a new direction. Perhaps it snatched at large insects such as dragonflies or crickets, or small vertebrates such as frogs or lizards. The lack of teeth and jaw fossils means that proposals about the diet of *Segisaurus*, however, must come from comparisons with other, better-known relatives, especially *Coelophysis*.

MELANOROSAURUS

Officially named in 1924 after its discovery site, for many years *Melanorosaurus* remained – along with *Plateosaurus* – one of the few large plant-eating dinosaurs known from the Late Triassic. More recent discoveries, however, especially those in South America, such as *Riojasaurus*, have helped to increase our knowledge of how this major early group of big dinosaurs, the basal sauropodomorphs, evolved and spread. In particular, the similarities between South African animals, such as *Melanorosaurus*, and those from South America may be a consequence of the adjacent positions of these two continents during the Triassic.

Melanorosaurus was fairly typical of the sauropodomorphs, although perhaps larger than most. It had a small head, long neck and tail, bulky body and four very sturdy limbs, for plodding rather than walking. Its limb-bone fossils are well known and their thickness suggests weight-bearing adaptations, over the four broad five-toed feet, for a total body load of 1 metric ton (1 ton) or more. The rear limbs were longer, so the body sloped down from the hips to the shoulders. Estimates of the dinosaur's total length vary from 7 to 12 meters (23 to 40 feet). *Melanorosaurus* probably craned its long neck to reach up into tree-sized plants, to crop the softer parts of the vegetation such as fern fronds, young conifer leaves, buds and shoots. Compared to *Plateosaurus*, it is less likely that *Melanorosaurus* could have raised its front legs off the ground, to support itself solely on its rear legs with the aid of its tail, as it reared to reach higher food sources.

DINO FACTFILE
Melanorosaurus

Meaning: Black Mountain reptile

Pronunciation: Mell-ann-ore-oh-sore-uss

Period: Late Triassic

Main group: Sauropodomorpha

Length: 10 meters (33 feet)

Weight: 1 metric ton (1 ton)

Diet: Plant matter, especially high-growing

Fossils: South Africa

LEFT *Melanorosaurus* may have possessed a longer, sharper claw on the first (innermost) digit of each foot, but the fossil evidence is not clear.

THECODONTOSAURUS

DINO FACTFILE

Thecodontosaurus

Meaning: Socket-toothed reptile

Pronunciation: Thee-coe-dont-owe-sore-uss

Period: Late Triassic

Main group: Sauropodomorpha

Length: 1–2 meters (3–6½ feet)

Weight: 10–20 kilograms (22–44 pounds)

Diet: Plants

Fossils: England, Wales

This dinosaur's name, referring to teeth set in sockets in the jawbone, should not cause confusion with the major group of reptiles known as thecodonts, but now described as archosauromorphs. Such similarity in names may seem irritating today, but *Thecodontosaurus* received its official title a long time ago, following the discovery of fragmented fossils in rock fissures (cracks) near Bristol in southwestern England. This was in 1843 – just after the name of the entire group, Dinosauria, had been coined. In those days, scientific views on prehistoric animals and how they should be classified were far different from modern systems.

Thecodontosaurus was a smallish plant-eating dinosaur that stood and moved mainly on its longer back legs. It could have held its shorter, weaker front legs off the ground, except when bounding along on all fours or perhaps when leaning forward or bending down to feed on surface-level vegetation. In this respect *Thecodontosaurus* was similar to a much better-known and more widespread relative, *Anchisaurus*. There were five digits on each "hand," the thumb being especially large-clawed, and four digits on each foot. The tail was long, the head and neck were relatively small, and the teeth were small and leaf-like, with serrated edges. Like *Anchisaurus*, *Thecodontosaurus* is regarded as an herbivorous basal sauropodomorph. It represents a "dead end" in evolution, for its group soon died out.

ABOVE Fossils associated with *Thecodontosaurus* suggest that it lived in a dry, scrub-and-bush habitat – a landscape common in the Late Triassic and Early Jurassic, around 200 million years ago.

RIOJASAURUS

First uncovered in the remote and windy Valley of the Moon, in the western Argentine province of La Rioja, fossils of this big plant-eater have since been found at other localities along the eastern foothills of the Argentine Andes. The first almost complete skeleton was excavated during the 1960s and named in 1969 by José Bonaparte, an eminent Argentine paleontologist. Another 20 or so specimens have since been located. *Riojasaurus* was one of the first dinosaurs to reach or even exceed 10 meters (33 feet) in length and 1 metric ton (1 ton) in bulk. It was a massive creature for its time, about 220 million years ago, and in many respects it foreshadowed the true giants, the sauropods, which became numerous and widespread during the Jurassic, the period that followed. But at the present time there is no evidence of a direct evolutionary link between *Riojasaurus* and the later sauropods.

The backbone of *Riojasaurus* was composed of large, sturdy vertebrae, both to carry its main body weight and to support its long neck and tail. The clawed feet on its elephant-sized legs were disproportionate, since those on the forelimbs were half the size of the rear pair. Perhaps the back legs took the main strain of the body weight, and *Riojasaurus* could even rear up on them, using its tail as a third support to avoid toppling backward. The teeth were small and leaf-shaped, suited to stripping and shredding foliage. This was swallowed without chewing, to be pulped in the massive stomach, perhaps with the aid of grinding stones, known as gastroliths ("stomach stones"), gulped down specially for this purpose.

DINO FACTFILE
Riojasaurus
MEANING: Rioja reptile (from its discovery site)

PRONUNCIATION: Ree-oh-ha-sore-uss

PERIOD: Late Triassic

MAIN GROUP: Sauropodomorpha

Length: 10 meters (33 feet)

Weight: 1 metric ton (1 ton)

Diet: Plants

Fossils: Argentina

BELOW *Riojasaurus* was one of the first truly quadrupedal dinosaurs, that is, moving for most of the time on four legs. It could perhaps rear up for a short time on the rear limbs, but the size and sturdiness of the bones are adapted to support a considerable bulk.

RIGHT *Plateosaurus* is shown in its "kangaroo" posture, tilted up on its rear legs and counterbalanced and supported by its thick-based, heavy, muscular tail. In this position it could reach foliage at heights of almost 5 meters (16 feet) above the ground.

PLATEOSAURUS

DINO FACTFILE

Plateosaurus

Meaning: Flat reptile

Pronunciation: Plat-ee-owe-sore-uss

Period: Late Triassic

Main group: Sauropodomorpha

Length: 6–10 meters (20–33 feet)

Weight: Up to 4 metric tons (4 tons)

Diet: Plants

Fossils: France, Germany, Switzerland

Dozens of fossilized skeletons, from various locations in Europe, make this dinosaur one of the best known from the Late Triassic period, some 220 million years ago. It was also one of the largest land creatures of the time, probably approaching 1 metric ton (1 ton) in weight. Fossil finds include the original specimens from which the animal was named and described in 1837 – even before the dinosaurs themselves had received recognition as a group – along with further discoveries in the early 1910s, the early 1920s, and again in the early 1930s. The area surrounding the city of Trossingen, 100 kilometers (80 miles) southwest of Stuttgart, Germany, yielded some particularly well-preserved specimens.

Plateosaurus was a powerful sauropodomorph with the typical features of small head, long and flexible neck, tubby body, sturdy limbs and a tail that made up almost half of its total length. The rear legs were considerably larger than the front pair, and probably took most of the weight when walking. *Plateosaurus* is often pictured rearing up like a giant kangaroo, propped back on its tail, its head reaching out on its long neck for plants 5 meters (16 feet) or more above the ground. There was a large claw on each thumb, which may have worked as a hook for pulling branches to the mouth – or as a spike to jab into enemies. The 120 or so small teeth were leaf-shaped, with serrations around the edges, ideal for snipping or cropping softer leaves and fronds from the tall vegetation of Late Triassic times, which included conifers, tree-ferns and cycads. Bones from numerous individuals have been found piled together in fossilized heaps, which may indicate that the members of a herd all perished together, or that floodwaters washed scattered individuals into one site in a valley or on a riverbank. Newer fossil finds suggest that all of the fingers had long claws, like the thumb.

BELOW *Efraasia* and *Sellosaurus* have been variously regarded as two separate kinds or genera of dinosaurs, as species within the same genus, or as exactly the same species with the variation in fossil specimens representing different-aged individuals. Opinion now tends to two separate genera. This reconstruction reflects the body proportions of the *Efraasia* specimens.

SELLOSAURUS/EFRAASIA

In 1909, Eberhard Fraas discovered fossils of a plant-eating dinosaur about 2.4 meters (8 feet) long. It was similar in proportions to sauropodomorphs such as *Plateosaurus*, which lived in the same region at around the same time. A scientific description of the remains proposed that they were a type of early sauropod. The name *Efraasia* was later bestowed in honor of the discoverer.

A year earlier, a similar sauropodomorph had been named *Sellosaurus* by another paleontologist, Friedrich Freiherr von Huene. (Von Huene was also to be the scientist behind the main accounts and descriptions of *Plateosaurus* itself, in the 1920s.) These remains eventually numbered mixed parts of about 20 skeletons, the largest nearing 7 meters (23 feet) in length. The general sauropodomorph similarities to *Plateosaurus* were confirmed by studying the fossils of both creatures in detail, and comparing the size and shape of the bones.

However, similarities between *Efraasia* and *Sellosaurus* gradually came to light, and it appeared that the former was likely a smaller version of the latter. The proportions were slightly different – for example, *Efraasia* had a shorter neck, compared to its overall length, than *Sellosaurus* did – but in dinosaurs as in living animals, the relative proportions of bodies change as they grow toward maturity. Further studies of the bones showed that *Efraasia* was perhaps a young *Sellosaurus*. Since the adult version had been named one year earlier, scientific convention determined that *Sellosaurus* became the official name. All specimens of *Efraasia* were for a time officially reclassified as *Sellosaurus*. Yet another recent study, however, shows the two are, after all, distinct dinosaurs. Fraas himself is also noted for studies of primate fossils from Egypt during the early 20th century.

DINO FACTFILE
Sellosaurus
Meaning: Saddle reptile

Pronunciation: Sell-owe-sore-uss

Period: Late Triassic

Main group: Sauropodomorpha

Length: 7 meters (23 feet)

Weight: 600 kilograms (1,325 pounds)

Diet: Plants

Fossils: Germany

Mussaurus

DINO FACTFILE

Mussaurus

Meaning: Mouse reptile

Pronunciation: Moo-sore-uss

Period: Late Triassic

Main group: Sauropodomorpha

Length: 3 meters (10 feet)

Weight: 150 kilograms (330 pounds)

Diet: Plants

Fossils: Argentina

Mussaurus was a sauropodomorph dinosaur – a bulky, four-legged plant-eater, with a small head, long neck and long tail, and similar in overall appearance to other sauropodomorphs. Why, then, did the Argentine paleontologists José Bonaparte and Martin Vince, who in 1979 named the 3-meter (10 feet), 150-kilogram (330-pound) beast, give it a name that means "mouse reptile"? *Mussaurus* was known only from the fossilized remains of babies, which are far from complete. A composite version from the fragments shows that they were, if not quite as small as real mice, then at least rat-sized – each around 20 centimeters (8 inches) in total length, with a long tail and a skull about the size of a human thumb. Some were hatchlings, just broken from their eggshells, when they perished; others were unhatched embryos, still in their shells when preserved.

The level of detail in these *Mussaurus* fossils, found in the 1970s in the Santa Cruz region of Argentina, is amazing. The jaws contain rows of teeth hardly larger than pinheads, and the ankle and foot bones are the size of rice grains. They are the smallest relatively complete dinosaur specimens of any type yet discovered.

More recently, fossils of adults have been positively identified, although they are mostly partial remains. The current estimate of the full-grown size, mentioned above, is based on these and the size ranges of other dinosaurs seen in the fossil record and the growth rates of today's reptiles. It is possible, however, that another dinosaur, *Coloradisaurus*, found in the same region and in the same rock layers, and dating from around 215 million years ago, could be the adult version. However, *Coloradisaurus* is, as yet, poorly known, as fossils of only the skull and jaws have been found.

BELOW An adult *Mussaurus* is usually reconstructed by applying typical sauropodomorph dinosaur growth rates and body proportions to the newly-hatched babies, which are the main fossil specimens known. However Argentinian fossils already described as *Plateosaurus* may actually be *Mussaurus* adults.

ANCHISAURUS

About the size of a large dog, *Anchisaurus* holds the honor of being the first dinosaur to be discovered from North America, specifically the Connecticut Valley, and to be officially described in the scientific literature on the basis of the fossils it left behind. That was in 1818, however, and the story has had several twists and turns since. For a time, the remains were thought to be from an ancient human being. By the 1850s, they were recognized as being a reptile, though not necessarily a dinosaur – the whole dinosaur group had received its official title and recognition only a few years earlier, in 1841. In 1885, Othniel Charles Marsh gave the name *Anchisaurus* to another set of fossils, this time from Massachusetts. In 1912, nearly a century after the remains were first described, they were finally identified as being *Anchisaurus*.

Anchisaurus lived about 195 million years ago. It had a typical sauropodomorph body, with a small head, and a long neck and tail. Its body and limbs were relatively slimmer, however, than those of bigger sauropodomorphs, like *Plateosaurus* or *Massospondylus*. It probably moved slowly on all fours, in a loping manner, like a kangaroo of today, nosing for plants on the ground. Nevertheless, *Anchisaurus* could perhaps rear up onto its two larger back limbs to run at speed. Each front foot had five digits, with the first bearing a large, curved claw, possibly for defense. The rear foot had four digits, each with a large, nail-like claw. Like many sauropodomorphs, *Anchisaurus* had small, leaf-like teeth with serrated edges, well suited to stripping plant matter such as leaves and fronds. Its habitat was a deep valley with many plant-fringed lakes.

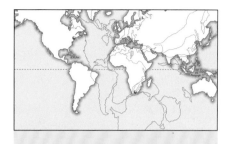

DINO FACTFILE
Anchisaurus
Meaning: Near reptile, close reptile
Pronunciation: Ann-kee-sore-uss
Period: Early Jurassic
Main group: Sauropodomorpha
Length: 2.5 meters (8 feet)
Weight: 35 kilograms (77 pounds)
Diet: Plants
Fossils: USA (Connecticut Valley, Massachusetts), possibly South Africa

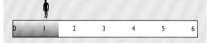

LEFT *Anchisaurus* was one of the smaller sauropodomorphs, also one of the most lightly built. It was probably able to trot or lope for considerable distances as it moved to new feeding areas of fresh plant growth.

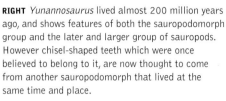

RIGHT *Yunannosaurus* lived almost 200 million years ago, and shows features of both the sauropodomorph group and the later and larger group of sauropods. However chisel-shaped teeth which were once believed to belong to it, are now thought to come from another sauropodomorph that lived at the same time and place.

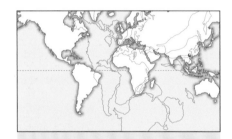

DINO FACTFILE

Yunnanosaurus

Meaning: Yunnan reptile

Pronunciation: You-nan-o-sore-uss

Period: Middle Jurassic

Main group: Sauropodomorpha

Length: 7–13 meters (23–42 feet)

Weight: 600–1,700 kilograms (1,320–3,740 pounds)

Diet: Plants

Fossils: Southern China

YUNNANOSAURUS

This medium-sized sauropodomorph was first described and named in 1942, by Young Chung Chien, a famous Chinese paleontologist known in the West as C.C. Young. Fossil specimens of some 20 individuals have been located in Yunnan Province, southern China. In general body shape and proportions, *Yunnanosaurus* resembles other, mostly earlier sauropodomorphs, such as *Plateosaurus*. Along with another similar sauropodomorph from the same area, *Lufengosaurus*, the discovery of *Yunnanosaurus* helped to demonstrate the almost worldwide distribution of the plant-eating sauropodomorph dinosaur group.

Like other sauropodomorphs, *Yunnanosaurus* had a small head, though with a relatively short snout, a long neck, a bulging body, sturdy legs with the rear pair slightly longer and stronger, and a long, tapering tail. It probably spent most of its days plodding slowly among forests of conifers, cycads and tree-ferns, swinging its long neck so that its

mouth could rake in soft leaves, shoots and buds. It could reach down to the ground when on all fours, or perhaps rear up onto its back legs and stretch its neck for food more than 5 meters (16½ feet) above.

Yunnanosaurus has been the subject of great debate because of its supposed teeth, which numbered more than 60 and were slightly chisel- or spoon-shaped. In this respect, *Yunnanosaurus* was more similar to the sauropods – the later, more massive plant-eaters (see pages 134–165) – than to the prosauropods, which had mostly leaf-shaped teeth. It is because of these spoon-like teeth that some experts have suggested that *Yunnanosaurus* was an early sauropod, but some of the chisel-like teeth may come from another dinosaur. The province of Yunnan has yielded many fossils of dinosaurs and prehistoric animals, including apes such as *Lufengpithecus* and the early humans *Homo erectus*.

MASSOSPONDYLUS

In the same way that *Plateosaurus*, from the Late Triassic, is well known from dozens of preserved individuals found in Europe, so is *Massospondylus*, which is from the Early Jurassic, with dozens of preserved individuals in southern Africa. Discovery sites include places in South Africa, Lesotho and Matabeleland in western Zimbabwe. Remains of *Massospondylus*, or a very similar dinosaur, have also been uncovered in Arizona, possibly making it an exceptionally widespread dinosaur.

Massospondylus was relatively slim and lightly built for a sauropodomorph dinosaur. Its head, in particular, seems tiny – simply a mouth at the tip of the long neck, rather than the enlarged, bulging body part usually found at a dinosaur's front end. Also, its teeth are quite pointed, their edge serrations are prominent, and the whole jaw and skull structure seems too delicate for biting and pulling off tough, fibrous plant food. During the 1980s, these features led to protracted discussions among experts on the nature of

Massospondylus's diet. Did it rake or tear off, and swallow, plant matter whole, in the usual sauropodomorph manner? Or was it really a meat-eater? In some ways, the long, serrated teeth resemble those of carnivorous dinosaurs. Perhaps *Massospondylus* snapped up small prey, or scavenged by tearing soft, rotting meat from decaying carcasses. Then further comparisons showed that similar long, serrated teeth are found in some of today's plant-eating lizards. Also found with *Massospondylus* fossils were gastroliths – polished pebbles swallowed into the guts to help grind up tough plant food.

RIGHT The jaws and teeth of *Massospondylus* show a curious mixture of features, some indicating herbivory but others suggesting a diet of small prey items or even carcass-scavenging. Recent reviews of the evidence point more to plant-eating.

DINO FACTFILE
Massospondylus

Meaning: Massive vertebrae, big backbones

Pronunciation: Mass-owe-spon-die-luss

Period: Early Jurassic

Main group: Sauropodomorpha

Length: 5 meters (16½ feet)

Weight: 350 kilograms (772 pounds)

Diet: Plants

Fossils: Southeastern and southern Africa, possibly southern USA

CHAPTER THREE

THE SMALL MEAT-EATERS

TODAY WE HAVE WILDCATS, STOATS, MONGOOSES, FOXES AND SIMILAR
MAMMALIAN PREDATORS. IN THE MESOZOIC ERA, THEIR ROLES AS SMALLER
BUT STILL DEADLY KILLERS WERE TAKEN BY A VARIETY OF DINOSAURS –
AND SINCE ANIMALS WERE BIGGER THEN, SOME OF THESE MINOR MEAT-
EATERS WERE LARGER THAN TODAY'S TIGERS AND BEARS!

SMALLEST TO SMALL

IN GENERAL, SMALL PREDATORS HUNT SMALL (OR AT LEAST SIMILARLY SIZED) PREY. THE DINOSAURS DESCRIBED IN THIS CHAPTER WERE MOSTLY LESS THAN 3 METERS (10 FEET) IN TOTAL LENGTH AND WEIGHED LESS THAN 100 KILOGRAMS (220 POUNDS) – ABOUT AS HEAVY AS A LARGE ADULT MAN. THIS WAS SMALL FOR THE DINOSAUR AGE, WHEN SOME OF THE LARGER PREDATORS WERE 70 TIMES HEAVIER. ALL MEAT-EATING DINOSAURS, LARGE AND SMALL, ARE KNOWN AS THEROPODS, "BEAST-FEET." MANY OF THE SMALLER MEMBERS OF THIS GROUP WERE SLIM, HOWEVER, OR EVEN ALMOST DAINTY, WITH LIGHTLY BUILT SKELETONS. IN PARTICULAR, THEIR REAR FEET WERE THREE-TOED AND SOME BONES WERE HOLLOW – VERY LIKE MODERN BIRDS. SOME ARE KNOWN AS COELUROSAURIDS, AND WERE AMONG THE SMALLEST AND LIGHTEST OF ALL THE DINOSAURS. WHAT THEY LACKED IN STRENGTH AND POWER WAS COMPENSATED FOR WITH SPEED AND AGILITY, AS THEY TWISTED AND DARTED AMONG ROCKS AND UNDERGROWTH IN PURSUIT OF PREY.

SMALL TO MEDIUM

Slightly larger than these mini-hunters, and generally later in the Age of Dinosaurs, were the dromaeosaurs, medium-sized meat-eaters known informally as "raptors." They were part of a larger group of predators, maniraptorans. One of the best-studied raptors is *Deinonychus*, which was lithe and agile, and powerful enough to tackle prey larger than itself, perhaps the size of a modern pig. Clues in the fossil record suggest that the raptors lived together in groups and hunted in packs, cooperating by using their relatively large brains. In fact, relative to their bodies, their brains were bigger than those of any reptiles, living and extinct.

LIKELY PREY

What did these hunters devour? Their equivalents today often feast on myriad small rodents, like mice, voles or lemmings, and small birds like finches. These did not exist during the early dinosaur age, though – then mammals and birds were probably scarce. Instead, the smaller predatory dinosaurs pursued invertebrates, such as cockroaches and other insects, grubs, slugs, worms and spiders. There were also numerous types of small non-dinosaur reptiles, especially lizards and others resembling them, and their eggs and babies could have been eaten too. Cooperative pack hunting brought much bigger victims within range, such as large plant-eating dinosaurs, weighing a metric ton (1 ton) or more.

LIVING DESCENDANTS

Beginning in the 1960s, scientific studies of raptors such as *Deinonychus* helped to expose as false the myth that all dinosaurs were slow and stupid. Suggestions gained force that they were fast and clever, and even might have been warm-blooded. From the 1980s, fossil finds, especially in China, have thrown us another surprise – dinosaurs with feathers, like *Sinornithosaurus* and *Microraptor gui*, the latter with clear impressions of feathers on all four limbs. The front limbs of these types were not modified as wings – the muscles were not strong enough for true flight – so the fluffy, filamentous feathers may have been for insulation. Again, this implies warm blood, and a likely ancestry to birds.

PREVIOUS PAGE One of the biggest "small" meat-eating dinosaurs was *Utahraptor* – some half a ton of fast, agile, powerful hunter. It was as heavy as today's biggest land carnivores, the brown or grizzly bears. It had the massive curved claw on each second toe characteristic of the "raptor"-type dinosaurs known as dromaeosaurs.

LEFT Dinosaur "wolves" on the prowl: *Velociraptor* and similar dromaeosaurs are now reconstructed as fast, lithe, agile, probably intelligent, pack-hunting killers.

SALTOPUS

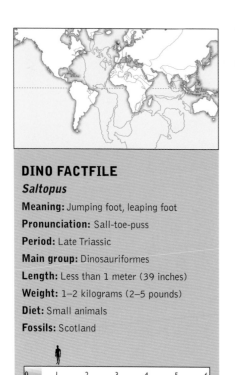

DINO FACTFILE

Saltopus

Meaning: Jumping foot, leaping foot

Pronunciation: Sall-toe-puss

Period: Late Triassic

Main group: Dinosauriformes

Length: Less than 1 meter (39 inches)

Weight: 1–2 kilograms (2–5 pounds)

Diet: Small animals

Fossils: Scotland

0	1	2	3	4	5	6

If a fairly complete skeleton of this dinosaur had been found, it might be famous today as one of the smallest dinosaurs-like fossils. But remains are too broken and incomplete to form a reasonable picture of *Saltopus*, and how it might have survived in the Late Triassic period, some 225–220 million years ago. What are believed to be preserved bones of one individual were found in the Elgin region of Scotland, an area well known for fossils. *Saltopus* is now generally regarded as a primitive dinosauriform, not a true dinosaur, but cloesely related to forms such as *Lagosuchus* from the Mid Triassic of Argentina.

The remains of *Saltopus*, scarce though they are, suggest that it was a very slight, lightly built theropod – a predatory dinosaur that walked and ran mainly on its two longer rear legs. Its length and height overall were probably less, and its build much slimmer, than those of a modern cat. Its hip region shows that four of the five sacral vertebrae (backbones) were fused to the pelvis (hipbone), unlike those of other small predatory dinosaurs of the time, such as *Procompsognathus*, which had five fused or sacral vertebrae. However, *Saltopus* had five digits at the end of each forelimb, a relatively primitive feature, although the fourth and fifth digits were tiny. The general evolutionary trend of theropods losing digits continued through the Age of Dinosaurs, eventually leading to forelimbs with just two digits. *Saltopus* must have been quick and agile, able to dart after small prey like insects and baby reptiles.

RIGHT *Saltopus* is one of the smallest dinosaurs known, but its fossils are too incomplete to permit a confident reconstruction. It was probably only 25 centimeters (10 inches) tall when in its upright "standing" pose.

PROCOMPSOGNATHUS

In 1913, German paleontologist Eberhard Fraas gave fragmentary remains uncovered near Wittenberge (north of Berlin, Germany) the name *Procompsognathus*. It may suggest that this dinosaur was some kind of predecessor to the small and well-known *Compsognathus* ("pretty jaw" or "elegant jaw"). Despite the fossils of both dinosaurs being found in the same general region, and the two being similar in shape, an enormous gap of 70 million years separates them: *Procompsognathus* dates from the Late Triassic period, some 220 million years ago, and *Compsognathus* dates from about 155–150 million years ago (see page 80). The similarity in the name is, therefore, purely symbolic and does not indicate that *Procompsognathus* was a direct or even indirect ancestor of the better-known *Compsognathus*.

Procompsognathus was probably somewhat larger than its much later part-namesake.

It was a lightweight, fast-running hunter of small prey like grubs, bugs and small vertebrates such as newly hatched reptiles. Its environment was dry, with sparse plant life forming scrubby bushland. The long rear legs attest to speed and agility, with only three of the four digits on each foot contacting the ground. The forelimbs were much shorter, but *Procompsognathus* had four strong digits on each of them, which it probably used for grabbing and perhaps tearing up victims.

The head was long and narrow, with a pointed snout, and the jaws had numerous small teeth, unsuited for heavy work such as gnawing carcasses. The tail was narrow and tapering, forming half the entire length of the creature. The structure of the caudal vertebrae (bones in the tail) suggests that the whole tail was relatively stiff, and could not be swished or whipped with flexibility like a length of rope.

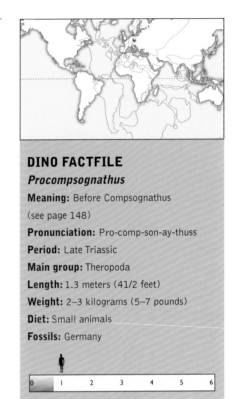

DINO FACTFILE
Procompsognathus

Meaning: Before Compsognathus (see page 148)

Pronunciation: Pro-comp-son-ay-thuss

Period: Late Triassic

Main group: Theropoda

Length: 1.3 meters (41/2 feet)

Weight: 2–3 kilograms (5–7 pounds)

Diet: Small animals

Fossils: Germany

0	1	2	3	4	5	6

RIGHT *Procompsognathus* was about the same weight as a pet cat of today, but much slimmer and more than twice a typical cat's nose-tail length. Its S-shaped neck allowed the head to dart in almost any direction.

COELURUS

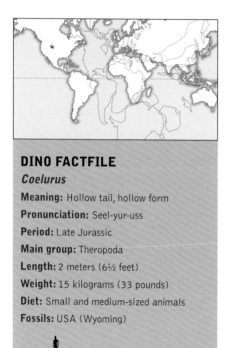

DINO FACTFILE
Coelurus
Meaning: Hollow tail, hollow form
Pronunciation: Seel-yur-uss
Period: Late Jurassic
Main group: Theropoda
Length: 2 meters (6½ feet)
Weight: 15 kilograms (33 pounds)
Diet: Small and medium-sized animals
Fossils: USA (Wyoming)

0		1	2	3	4	5	6

This dinosaur's name – meaning "hollow form" in Latin – refers to its tube-like bones, which were thinly walled with chambers inside, saving weight while preserving much of their strength – a feature that other small theropod dinosaurs shared with today's birds. *Coelurus* has lent its name to several groupings of theropod dinosaurs; generally similar types of small predators have been referred to as "coelurosaurs," a convenient but loose term for a mixed bag. More precisely, though, the name Coelurosauria has been applied to small theropods surviving from Late Jurassic times through most of the Cretaceous period following. The family had a worldwide distribution, and it included such well-known forms as *Compsognathus* and *Orthitholestes*, as well as many more obscure types. But recent views have described the coelurosauria as a larger, more encompassing group that gave rise to several different subgroups, such as the huge tyrannosaurs, the ostrich-like ornithomimosaurs, and maniraptorans such as *Deinonychus*.

(*Coelurosauravus* was a different type of reptile, a lizard-like glider, see page 38.)

Despite this fame, *Coelurus* itself is poorly known. It was used as the basis for grouping similar dinosaurs because it was one of the first of these general types to receive an official scientific name. In 1879, Othniel Charles Marsh, an eminent American dinosaur-hunter, coined the name Coelurus for remains 155–145 million years old found in Wyoming. A composite picture of *Coelurus* shows that it had a small, low head about 20 centimeters (8 inches) long, a flexible neck and a long, slim tail. The three large, strong, clawed digits on each forelimb must have had a powerful grasping grip. The femur (thighbone) measures some 55 centimeters (22 inches) in length, giving clues to the overall proportions of a light but strongly built theropod that moved on its rear legs. It probably fed on large insects, small vertebrates such as lizards or frogs and, perhaps, some of the small mammals of the time in the Late Jurassic forests and swamps of this American region.

RIGHT The strong fingers and sharp claws on the forelimbs of *Coelurus* would have been useful tools for scrabbling after and grabbing small prey items like insects and worms.

ORNITHOLESTES

Ornitholestes was given its name – "bird robber" – because it was thought that it may have chased and eaten early types of birds, like *Archaeopteryx*. These lived at about the same time, 150 million years ago, but their fossil sites are separated by thousands of kilometers. Only one main specimen of *Ornitholestes* is known, an almost complete skeleton recovered in 1900 from the famous site of Bone Cabin Quarry near Como Bluff, Wyoming. The fossils were studied and named in 1903 by the legendary paleontologist Henry Fairfield Osborn, director of the American Museum of Natural History, with a follow-up report of further studies in 1916. Only a handful of very limited specimens, such as parts of a forelimb, are known from other individuals.

Ornitholestes is usually viewed as a coelurosaurian, a cousin of *Coelurus* (see opposite). It was a lightweight, speedy theropod (predatory, or meat-eating dinosaur) that walked and ran on its slim but strong and long back legs. Its forelimbs were also long and powerful, with relatively massive "hands" with amazingly lengthy digits, comparable in size to the forearms. Each of the three digits had a sharply hooked claw, suggesting that *Ornitholestes* used them to catch and tear up its victims. The jaws could open wide to reveal small, sharp, well-spaced teeth, although only in the front half – the rear of each jaw was toothless. Two other features of *Ornitholestes* are also notable. Some reconstructions show a thin flange of bone on the snout, like a rounded nose crest, flattened from side to side which was perhaps a visual sign of maturity; and the tail of *Ornitholestes* was exceptionally long and whippy, forming more than half the total length of this dinosaur. The teeth were slightly unusual – those at the front of the mouth were almost conical in shape, while those farther back were more blade-like.

DINO FACTFILE
Ornitholestes

Meaning: Bird robber, bird thief
Pronunciation: Or-nith-owe-less-teez
Period: Late Jurassic
Main group: Theropoda
Length: 2.2 meters (7½ feet)
Weight: 15 kilograms (33 pounds)
Diet: Small and medium animals
Fossils: USA (Wyoming)

COMPSOGNATHUS

DINO FACTFILE

Compsognathus

Meaning: Pretty jaw, elegant mouth

Pronunciation: Comp-son-nay-thuss

Period: Late Jurassic

Main group: Theropoda

Length: 1.3 meters (4½ feet)

Weight: 3 kilograms (6½ pounds)

Diet: Small animals

Fossils: Germany, France

Among dinosaur afficionados, this tiny theropod has an enormous reputation as one of the smallest dinosaurs known from reasonably complete remains. There are two main fossil specimens. The smaller one, which has a total length of 70 centimeters (27½ inches), was perhaps a partly grown individual. It was excavated in the late 1850s in the Riedenberg area of Bavaria in southern Germany. The larger and probably full-grown individual was uncovered in 1972 from Var, near Nice, in southern France. It has an overall length of some 1.3 meters (4½ feet).

Compsognathus was not only small, it had an extremely light build, so it probably weighed just 2–3 kilograms (5–7 pounds). It was long thought that its hands had just two fingers, with slightly curved claws, and this is reflected in restorations and illustrations. However, new evidence shows the hands were probably three-fingered, with the first digit or thumb larger and thicker than the other two. Its head was long and low; the skull was mainly struts with spaces for flesh between them, rather than large plates of bone; and the relatively small jaws could be described as "elegant" (hence the dinosaur's name). The teeth were tiny and evenly spaced. The rear legs were also slim, with relatively short thighs and shins, but very long feet – the proportions of a rapid runner. Both the neck and tail were also long and their joints show they were flexible.

The overall impression of *Composognathus* is of a fast, lean, agile creature that could dart and twist at speed when chasing prey, dash into the undergrowth, or hide in narrow rock crevices to escape enemies such as bigger dinosaurs. There is evidence of diet in the German specimen: fossilized remains of a small lizard, *Bavarisaurus*, were found preserved within the body of *Compsognathus*.

LEFT The body of *Compsognathus* was about the same length and weight as a domestic cat today.

BELOW The snout shape and proportions of the arms and legs are reasonably known from the few fossils of *Dromaeosaurus* discovered. The rest of the reconstruction relies on information borrowed from others in its group. Following its initial discovery, this dinosaur was thought to be a larger version of *Coelurus*.

DROMAEOSAURUS

The dromaeosaurs, or "running reptiles," were named after this dinosaur, which was one of the first in the group to be described but is still one of the least understood. Barnum Brown, a respected fossil-finder of his time, dug up the first remains of *Dromaeosaurus* near Alberta's Red Deer River in 1914. Together with William Diller Matthew, Brown named this dinosaur in 1922, but on scanty evidence only – some skull and lower jaw parts, plus a few limb and foot bones. The situation changed drastically in the 1960s with the discovery of *Deinonychus* (see page 83) and subsequent discussions about intelligence, warm-bloodedness and, recently, whether the covering was feathers and not scales. By comparing the detailed fossils of *Deinonychus* with the less conclusive material for *Dromaeosaurus*, scientists were able to establish the *Dromaeosaurus* group as fast, powerful, predatory dinosaurs, but still under

the original name of dromaeosaurs. The more familiar or colloquial term for these dinosaurs is "raptors", since the group also includes *Velociraptor*, *Utahraptor*, *Microraptor* and others.

Working backward from today's richer picture of the dromaeosaur group helps to fill some gaps in knowledge about *Dromaeosaurus* itself. It had a big head with large eyes, a tall and rounded snout, and powerful jaws bristling with fang-like teeth. The forelimbs were probably smaller than the rear limbs, but still powerful, and with sharply clawed digits. The rear limbs were also strong, suitable for running and leaping. The second digit of each foot bore the huge, curved "sickle claw" that is a major feature of the group. In overall size, *Dromaeosaurus* was comparable to *Velociraptor* (see page 84), being smaller than *Deinonychus* and especially *Utahraptor* (see page 82). It lived 75–72 million years ago.

DINO FACTFILE

Dromaeosaurus

Meaning: Running reptile, swift reptile

Pronunciation: Drom-ay-owe-sore-uss

Period: Late Cretaceous

Main group: Theropoda

Length: 1.7 meters (5½ feet)

Weight: 15 kilograms (33 pounds)

Diet: Animals, carrion

Fossils: Midwestern USA, Canada (Alberta)

| 0 | 1 | 2 | 3 | 4 | 5 | 6 |

UTAHRAPTOR

DINO FACTFILE

Utahraptor

Meaning: Utah thief, Utah hunter
(from its discovery site)

Pronunciation: You-taw-rap-tore

Period: Early Cretaceous

Main group: Theropoda

Length: 5–6 meters (16–20 feet)

Weight: 500 kilograms (1,100 pounds)

Diet: Larger animals

Fossils: USA (Utah)

0	1	2	3	4	5	6

This hunter is one of the most recently discovered and largest of the dromaeosaurs, or "raptors." It shot to fame in the early 1990s as a result of fact following fiction. The clever, co-operative dinosaurs of the 1993 movie *Jurassic Park* are based on smaller dromaeosaurs, such as *Velociraptor* and *Deinonychus*, but to make them a match for human adversaries they were enlarged to slightly more than the height of an adult person and to several meters (yards) in length. During production of the movie, in 1991, fossil remains of just such a raptor were uncovered in eastern Utah, giving a factual basis for *Jurassic Park's* fearsome monsters.

Several further part-specimens of *Utahraptor* have been identified in the past few years at various North American sites. Combined with knowledge from other raptors, *Utahraptor* is reconstructed as a powerful predator, fairly light and fast for its overall length and height, with rows of sharp, curved fangs, each around the size of a human thumb, in its jaws. It was twice the length of *Deinonychus* (see opposite) and weighed perhaps ten times more. Like other dromaeosaurs, it possessed a huge "sickle claw" on the second digit of each hind foot, which could be flicked around in a slashing arc.

At more than 20 centimeters (8 inches) long, this claw was longer than most human hands. Presumably *Utahraptor* kicked and sliced at big prey to gash them open. Its fossils date to the Early and mid-Cretaceous period – 120–110 million years ago – making it one of the earliest known dromaeosaurs. It was probably a hunter of weaker plant-eating dinosaurs, such as sauropods or ornithopods, able to tackle prey larger than itself. This dinosaur also throws new light on how the raptor group may have evolved. The main fossils come from rocks known as the Cedar Mountain Formation in central Utah, and the name was given in 1993 by James Kirkland, Robert Gaston and Donald Burge.

LEFT No feathers have been found associated with *Utahraptor* remains, but as a dromaeosaurid it may have had some kind of feathery covering.

DEINONYCHUS

In 1964, John Ostrom, Grant Meyer and a team of excavators were exploring a new fossil site in southern Montana. Over the next few years, they recovered many specimens, but most exciting were the remains of a medium-sized theropod (predatory, or meat-eating dinosaur). Several good skeletons from 115–110 million years ago rendered a detailed reconstruction of this hunter, *Deinonychus*, with its powerful yet agile physique, wide and gaping jaws armed with saw-edged fangs, large strong "hands" for a vice-like grip, and straight, stiff tail. The vicious extra-large "terrible claw" that gives this dinosaur its name was on the second digit of each foot, and could be flicked around in a slicing motion like a knife. Further remains were uncovered in Wyoming, and the study of these remarkable finds continued for several years.

In 1969, John Ostrom's reports on *Deinonychus* caused a sensation. Suddenly, it appeared that not all dinosaurs were cold-blooded, slow and stupid! Several lines of evidence suggested that *Deinonychus* and its kin were fast movers, with great leaping ability, quick reactions and relatively big brains. It even was suggested that they were capable of learned, intelligent behavior, and perhaps, were warm-blooded, too. Although debate continues, on the issues of intelligence and warm-bloodedness in particular, the perception of dinosaurs among the general public, and certain scientists, was revolutionized forever. One interpretation of *Deinonychus* fossils *in situ* (as they were found) suggests that raptors coordinated their attacks on larger prey. The site includes the remains of a potential victim, a one metric ton ornithopod dinosaur named *Tenontosaurus*. Did the hunters gather to leap upon and slash open the plant-eater, as a pack of wolves today might surround a deer, or a pride of lionesses bring down a wildebeest?

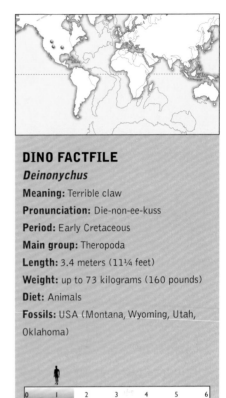

DINO FACTFILE
Deinonychus
Meaning: Terrible claw
Pronunciation: Die-non-ee-kuss
Period: Early Cretaceous
Main group: Theropoda
Length: 3.4 meters (11¼ feet)
Weight: up to 73 kilograms (160 pounds)
Diet: Animals
Fossils: USA (Montana, Wyoming, Utah, Oklahoma)

| 0 | 1 | 2 | 3 | 4 | 5 | 6 |

LEFT Although no *Deinonychus* remains have been found with feathers, it is reconstructed here as a dromaeosaurid with a feathery body covering and feathers on the arms.

RIGHT The head crest of *Oviraptor philoceratops* is shown clearly in this illustration. *Oviraptors* were one of the most bird-like of the non-avian dinosaurs which probably had an extensive covering of feathers.

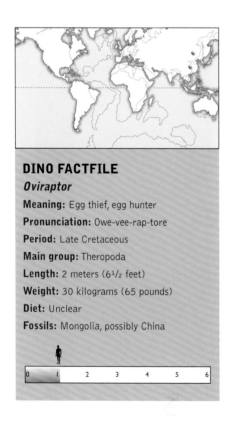

DINO FACTFILE
Oviraptor

Meaning: Egg thief, egg hunter

Pronunciation: Owe-vee-rap-tore

Period: Late Cretaceous

Main group: Theropoda

Length: 2 meters (6½ feet)

Weight: 30 kilograms (65 pounds)

Diet: Unclear

Fossils: Mongolia, possibly China

0	1	2	3	4	5	6

OVIRAPTOR

This dinosaur was given its name, meaning "egg thief," because one set of its fossils was found associated with remains of dinosaur eggs. George Olsen made the find in 1923, during one of the expeditions to Asia organized by the American Museum of Natural History. Experts concluded that this *Oviraptor* perished while raiding the nest of another dinosaur, and the strange head and jaws of this dinosaur support such an idea. The skull was tall, with deep jaws shaped like the pointed beak of a bird like a parrot. The jaws lacked teeth but were suited to exerting great pressure along their edges to crack hard objects, like nuts – or eggs. Also interesting was the tall, thin, curved crest on the snout, which varied between the two species of *Oviraptor*: one, *Oviraptor philoceratops*, had a snout crest shaped like a parallelogram (a skewed or distorted rectangle); the other, *Oviraptor mongoliensis*, had a taller, more rounded crest (see also *Ajancingenia*, opposite). The rest of *Oviraptor's* body was fairly typical of many small theropods – long, slim, rear legs for running, and large forelimbs, each ending in three elongated, powerful digits tipped with sharp claws. The neck and tail, however, were less lengthy than in many comparable theropods.

The situation became clearer in the 1990s with further discoveries of *Oviraptor* fossils, in Mongolia and China, again associated with egg remains. But the evidence this time was more of a dinosaur tending its own nest, rather than stealing from the nests of others. In one find, the preserved skeleton of a tiny *Oviraptor* embryo was lying in fragments of shell. In another, it appeared that an *Oviraptor*-type adult had died while extending its forelimbs over 22 eggs in the nest, perhaps as protection against a rainstorm or a predator. However, there are disputes over whether these newer finds represent *Oviraptor* or another similar genus (see also *Protoceratops*, page 249).

AJANCINGENIA

This dinosaur is usually called an oviraptorid, meaning that it has many similarities with, and may be a close cousin of, *Oviraptor* (opposite). *Ajancingenia* was perhaps slightly smaller, nearer 1.5 meters (5 feet) in total length. Most of its known bodily features are reminiscent of *Oviraptor*, and it lived at about the same time, around 80 million years ago, and in the same region, now Mongolia. It received its official name in 1981. Like *Oviraptor*, *Ajancingenia*'s diet remains something of a mystery. It may have been an omnivore, pecking at and cracking open all kinds of food, including bugs, eggs, hard-cased animals like shellfish or snails, other small animals and even roots and seeds. Or it may have scavenged meat and bone from carcasses, as vultures and condors do today, or pecked at vegetation. The beak-like jawbone was probably covered with a horny layer or sheath, as in birds today, maybe providing an

even more sharply edged and hook-shaped eating tool.

Oviraptor is the better-known theropod. Certain fossil skulls with deep, toothless, parrot-like, beaked jaws similar to an *Oviraptor*'s, but with very small snout crests or no crest at all, were once identified as young *Oviraptor*. The reasoning was that features such as crests and horns, in prehistoric creatures as in today's animals, would be relatively very small in juveniles and grow faster as the individual matured. However, other details of these skulls led to some of them being assigned to the newer genus *Ajancingenia*. In recent years renewed studies of the fossils of *Ajancingenia*, coupled with new knowledge about how beaks work in living birds, favors the plant-eating view.

BELOW The powerful hooked beak of *Ajancingenia* could have tackled many kinds of hard foods, from nuts and seeds, to the stringy gristle and marrow-filled bones of small mammals. One suggestion is that *Ajancingenia* hunted in shallow water for crustacean animals such as freshwater shrimps and crayfish. Another is an herbivorous diet of tough plant parts like roots and wood-cased, sappy stems.

ANIMAL FACTFILE
Ajancingenia
Meaning: From the area of its discovery, Ingeni-Khobur Depression in Mongolia
Pronunciation: A-jan-sin-gen-ee-a
Period: Late Cretaceous
Main group: Theropoda
Length: 1.5–2 meters (5–6½ feet)
Weight: 25 kilograms (55 pounds)
Diet: Uncertain
Fossils: Mongolia

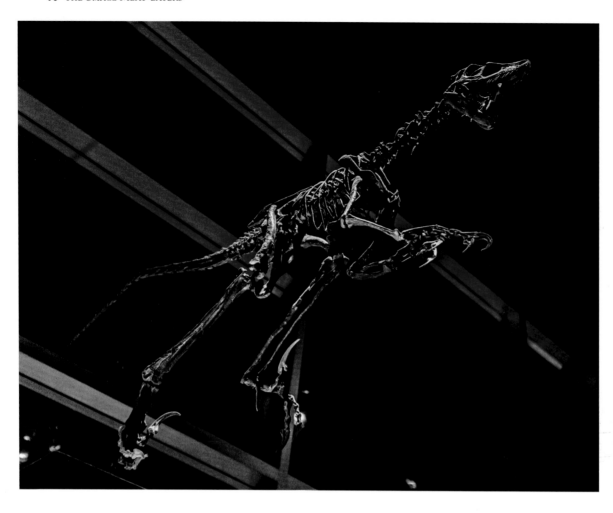

LEFT A fine action-posed skeleton of *Saurornitholestes* from the Royal Tyrrell Museum in Alberta, Canada, near the region of its discovery.

SAURORNITHOLESTES

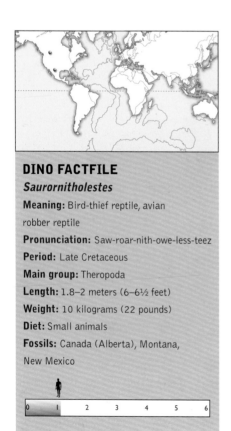

DINO FACTFILE

Saurornitholestes

Meaning: Bird-thief reptile, avian robber reptile

Pronunciation: Saw-roar-nith-owe-less-teez

Period: Late Cretaceous

Main group: Theropoda

Length: 1.8–2 meters (6–6½ feet)

Weight: 10 kilograms (22 pounds)

Diet: Small animals

Fossils: Canada (Alberta), Montana, New Mexico

The fast-moving, meat-eating *Saurornitholestes* was a member of the dromaeosaur or "raptor" group that lived in North America during the last phase of the Cretaceous Period, its fossils dated to 75–73 million years ago. This was a time when the great predatory dinosaurs, such as the fearsome *Albertosaurus* and the even mightier *Tyrannosaurus*, roamed what is now North America. *Saurornitholestes* was hundreds of times smaller than these giants, and would have stood only waist-high to an adult human being. Nevertheless, it was just as deadly to its victims, which were probably small vertebrates like lizards, snakes or frogs, and perhaps birds, as well as mammals about the size of rats, that are known to have been present in the region around this time.

Saurornitholestes bore some similarities to *Velociraptor* (see page 84), and has been viewed as its North American counterpart. Hans-Dieter Sues named *Saurornitholestes* in 1978, more than 50 years later than *Velociraptor* was named. The main fossils

recovered include parts of the skull, some teeth, and parts of forelimb bones. It is a reasonable assumption that *Saurornitholestes* was bipedal, moving only on its long, strong but slender, rear limbs. Its total length approached 2 meters (6½ feet). Estimates of its build and weight vary, due to the incompleteness of its remains, from five kilograms (11 pounds) to four times that much. Another, earlier suggestion was that *Saurornitholestes* was more like *Troodon* (see page 84), with powerful grasping hands, and perhaps a large brain capable of learning and relatively intelligent behavior. Further studies showed greater similarities with *Velociraptor* than with *Troodon*.

CHIROSTENOTES

This powerfully built theropod dinosaur was long a mystery, known only from fossilized bones discovered in Alberta's Red Deer River region, and named by American fossil expert Charles Gilmore in 1924. The find included bones from its forelimbs, each of which had three extremely elongated, clawed digits, the middle one being even longer than the other two. For many years, there was very little further information on these strangely proportioned remains of *Chirostenotes*. There were attempts to link them to some teeth and part of a lower jaw, found some miles away in the same rock layers, and dating back almost to the end of the Cretaceous period. These would fill out the picture and assign *Chirostenotes* to the caenagnathid oviraptosaurs group, along with *Caenagnathus* and *Oviraptor*. Other experts have linked oviraptorosaurs such as *Chirostenotes* with the therizinosaurs but this has been challenged.

In 1932 Charles Sternberg named another group of fossils Macrophalangia ("big toes"). They were noted as being very similar to, and have since been reclassified as, *Chirostenotes*. Also, parts of other skeletons have become involved, including one that had lain largely unprepared in a museum, still in rock as dug from the ground, for 60 years. These "new" fossils provided parts of the skull, pieces from most sections of the long spinal column (backbone), and parts of the hip region. One current view is that *Chirostenotes* may have been more similar to *Oviraptor*, with a bird-like head, a beak like a parrot's, sturdy rear limbs and powerful forelimbs. The mystery has yet to be conclusively solved.

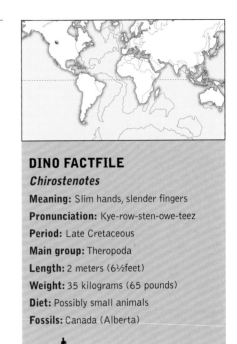

DINO FACTFILE
Chirostenotes

Meaning: Slim hands, slender fingers
Pronunciation: Kye-row-sten-owe-teez
Period: Late Cretaceous
Main group: Theropoda
Length: 2 meters (6½ feet)
Weight: 35 kilograms (65 pounds)
Diet: Possibly small animals
Fossils: Canada (Alberta)

0	1	2	3	4	5	6

LEFT This reconstruction of *Chirostenotes* follows the modern view that it was an oviraptorosaurid, with a deep, hooked, beak-like mouth and tall, thin skull crest. There have been several other possibilities over the years, including the suggestion that Ingenia was a type of dromaeosaur or "raptor" like Deinonychus.

Avimimus

The idea that some dinosaurs had body coverings of feathers, not scales, has made a huge impact in the past few years. An earlier suggestion that this might have been the case came in 1981, when Sergei Mikhailovich Kurzanov, a Russian dinosaur expert, described and named *Avimimus*. He based his description on fossils found in the Omnogov region of Mongolia during the extensive expeditions mounted in the Gobi and surrounding areas in the 1970s jointly by Soviet and Mongolian investigators.

Kurzanov identified several close similarities between *Avimimus* and birds, including the toothless beak; long skull; slim and flexible neck; muscle scars on the humerus (upper forelimb bone); arm joints that allowed the forelimb to fold like a wing (see page 75); a deep, compact body; and fused bones in the upper foot. One piece of evidence Kurzanov highlighted was a ridge running along the ulna, one of the bones of the forelimb. Unknown in other theropods, this ridge happened to be in the same position where a modern bird's equivalent bone would have a row of tiny knobs, like pimples. They are called papillae and are small mounds where the muscles that move (tilt and twist) the feathers are anchored to the bone. Kurzanov's conclusion was that *Avimimus* had feathers, at least along this part of the forelimb. No imprints, however, or signs of feathers were found among the fossilized remains. *Avimimus* thus blazed a trail, of sorts, for the notion of feathered dinosaurs. From the mid 1990s, discoveries of feathered dinosaurs came thick and fast, and the concept is now generally accepted.

Avimimus probably ran at speed in the open countryside of the region, about 83 million years ago, snapping up small animals with its powerful beak. It remains something of a puzzle, and the evidence for its feathers is still conjectural. But even with feathers, the forelimbs are too small and weak for powered, sustained flight, so perhaps the feathers performed another function. They may have helped to insulate the warm-blooded body, or worked as some kind of trap for flying prey such as dragonflies.

DINO FACTFILE

Avimimus

Meaning: Bird mimic, bird pretender

Pronunciation: Aye-vee-mim-uss

Period: Late Cretaceous

Main group: Theropoda

Length: 1.6 meters (5½ feet)

Weight: 10–15 kilograms (22–33 pounds)

Diet: Small animals, perhaps seeds and plants

Fossils: Mongolia, China

RIGHT The presence of feathers on the bird-like *Avimimus* is now widely accepted, but most paleontologists do not believe this dinosaur could fly.

ABOVE *Sinosauropyteryx* probably grabbed smaller creatures like mammals and lizards as prey. Its feathery covering resembled the fine, hairy "down" which baby birds possess to keep their bodies warm.

SINOSAUROPTERYX

The rural Chinese province of Liaoning, north of Beijing, has yielded some of the most exciting dinosaur finds since about 1994. One is *Sinosauropteryx*, which in some respects is a fairly standard *Compsognathus*-like theropod dinosaur from about 120 million years ago. It was small and lightly built, with long rear limbs for walking and running, short forelimbs, and a long tail, which helped to balance the body when *Sinosauropteryx* was sprinting. But there was a surprise. The very finely grained rocks in which the remains were found had allowed detailed preservation, including impressions that looked like feathers. These were not the fully formed, wide-vaned feathers that modern birds use for flight and outer body covering, but smaller, downier or hair-like "plumes," each about ½ centimeter (¼ inch) long. The fossils showed these feather traces mainly on the animal's neck and shoulders, and also along the back and parts of the tail.

The first discovered specimen of *Sinosauropteryx* was probably a juvenile, about 55 centimeters (22 inches) in total length, half of this being the tail. Chinese fossil experts Ji Qiang and Ji Shu-An described and named it in 1996. Soon after, paleontologists uncovered another larger and probably fully-grown specimen. It too had impressions of feathers. What looked like the remains of a small mammal, with jaws and teeth and other parts, were preserved with it, and are probably evidence of the dinosaur's diet.

The role of the feathers has been much discussed. They might have been for insulation, to retain body heat, which would imply that *Sinosauropteryx* was warm-blooded – a view gaining new acceptance. They may have been brightly colored, perhaps to attract a mate at breeding time, or dull in color, to blend in with the surroundings for camouflage.

DINO FACTFILE
Sinosauropteryx

Meaning: China's winged or feathered reptile

Pronunciation: Sye-no-saw-op-tur-icks

Period: Early Cretaceous

Main group: Theropoda

Length: 1 meter (39 inches)

Weight: 0.5 kilograms (1¼ pounds)

Diet: Small animals

Fossils: China

RIGHT The fanned, vaned feathers of *Caudipteryx* were located on the forelimbs and tail. Their size and detailed shape, coupled with the size and muscular power of the forelimbs, show that this dinosaur was not capable of flight. The function(s) of the feathers remain a mystery.

CAUDIPTERYX

DINO FACTFILE
Caudipteryx
Meaning: Tail wing, tail feather
Pronunciation: Cawd-ip-tur-icks
Period: Early Cretaceous
Main group: Theropoda
Length: 80 centimeters (31 inches)
Weight: 2.5 kilograms (6 pounds)
Diet: Varied, perhaps animals and plants
Fossils: China

This creature has been the subject of great discussion since the description of its fossils, from Liaoning Province in China, in 1998. It has been identified variously as a very unusual offshoot of the main group of small theropods, or as a flightless descendant of as-yet-unknown dinosaurs, or even a descendent of birds that evolved from flying to flightless. *Caudipteryx* lived slightly later than *Archaeopteryx*, the earliest fully flying bird, so it could not have been an ancestor to that group. Likely it was a member of a group of dinosaurs that left no descendants, whether among reptiles or among birds.

The mix of features in this animal is certainly confusing. Some of its skeleton is similar in structure and proportions to a generalized small predatory dinosaur. But the tail is extremely short, and the forelimbs are too, although *Caudipteryx* had three long, clawed digits on each, just as did many other dinosaurs. The head is long and the mouth

has a curved beak, like *Oviraptor* (see page 88). There are teeth at the front of the upper jaw, but they are sharp and stick out slightly, almost like a fringe. The legs are long and slim for fast movement, and some of their bones and joints are again reminiscent of *Oviraptor*, while other parts are said to be more like a typical (modern) bird's legs.

Perhaps the weirdest feature is the feathers. On the forelimbs and tail these have vanes and quills, generally like a bird's flight feathers. Those at the end of the tail are up to 20 centimeters (8 inches) long and spread out in a fan shape. Yet the feathers were not shaped in detail like true flight feathers, and the size and power of the forelimbs show that *Caudipteryx* was not capable of flying. The main body seems to have been covered in fluff or fibrous downy feathers, like *Sinosauropteryx* (see page 93).

THERIZINOSAURUS

In the late 1940s, a joint Soviet–Mongolian fossil-hunting expedition to the Gobi Desert yielded some amazing bony claws of huge size. They were thought to come from a dinosaur or similar large beast, and this otherwise unknown animal was named *Therizinosaurus* – "scythe reptile" – in 1954. More claws turned up in Central Asia during the 1950s and 1960s, as well as parts of a forelimb skeleton and a few fragments of hind limb. Then, finds in China led experts to conclude that the bones belonged to a group of similar dinosaurs, which became known collectively as therizinosaurs and which include the 1993 find, *Alaxasaurus*, and *Beipiaosaurus*, found in 1996. These later finds helped to fill in parts of the picture – and the results are truly astonishing. *Therizinosaurus* was an enormous theropod dinosaur, meaning that it fits in with the group of meat-eaters, yet it may have lived more like a giraffe or a gorilla, consuming only plants.

Therizinosaurus dates to 75–70 million years ago and was one of the later representatives of its group. The three digits on the forelimb each had a massive claw, slightly curved and flattened, and tapered to a sharp point. But the first digit bore the largest claw – more than 60 centimeters (23 inches) in length – and the whole forelimb was 2.5 meters (8 feet) long. The neck was immense, the head small with a beaked mouth, the body deep, the hips wide, and the rear limbs sturdy, with broad, short feet each ending in four digits. *Therizinosaurus* may have been huge, more than 10 meters (33 feet) in length or height, and covered in downy feathers.

Therizinosaur behavior is hotly debated. Perhaps they craned their long necks to peck and grab at fruit and other vegetation in trees. The claws may have been used as rakes to gather food, as defensive weapons, or as signs of social status and sexual maturity (like a walrus's tusks), or to rip open termite and ant nests, in the manner of the great-clawed giant anteater today. Other "scythe reptiles" included *Segnosaurus*, *Nanshiungosaurus*, *Erlikosaurus* and *Enigmosaurus*. The evidence for a feathery covering is mainly from fossils of *Beipiaosaurus*.

DINO FACTFILE
Therizinosaurus
Meaning: Scythe reptile
Pronunciation: There-iz-in-owe-sore-uss
Period: Late Cretaceous
Main group: Theropoda
Length: 10-plus meters (33-plus feet)
Weight: About 1 metric ton (1 ton)
Diet: Perhaps plants
Fossils: Central and East Asia

LEFT One of the strangest of all dinosaurs, *Therizinosaurus* is sometimes reconstructed with a scaly covering, as here, and sometimes with feathers. The largest of the "scythe" claws were each as long as a human arm and hand.

ARCHAEOPTERYX

BIRD FACTFILE
Archaeopteryx
Meaning: Ancient wing
Pronunciation: Ark-ee-op-tur-icks
Period: Late Jurassic
Main group: Avialae
Length: Beak to tail 60 centimeters
(24 inches)
Wingspan: 70 centimeters (28 inches)
Diet: Insects and other small animals
Fossils: Germany

Almost every year, prehistory records are broken as yet bigger, earlier or stranger creatures are discovered and described. The time may come when *Archaeopteryx* loses its perch, but for now it remains the earliest known representative of the birds – a group whose definition becomes more blurred with every year. *Archaeopteryx* is known from 11 fossils, one being just a feather, and another being a spectacular and beautiful specimen showing the whole creature with outstretched wings, feathers, skull, body, legs and tail in glorious detail. It was preserved in very finely grained limestone in the Solnhofen region of Bavaria in southern Germany. *Archaeopteryx* was given its name, meaning "ancient wing," by Hermann von Meyer, a

German paleontologist, in 1861.

For a long time, two other partial specimens of *Archaeopteryx* were long identified as small meat-eating or theropod dinosaurs, similar to *Compsognathus*, which lived around the same time and has been found in the same region. They were reassigned to *Archaeopteryx* in the 1950s and 1970s. This emphasized the similarity between certain theropods, especially the dinosaurs called raptors, and the bird group, as described on page 75. *Archaeopteryx* was a patchwork of features reptilian and avian. The latter included its beak-like mouth, forelimbs modified as wings, long feathers, and feet suited to perching, with a reversed hallux (rear-facing big toe). On the reptilian side, it had teeth in its jaws, claws on its three wing fingers, and a long tail of vertebral bones. Its feathers were not fluffy down but were fully adapted for flight, each with a central shaft and asymmetric vane, as in birds today. *Archaeopteryx* could probably fly, but not with the grace, agility or endurance of modern birds, as it ran, flapped and snapped at insects and similar small creatures.

RIGHT The feathers of this first known bird are fully designed for flight, and no earlier evidence has been found of part-evolved versions of *Archaeopteryx* – although there are many later specimens with a variety of feather designs.

CONFUCIUSORNIS

Named in honor of Confucius, the philosopher and teacher whose ideas have been dominant in China for two thousand years, this magpie-sized bird lived during the Early Cretaceous period, over 120 million years ago. There are some similarities between *Confuciusornis* and the much earlier *Archaeopteryx* (opposite). *Confuciusornis* retained reptilian skeletal features, such as clawed fingers and the detailed structure of its wrists and hips, but it had also developed avian (bird-like) features. It had no teeth in the horn-covered beak, but it did have sturdy clavicle bones (colloquially known in modern birds as the "wishbones") in the shoulders. Its tail was not a row of 20-plus vertebral bones, as in *Archaeopteryx*, but a short lump of fused-together bones, like the feature known in modern birds as the pygostyle (or "parson's nose").

Based on numerous and varied fossils from Liaoning (see page 98), it seems that *Confuciusornis* lived in colonies, was an able flier, and was adept at perching in trees. Although it lacked tailbones, it did have a tail. Feather impressions show that some individuals had very elongated tail feathers, shaped like long-stemmed paddles, while others lacked these and had rear ends covered in "normal" body feathers as in most modern birds. It is difficult to imagine a practical physical use for the long trailing tail feathers, whether for finding food or for avoiding enemies, so it is tempting, instead, to assume that the feathers were for visual display. In today's bird species, it is almost always the male that has extravagant plumage, which it uses to attract a female at breeding time. Perhaps the two types of *Confuciusornis* specimens represent males and females.

ABOVE *Confuciusornis* fossils resemble those of *Archaeopteryx* (one example is shown above) but are not so complete or detailed. The long bony tail of the latter was not present, replaced by a small lump of bone as in modern birds.

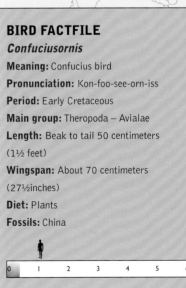

BIRD FACTFILE
Confuciusornis

Meaning: Confucius bird

Pronunciation: Kon-foo-see-orn-iss

Period: Early Cretaceous

Main group: Theropoda – Avialae

Length: Beak to tail 50 centimeters (1½ feet)

Wingspan: About 70 centimeters (27½inches)

Diet: Plants

Fossils: China

0 | 1 | 2 | 3 | 4 | 5 | 6

LIAONINGORNIS AND PROTARCHAEOPTERYX

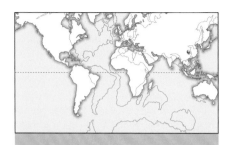

BIRD FACTFILE
Liaoningornis
Meaning: Liaoning bird
(from its discovery region)
Pronunciation: Lee-ah-hoh-nin-orn-iss
Period: Early Cretaceous
Main group: Theropoda – Avialae
Length: Beak to tail 10 centimeters
(3 inches)
Diet: Likely omnivorous
Fossils: China

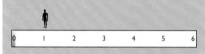

Since the 1990s, the province of Liaoning, in northeastern China, has been one of the "hot spots" for the discovery of fossils from the Age of Dinosaurs. They include *Confuciusornis* (see previous page), *Liaoningornis* and *Protarchaeopteryx*. At one site it seems that a disaster – probably a volcanic eruption – killed almost everything in the area, providing a "snapshot in time." At first, some experts dated the fossils as Late Jurassic, perhaps 150 million years old. Others, however, have estimated that they come from the Early Cretaceous period, 130–120 million years ago. In any case, the discoveries have caused intense debate. In particular, the fossils of both *Liaoningornis* and *Protarchaeopteryx* are difficult to interpret, and challenge many established ideas about reptiles and birds.

Liaoningornis was an early bird much the same size as a modern sparrow. It had a very deep keel – the flange on the sternum (breastbone) that anchors the main wing-flapping flight muscles. This feature and other details suggest that *Liaoningornis* was more like modern birds, and did not belong in the more ancient groups that include *Archaeopteryx* and *Confuciusornis*. If so, *Liaoningornis* may be the earliest truly "modern" bird. At first *Protarchaeopteryx* was also regarded as a bird and, as its name suggests, it had features that seemed to indicate that it was some kind of predecessor of *Archaeopteryx* (see page 96). It lived much later than *Archaeopteryx*, however, and it was probably not a bird, but an oviraptorosaurian dinosaur. This theropod (meat-eater) was unable to fly but possessed feathers on its arms, most of its body, and fanned out from its short tail. Perhaps they were for insulation of the warm-blooded body and/or for visual display during courtship (see page 94).

BIRD FACTFILE
Protarchaeopteryx
Meaning: Before Archaeopteryx
Pronunciation: Prote-ark-ee-op-tur-icks
Period: Early Cretaceous
Main group: Theropoda
Length: 70 centimeters (28 inches)
Diet: Probably small prey or omnivorous
Fossils: China

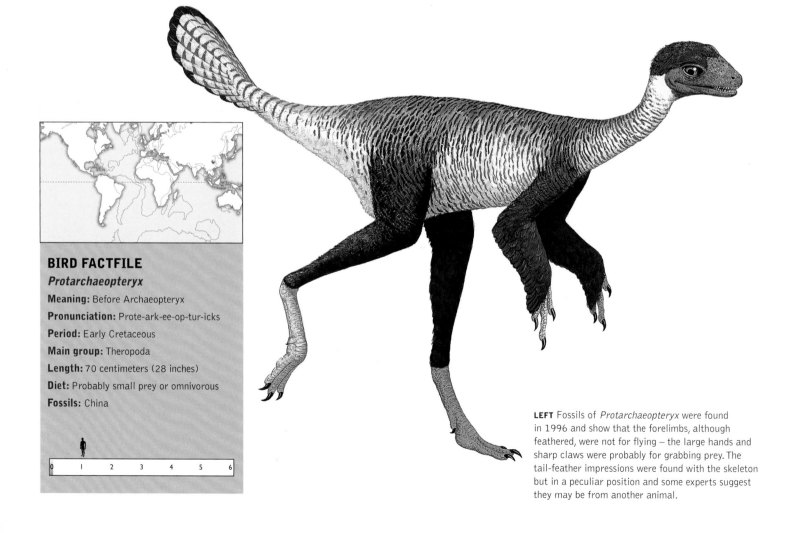

LEFT Fossils of *Protarchaeopteryx* were found in 1996 and show that the forelimbs, although feathered, were not for flying – the large hands and sharp claws were probably for grabbing prey. The tail-feather impressions were found with the skeleton but in a peculiar position and some experts suggest they may be from another animal.

ABOVE The all-important alula (bastard wing) of *Eoalulavis* is the small tuft toward the end of the leading edge of each main wing, supported by clawed digits. This feature is of great significance since it shows this small bird was an adept flier.

EOALULAVIS

This very small bird, similar in size to today's sparrow, was described in 1996 from fossils found in Spain. It is noted for being the earliest known type of bird to possess an alula, a feather or small feather group on the front or leading edge of the wing, positioned in the "thumb" region where the main leading edge angles back, as the bony skeletal part gives way to the large wingtip feathers. The alula is sometimes known as the "bastard wing" and is supported by the thumb (first digit) bone. The alula helps to adjust the airflow over the wing, especially at low speeds, giving much greater control of flight. (Airplanes extend flaps at the leading and also the trailing edges of their wing at low speeds, such as when landing, for the same effect.) All birds today retain the alula.

The fossil site of *Eoalulavis* consisted of a "pocket" of limestone rocks called Las Hoyas near Cuenca in Central Spain. Most of the remains found there date to around 115

million years ago and include dinosaurs, fish, amphibians, insects and crustaceans, which all lived in and around a lake.

Eoalulavis seems to have been on a side-branch of the main evolutionary groups that led to modern birds. Like *Iberomesornis* (page 100), it belongs to a subgroup known as the enantiornithes, or "opposite birds," meaning they had an arrangement of bones in the shoulder and chest, including the scapula (shoulder blade) and coracoid (wishbone), oriented in a pattern which mirrors that of modern birds. *Eoalulavis* probably lived much like a modern sparrow, in the Early Cretaceous period, hopping and flapping, and pecking at a variety of foods. Its large breast-bone had a broad area for anchoring the pectoral muscles, which pull the wings down strongly on their power stroke, showing that this little bird was a strong and able flier. The enantiornithes are believed to have become extinct around 70 million years ago.

BIRD FACTFILE
Eoalulavis

Meaning: Dawn little wing bird
Pronunciation: Ee-owe-all-you-lav-iss
Period: Early Cretaceous
Main group: Theropoda – Avialae
Length: 15 centimeters (6 inches)
Weight: About 50 grams
(2 ounces)
Diet: Omnivore
Fossils: Spain

| 0 | 1 | 2 | 3 | 4 | 5 | 6 |

ABOVE *Iberomesornis* could flap and flutter among the branches with reasonable ease as it searched for small creatures such as insects, which it grabbed in its spike-toothed beak.

IBEROMESORNIS

BIRD FACTFILE
Iberomesornis

Meaning: Iberian intermediate or middle bird

Pronunciation: Eye-bur-oh-mez-or-niss

Period: Early Cretaceous

Main group: Theropoda – Avialae

Length: Beak to tail 15 centimeters (6 inches)

Diet: Small animals such as insects, grubs

Fossils: Spain

One of the smaller birds from the dinosaur age, *Iberomesornis* was hardly the size of a sparrow or robin today, at 15 centimeters (6 inches) from tip of beak to end of tail. It was named in 1992 by José Luis Sanz and José Bonaparte after the fossil region of Spain, on the Iberian Peninsula of southwestern Europe, where it was found. Exactly where *Iberomesornis* fits in the scheme of bird evolution is debatable, since many early groups of birds seem to have been "dead ends," with no modern survivors.

One bird group is named the ornithothoraces, and their characteristic feature was the alula, a small tuft of feathers at the front or leading edge of the wing, which greatly aided low-speed flight and aerial agility – see *Eoalulavis* (page 99) for a fuller explanation. The alula is prominent in many modern aerobatic birds rather than high-soarers.

A subgroup of the ornithothoraces was the enantiornithes, which includes *Iberomesornis* and *Eoalulavis*. These were Cretaceous birds that showed some evolutionary change, especially during the early and middle part of that period, but which then seem to have died out. They differed from modern birds in the structure of their shoulder and chest regions, where the strut-like coracoid bone and the scapula or shoulder blade are positioned the other way around or opposite to modern birds – enantiornithes means "opposite birds." There are also differences from modern birds in the orientation of the bones that make up the hip. Most of the enantiornithes were toothless, but Iberomesornis had tiny, spiky teeth in its small bill. It was probably a reasonable flier and may have eaten small creatures like worms, grubs or bugs.

HESPERORNIS

One of the largest birds known to have lived during the dinosaur age was *Hesperornis*. It was given its name, which means "western bird," by Othniel Charles Marsh in 1872, after its fossil sites near the Smoky Hill River in Kansas. This makes it one of the earliest birds to receive a scientific name. *Hesperornis* dates from near the end of dinosaur times, the Late Cretaceous period. It stood at least 1 meter (39 inches) tall, and some estimates go as high as a modern adult human, at 1.8 meters (6 feet). It may seem odd that after millions of years developing flight in birds generally, *Hesperornis* had lost this ability, although its remains – which include almost all parts of the skull and skeleton in various specimens – show that it was descended from flying ancestors.

Hesperornis was a swimmer rather than a flier or runner. Its strong legs and large feet were set far back on the body, giving it an upright waddling stance on land, like the birds called divers or loons today. This structure is excellent for swimming, as the webbed feet provide pushing power at the rear of the body for maximum propulsive efficiency. The keel or flange of the sternum (breastbone), which anchors powerful wing-flapping muscles in flying birds, had almost disappeared in *Hesperornis*. So had the wing bones – the very small, almost stub-like wings may have been used for steering as *Hesperornis* swam. The neck was long and strong, and so were the skull and jaws, which were equipped with tiny teeth suited to gripping wriggling prey. *Hesperornis* may have swum along the shores of the shallow seas that covered Late Cretaceous Kansas, using its flexible neck and powerful bill to grab a variety of sea creatures.

BELOW *Hesperornis* probably had a lifestyle similar to those of modern penguins, swimming rapidly underwater after fish and other small sea creatures. In size it was at least as tall as the largest type of penguin, the emperor. However penguins swim by flapping their wings, but Hesperornis used its large webbed feet.

BIRD FACTFILE
Hesperornis

Meaning: Western bird

Pronunciation: Hess-purr-orn-iss

Period: Late Cretaceous

Main group: Theropoda – Avialae

Standing height: 1.8 meters (6 feet)

Diet: Fish, water animals

Fossils: USA (Kansas), Canada, Russia

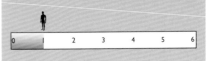

CHAPTER FOUR
THE GREAT PREDATORS

THE MOST MASSIVE MEAT-EATERS TO STALK THE EARTH, SUCH AS
ALLOSAURUS, TYRANNOSAURUS, AND GIGANOTOSAURUS, CAN STILL
BE FRIGHTENING MORE THAN 65 MILLION YEARS AFTER THEIR DEMISE.

THE BIGGEST MEAT-EATERS

THE THEROPOD GROUP INCLUDES ALL PREDATORY DINOSAURS, LARGE AND SMALL. AMONG THE SUBGROUPS WERE SEVERAL THAT BOASTED THE LARGEST LAND HUNTERS THE WORLD HAS EVER SEEN. IT IS WORTH NOTING, HOWEVER, THAT EVEN MORE GIGANTIC PREDATORS, SUCH AS THE PLIOSAUR *LIOPLEURODON*, EXISTED IN THE PREHISTORIC SEAS, AND THAT THERE ARE SIMILARLY VAST HUNTERS ROAMING THE OCEANS TODAY – THE SPERM WHALES – WHICH WOULD OUTWEIGH THE GREATEST PREDATORY DINOSAURS SEVERAL TIMES OVER.

HOW BIG WAS BIG?

The big theropod dinosaurs were several times larger than the record-holding land hunters of today, such as the grizzly bear or the Siberian tiger, which weigh less than 1 metric ton (1 ton) each. The well-known *Tyrannosaurus* of North America weighed more than 5 metric tons (5 tons), while *Giganotosaurus*, whose fossils were discovered much more recently in South America, was another metric ton or two heavier. Recently excavated fossils, also from South America, hint at even greater sizes.

GROUPS OF GREAT HUNTERS

The big meat-eaters came from several dinosaur subgroups. One was the ceratosaurs, such as *Dilophosaurus* and *Carnotaurus*, and *Ceratosaurus* itself. The name ceratosaur means "horned reptile," but not all ceratosaurs had horns, and plenty of other non-ceratosaurs did. These predators were successful mainly in the Jurassic period, but faded thereafter in the northern continents. The tetanurans, or "stiff tails," such as *Eustreptospondylus*, *Megalosaurus*, *Spinosaurus* and *Allosaurus* took their place. Later in the Age of Dinosaurs came even bigger tetanurans, such as *Giganotosaurus* and, at the very end, *Tyrannosaurus* (see pages 109 and 118).

HUNTERS OR SCAVENGERS?

Much of the debate today concerns whether these great beasts were primarily hunters or scavengers. If they were scavengers, they might have followed the great herds of huge plant-eating dinosaurs, to feast on any easy victim – the dead or dying, old or young, sick or injured. If they were hunters, did they ambush or pursue their prey? Did they stalk and then lie in wait to charge at a surprised victim, or doggedly chase the victim until it tired and slowed down? The evidence from fossilized footprints shows that dinosaurs like *Tyrannosaurus* could run as well as walk. But it is not clear whether they pounded along slowly and deliberately, or sprinted at higher speed. Estimates of their top speed range from less than 20 to more than 50 kilometers (10 to 30-plus miles) per hour. The teeth and skulls of many big meat-eaters certainly seem very strongly built, able to withstand the stresses caused by a struggling prey, while their necks, too, were powerful structures, capable of jerking and twisting their heads as, perhaps, they wrenched off great chunks of flesh.

OPPORTUNISTIC APPETITES

Perhaps, in life, the great predatory dinosaurs did not have to decide among ambush, pursuit or scavenging. Like hyenas, jackals and wolves today, they may have simply taken advantage of any opportunity that came their way. Recent discoveries of *Tyrannosaurus* fossils suggest that they lived as families or larger groups. The prospect of a ravenous pack of these flesh-eaters, some ambushing, some pursuing, others, perhaps the young, scavenging, is truly awesome.

PREVIOUS PAGE Each tooth of *Tyrannosaurus* was 15 centimeters (6 inches) long, back-curved and serrated-edged. The uneven nature of the teeth was due to the pattern of renewal – when a particular tooth was broken or lost, a new one grew in its place, so the jaws always had a mixture of teeth in different stages of growth. This pattern is seen in living reptiles such as crocodiles. There was no "whole set" replacement as there is in mammals such as ourselves.

LEFT A hungry *Megalosaurus* pounces on a hapless sauropod. *Megalosaurus* was a meat-eating predator that lived around 166 million years ago.

BELOW *Eustreptospondylus*, like many large meat-eating dinosaurs, was originally confused with *Megalosaurus*. It is now considered to be an early or primitive member of the spinosaur group, which has come to prominence since about 1990 with the discovery of several new members, including *Suchomimus* (see page 123).

EUSTREPTOSPONDYLUS

A medium-to-large predator with a speedy-looking appearance, *Eustreptospondylus* fossils were studied in 1841, the same year that the group Dinosauria itself received its official name, and by the same comparative anatomist, Richard Owen. Its original name, however, was not *Eustreptospondylus* at all, but *Megalosaurus*, a term that was already in general use for a variety of large reptilian carnivores. More than a century later, in 1964, Alick Walker, a British fossil expert, reviewed the two sets of "*Megalosaurus*" fossils and showed that one partly grown, well-preserved but incomplete specimen from near Wolvercote in Oxfordshire, England, deserved its own identity. Suggestions for calling it *Streptospondylus* were made, but the name was already suggested for another fossil reptile. So it was called *Eustreptospondylus*, in reference to the curved surfaces of the vertebral bones in its backbone. It may be synonymous with *Magnosaurus* and is generally grouped as a

megalosaurian. It has some similarities with the great North American theropod of about the same time period, *Allosaurus*, but also with *Spinosaurus*.

Eustreptospondylus lived some 170 million years ago and was long, lean and probably mean. The large head, with weight-saving gaps in the skull bones, bore a huge mouth. The teeth were long and sharp, with serrated edges, yet they were not especially large. The small forelimbs each had three digits, and the powerful back legs had sturdy bones and big bird-like feet, with three digits on the ground and one above it in the rear. The tail was fairly narrow at the base and tapered slowly to form almost half of the animal's total length. Its prey may have included armored plant-eaters like *Sarcolestes* and sauropods like *Cetiosaurus*.

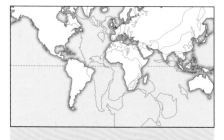

DINO FACTFILE
Eustreptospondylus

Meaning: Well or sharply curved vertebrae, true reversed backbone

Pronunciation: You-strep-toe-spon-die-luss

Period: Mid- to Late Jurassic

Main group: Theropoda

Length: 6 meters (20 feet)

Weight: 500 kilograms (1,100 pounds)

Diet: Animals

Fossils: England

CARNOTAURUS

Carnotaurus was a large Cretaceous theropod or predatory dinosaur with many unusual features. José Bonaparte, an eminent Argentine expert on dinosaurs, named it in 1985 from almost complete skeletal remains excavated in the fossil-rich region of Chubut, Argentina. Studies showed that *Carnotaurus* was a cousin of *Abelisaurus*, also named by Bonaparte and colleagues in 1985. The abelisaurids were a group of primitive theropods that nonetheless had a long history through the Cretaceous period. The prey of *Carnotaurus* may have been young or old or sick herbivores, like the sauropod *Chubutisaurus*, known from fossils from about the same time and place. However the peculiar jaw proportions make views on diet very varied.

Carnotaurus had a small conical projection, like a short cow's horn, above each eye. The eyes themselves were relatively small but – unusually among dinosaurs – they looked partly forward rather than largely sideways, giving

Carnotaurus stereoscopic, or binocular, vision for accurate assessment of distance. The snout was short and deep, giving the face a bull-nosed appearance, with powerful jaw muscles. The lower jaw, however, was strangely shallow and not very sturdy, and the teeth were smaller and weaker than would be expected in such a large head. The forelimbs were almost laughably tiny, even smaller than those of *Tyrannosaurus* (see page 118). The tail was lengthy and tapered very gradually. Accompanying the remains, which are dated at 100–95 million years old, were skin impressions showing a rough hide with rows of low, lumpy scales along the sides and back, and also rounded, disc-like scales.

ABOVE The strange "wing"-like brow horns, and the slim or shallow lower jaw compared to the tall or deep upper skull, mark out *Carnotaurus* as an unusual large theropod from the abelisaurid group.

DINO FACTFILE

Carnotaurus

Meaning: Carnivorous bull, meat-eating bull

Pronunciation: Kar-noe-tore-uss

Period: Late Cretaceous

Main group: Theropoda

Length: 8–9 meters (26–30 feet)

Weight: 1.4 metric tons (1.5 tons)

Diet: Animals

Fossils: Argentina

0	1	2	3	4	5	6	7	8

DILOPHOSAURUS

This medium-to-large carnivore is one of the few of its general type that is well known from plentiful remains. The fossils date to as far back as the Early Jurassic period, almost 200 million years ago, making it one of the earliest big predatory dinosaurs. It is probably related to the ceratosaurians (see opposite). Fossils have been found in Arizona and, possibly, in the Yunnan region of China. Among the American specimens are three individuals preserved together – they may have been a hunting pack. American paleontologist Sam Welles named this dinosaur, but it took two attempts. The three Arizona specimens were excavated in 1942, after a member of the Navajo nation, Jesse Williams, guided experts to their remains. Later, Welles studied them, and in 1954 he described them as a new species of *Megalosaurus*. Then, in 1964, further discoveries of fossils of these crested types of dinosaur, some by Welles himself, led him to distinguish the creatures from *Megalosaurus*. In 1970 he created the new name *Dilophosaurus*.

At 6 meters (19½ feet) long, *Dilophosaurus* was relatively slim and probably weighed less than half a metric ton (½ ton). The name refers to the two prominent crests on the head. Each is a curved bony ridge, like one-third of a dinner plate and barely as thick, projecting at an angle above the eye. These crests were so thin and fragile that they were probably for visual and symbolic, rather than physical, use, perhaps as a sign of gender and/or maturity. Trackways (fossilized sets of footprints) assigned to *Dilophosaurus* show just its claws making impressions, and with a stride of some 2 meters (6½ feet). A version of *Dilophosaurus* is seen in the movie Jurassic Park, but, unlike the cinematic monster, the real thing probably did not spit poison or have a neck frill.

DINO FACTFILE
Dilophosaurus

Meaning: Two-ridged reptile, double-crested reptile

Pronunciation: Die-loaf-owe-sore-uss

Period: Early Jurassic

Main group: Theropoda

Length: 6 meters (20 feet)

Weight: 400 kilograms (880 pounds)

Diet: Animals

Fossils: USA (Arizona)

RIGHT *Dilophosaurus* was among the largest carnivores of its time and had a pair of rounded crests on its skull.

CERATOSAURUS

Allosaurus was the greatest predator in Late Jurassic North America, but *Ceratosaurus* was its lesser rival. Named for the thin, jutting horn on its nose – and also showing a ridge-like crest above each eye – this theropod was a meter or two (3½ to 6½ feet) smaller all-around than *Allosaurus*. Yet it was still a formidable hunter, with a weight approaching 1 metric ton (1 ton) – heavier than any bear, big cat or other terrestrial carnivore of today.

The great American fossil-hunter Othniel Charles Marsh named *Ceratosaurus* in 1884. Marsh was struck by the tall upper and lower spine-like extensions of the caudal vertebrae (tailbones). He compared this tail shape to that of a crocodile and suggested that *Ceratosaurus* might have been a fine swimmer in swamps of 150 million years ago.

Established so early in the scientific history of dinosaurs, *Ceratosaurus*'s name was given to one of the major subgroups of the theropods (bipedal predators) – the Ceratosauria – which groups together over 20 species. This is the earlier counterpart of another great theropod group, the Tetanurae, and includes *Coelophysis* and *Dilophosaurus* (see opposite). Despite some primitive features in the hips and other parts, including four digits on each forelimb rather than three and then two as in later theropods, *Ceratosaurus* must have been an able predator. It sported huge fang-like teeth and powerful rear limbs for fast running. Fossils of individuals have been found with more plentiful remains of several *Allosaurus*, suggesting that the former was a lone hunter while the latter roamed in packs. *Ceratosaurus* fossils have also been identified in Portugal and possibly in East Africa too.

ABOVE The curious nose horn of *Ceratosaurus* has stimulated great discussion but no clear consensus on its use. It was probably too small and weak to be a weapon, and so may have been a sign of maturity and readiness to breed, or possessed by one sex only.

DINO FACTFILE

Ceratosaurus

Meaning: Horned reptile

Pronunciation: Se-rat-owe-sore-uss

Period: Late Jurassic

Main group: Theropoda

Length: 6 meters (20 feet)

Weight: 700–850 kilograms (1540–1875 pounds)

Diet: Animals

Fossils: USA (Colorado, Utah, Wyoming), Portugal

| 0 | 1 | 2 | 3 | 4 | 5 | 6 | 7 | 8 |

ALIORAMUS

Known largely from just a partial skull and partial foot bones, this medium-sized predator is regarded as an unusual cousin of the last major group of dinosaur meat-eaters, the tyrannosaurs. It lived at the end of the dinosaur age, 70–65 million years ago. It was named in 1976, from fossils found in Mongolia by Sergei Mikhailovich Kurzanov, a Soviet expert on fossils who has also attracted attention with his studies and opinions on the much smaller and possibly feathered theropod, *Avimimus* (see page 92).

While the lack of fossils of leg or body bone makes it difficult to determine actual size, it is thought that *Alioramus* was far smaller than its great tyrannosaur cousins, but still a huge and powerful hunter, much larger than most land carnivores of today. Some experts conjecture that it probably reached 6 meters (20 feet) in total length and about 1.5 metric tons (1.5 tons) in weight. Its fossil foot bones show that it was lighter and probably faster than the bigger theropods. Some expert estimates for its running speed are in excess of 40 kilometers (25 miles) per hour. The body structure and proportions were fairly typical of tyrannosaurs, with tiny arms, long and strong rear legs and a long, stiff tail.

The head, however, was more unusual. The head shape is known from the partial skull, which was long and shallow with a lengthened snout rather than tall and with a shorter snout, as in most tyrannosaurs. Also, there were bony projections, including four small bump-like "horns" in a row along the center of the nose, and another pair higher up, one near each eye. *Alioramus* may not have been the dominant predator of its world. It probably shared its time and place, the Late Cretaceous of East Asia, with the much larger species of tyrannosaur formerly known as *Tarbosaurus*.

ABOVE Alioramus is distinguished from most other tyrannosaurs by its long shallow snout, small bony projections on the nose and above the eyes, and its relatively small size compared to its huge cousins.

LEFT *Albertosaurus* was a bipedal predator that balanced its heavy head and torso with a long tail.

ALBERTOSAURUS

A similar but smaller cousin of *Tyrannosaurus*, *Albertosaurus* roamed what is now northwestern America during the Late Cretaceous period, near the end of the dinosaur age but before its great cousin. *Albertosaurus* had all the typical features of a larger meat-eating dinosaur: long, sharp teeth in strong jaws; a large, deep-snouted head; thick neck and deep chest; small and apparently useless forelimbs with two clawed digits each; very powerful rear legs with three long, clawed digits on each foot; and a long, thick-based, tapering tail. The teeth numbered about 16 in the lower jaw and slightly more, 18 or 19, in the upper. As in most other big hunting dinosaurs, the teeth had wavy or serrated edges, useful for sawing and slicing though flesh in the manner of a steak knife.

At one site, about nine *Albertosaurus* individuals of different ages were preserved together, suggesting that they may have lived in a group.

Albertosaurus was named by Henry Fairfield Osborn, then head of the American Natural History Museum, in 1905, the year that the Canadian province it is named after was formed. But the fossils, including two partial skulls, were discovered earlier than that, in about 1884 and 1890–91, in the Red Deer River region of what was to become Alberta. They had already been named *Laelaps* and then *Dryptosaurus* before Osborn reclassified them. In 1913, a well-preserved skeleton of a similar creature was found, and named *Gorgosaurus*. In 1970, Dale Russell reviewed the situation and concluded that the specimens known as *Gorgosaurus* were really juveniles of *Albertosaurus* or a smaller species. Recently, in another swing of the pendulum, the name *Gorgosaurus* has resurfaced again as applicable to the earlier species of *Albertosaurus*, *Albertosaurus libratus*. This leaves the main species as before, *Albertosaurus sarcophagus*.

DINO FACTFILE
Albertosaurus

Meaning: Alberta reptile

Pronunciation: Al-bert-owe-sore-uss

Period: Late Cretaceous

Main group: Theropoda

Length: 9 meters (30 feet)

Weight: 1.5 metric tons (1.5 tons)

Diet: Animals

Fossils: Western North America

Carcharodontosaurus

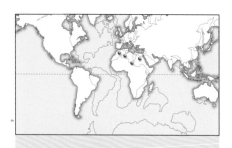

DINO FACTFILE

Carcharodontosaurus

Meaning: Shark tooth reptile

Pronunciation: Kar-kar-owe-don-toe-sore-uss

Period: Early–Late Cretaceous

Main group: Theropoda

Length: 13 meters (43 feet)

Weight: 7–8 metric tons (7–8 tons)

Diet: Large animals

Fossils: Algeria, Morocco, Egypt, Niger

Part of this dinosaur's name will be familiar to people who know about sharks, since the scientific name of the great white shark is *Carcharodon carcharias*. This "shark-tooth reptile" vies with *Giganotosaurus* as the largest meat-eater ever to prowl on land. *Carcharodontosaurus* has undergone a spectacular renaissance as the result of studies of fossils found in North Africa in 1996 by Paul Sereno and his colleagues from the University of Chicago (see also *Suchomimus*, opposite). The fossils represent a theropod maybe 13 meters (43 feet) long and over 7 metric tons (7 tons) in weight, outsizing *Tyrannosaurus*. Yet *Carcharodontosaurus* has a long history despite recent fame. It was originally named by Ernst Stromer von Reichenbach in 1931, from a partial skull and other remains found in the Sahara in 1927. Like many other fossils of large meat-eating theropods, these at first had been attributed to *Megalosaurus*. Unfortunately, these earlier finds were lost during World War II (see *Spinosaurus*, page 117). Sereno's 1996 find revived the dinosaur's reputation and rewrote the record books. New fossil finds in South America since 2000, although scarce and fragmentary, have suggested that there could have been even bigger meat-eaters and so the situation may change again.

Carcharodontosaurus in Africa was similar in some ways to *Giganotosaurus* of South America. Both are classified as mid-Cretaceous "remnants" of the theropod group that included *Allosaurus* and had enjoyed most success earlier in the Late Jurassic period. Links are seen in parts such as the three digits on each forelimb, contrasting with the two digits of later giant theropods like *Tyrannosaurus*. *Carcharodontosaurus* was heavily built, with very sturdy bones, and its skull was as long as many human beings today are tall – 1.6 meters (5 feet). The teeth are truly fearsome, tapering triangles some 20 centimeters (8 inches) long with serrated edges, far larger and stronger than the teeth of any shark.

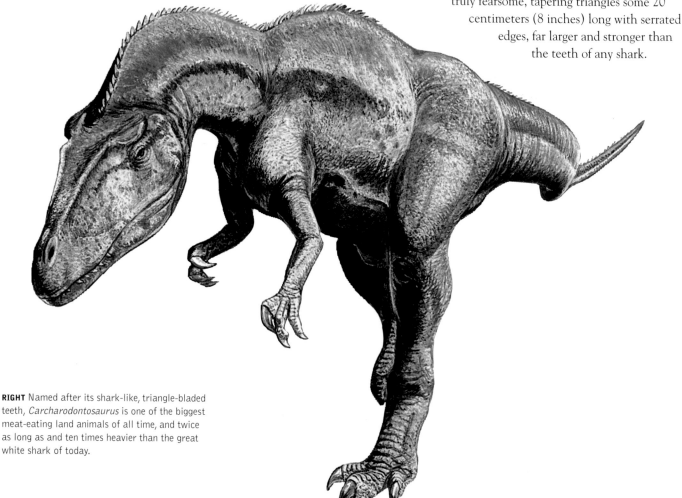

RIGHT Named after its shark-like, triangle-bladed teeth, *Carcharodontosaurus* is one of the biggest meat-eating land animals of all time, and twice as long as and ten times heavier than the great white shark of today.

LEFT The long, low snout of *Suchomimus* is similar to that of *Baryonyx* and several kinds of modern crocodiles. It is suited to swishing sideways fast through the water and grabbing slippery, wriggling prey such as fish.

SUCHOMIMUS

After discovering a new specimen of *Carcharodontosaurus* (opposite), Chicago-based paleontologist Paul Sereno and his team scored another success in 1997, with the discovery in the Sahara, around Tenere, in Niger, of fossils that represented about two-thirds of the skeleton of a huge meat-eater. This was named *Suchomimus*, "crocodile mimic," after the shape of its head. But unlike most great theropods (meat-eaters), *Suchomimus* had a very long, low snout and narrow jaws studded with some 100 teeth, not very sharp and curving slightly backward. The tip of the snout was enlarged and carried a "rosette" of longer teeth. The animal is reminiscent of crocodilians that eat mainly fish, such as the living gharial, a type of large crocodile with a very long, slim snout, from the region of India. *Suchomimus* also had tall extensions of its vertebrae which may have held up some kind of low flap, ridge or sail of

skin, as seen in much more exaggerated form in *Spinosaurus* (see page 117). The overall impression is of a massive and powerful creature that ate fish and meat 100 million years ago, when the Sahara was a lush, swampy habitat. *Suchomimus* has been placed in the spinosaur group of predators.

Apart from the back ridge, *Suchomimus* was very similar to *Baryonyx* (see page 110), which also had strong forelimbs and a huge sickle-curved claw on its "thumb." And, as with *Baryonyx*, the claw was the first fossil part to be noticed by paleontologists. *Suchomimus* was considerably larger than *Baryonyx*, but the latter might almost have been a juvenile of the former. Detailed study shows that the specimen of *Suchomimus* was itself not fully grown when it died.

DINO FACTFILE

Suchomimus

Meaning: Crocodile mimic

Pronunciation: Soo-koe-mim-uss

Period: Early Cretaceous

Main group: Theropoda

Length: 11 meters (36 feet)

Weight: 27 metric tons (3 tons)

Diet: Animals, perhaps fish

Fossils: Sahara (Niger)

| 0 | 1 | 2 | 3 | 4 | 5 | 6 | 7 | 8 |

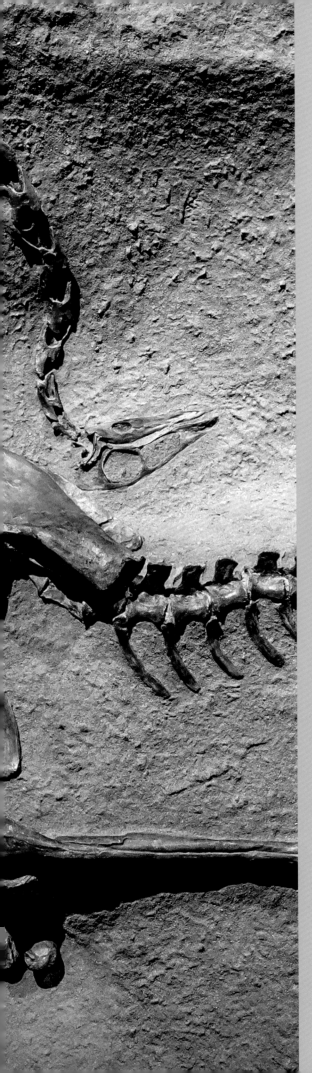

CHAPTER FIVE

OSTRICH DINOSAURS

Among the strangest groups of dinosaurs were the ornithomimosaurs. Most had no teeth at all, and pecked at food with beaks.

LIKE A BIRD'S BEAK

SEVERAL KINDS OF DINOSAURS HAD BEAK-LIKE FRONTS TO THEIR MOUTHS, INCLUDING LARGE-SIZED PLANT-EATERS LIKE *TRICERATOPS* AND *STEGOSAURUS*. BUT AMONG THE MEAT-EATERS, ONLY THE ORNITHOMIMOSAURS EVOLVED THIS FEATURE. THEIR NAME, WHICH MEANS "BIRD MIMIC REPTILES," REFERS PARTLY TO THE PRESENCE OF A BEAK. IN FOSSILIZED REMAINS, THIS CONSISTS OF BONES FORMING THE UPPER AND LOWER JAWS, WHICH ARE LONG AND LOW, LIKE A PAIR OF NEEDLE-NOSE PLIERS. TEETH WERE ENTIRELY ABSENT IN MOST TYPES (BUT SEE BELOW). IN LIFE, THE JAWBONES WOULD HAVE BEEN COVERED WITH HORN SHEATHS, AS IN MODERN BIRDS. THE HORN GREW SLOWLY AND REPAIRED ITSELF, PROTECTING THE BONE WITHIN. IT MIGHT ALSO HAVE FORMED SHARP EDGES OR RIDGES ALONG THE JAWS, SO THAT THEY COULD BE USED TO CUT RATHER THAN SIMPLY SQUASH FOOD.

MORE LIKE AN OSTRICH

The beaks of birds vary hugely in size and shape. Among those of living birds, the beaks most like those of ornithomimosaurs belong to ostriches. Indeed, not only the beak, but the head, neck and rear limbs of an ornithomimosaur all resembled those of a modern ostrich. One of the best-known ornithomimosaurs is named *Struthiomimus*, meaning "ostrich mimic," and the whole group is often called the ostrich dinosaurs. It is important not to be misled by this. The similarities between ostrich dinosaurs and ostriches are accidents of evolution, not signs of any close relationship, and there are important differences between them and the bird after which they are named; after all, they were prehistoric reptiles, not modern birds. An ostrich's forelimbs are wing-like, while ostrich dinosaurs had sizably long arms that dangled below the body and were tipped with sharply clawed digits that could scratch, dig and grab. Finally, no modern bird has the long series of tailbones possessed by dinosaurs. While today's ostrich body is covered with feathers, there is, so far, no good fossil evidence either way as to whether ostrich-dinosaurs had scales, like most other reptiles, or feathers, like some dinosaurs and all birds.

BEHAVIOR PATTERNS

In spite of the differences, the similarities suggest that ostrich dinosaurs lived in ways similar to ostriches today. They probably strode across the landscape, their large eyes held well above the ground by the long legs and neck, scanning for food and enemies. If danger appeared, an ostrich dinosaur would use its chief method of survival – it would run. The bones of their limbs, and reconstructions of their muscles, indicate that ornithomimosaurs were probably the fleetest of all dinosaurs. Some could equal or even exceed the speed of a modern ostrich, which has been measured at around 80 kilometers (50 miles) per hour. If an ornithomimosaur detected food, it might peck it up using its long neck and head. Alternatively, its front limbs could grab small prey, such as lizards and baby dinosaurs. Ostriches today are master omnivores. They eat almost anything, including leaves, stems, shoots, buds, eggs, insects, grubs and other small animals. Ostrich dinosaurs may well have done the same.

EVOLUTION

Ostrich dinosaurs were one of the last groups of dinosaurs to appear. The ornithomimosaurs are grouped with maniraptorans as maniraptoriform theropods. Most lived toward the end of the Cretaceous period, and most of their fossils have been found on northern land masses – North America, Europe and East Asia. One of the earlier types was *Pelecanimimus*, from Europe. It still had teeth – more than 60 at the front of the upper jaw, and 140 below them in the lower jaw, but all of them tiny. This shows how ostrich dinosaurs gradually lost the normal dinosaur teeth as their beaks took over. The group seems to have been evolving still and spreading when the great extinction brought them to an abrupt end (see pages 291–293).

PREVIOUS PAGE The typical ornithomimosaur features of inadequate-looking head, gangly front limbs, long and powerful rear limbs, and lengthy tail are all apparent in this fossilized skeleton.

LEFT The *Dromiceiomimus* dinosaur with its young in a prehistoric woodland. This herbivorous ornithomimid (ostrich-like) theropod lived during the Late Cretaceous Period (around 100-66 million years ago), in what is now North America.

ORNITHOMIMUS

The scientific history of ostrich dinosaurs began with a "big bang" in 1890, when Othniel Charles Marsh, eminent paleontologist and prolific namer of dinosaurs, named three species of this genus from fossils unearthed a year or two earlier by George Cannon in Denver, Colorado, and by John Bell Hatcher in Montana. Marsh suspected that these creatures were bird-like reptiles and probably ornithopods, from the same main group of dinosaurs as the much larger *Iguanodon*. Two more species followed in 1892, but by then Marsh had realized that these dinosaurs were probably theropods, that is, bipedal predators. After more finds and some confusion with the related *Struthiomimus*, *Ornithomimus* assumed its place as the founding member of a newly classified group, the ornithomimosaurs ("bird mimic reptiles"), or ostrich dinosaurs.

Ornithomimus had all the features that are typical of the group: slim build; hollow bones; long low skull; toothless beak; big eyes and

brain; strong front limbs with three clawed and grasping fingers; extremely long, slender rear legs powered by strong hip muscles; very long metatarsals (foot bones); three big digits on each foot on the ground; and a long, thin tail with up to 40 caudal vertebrae (backbones). It was one of the larger members of the group, at 4 meters (13 feet) or more in total length, slightly larger than *Struthiomimus*. Its fossils have been provisionally identified in Mongolia, as well as on the North American continent. Like most ostrich dinosaurs, it was probably an omnivore, pecking and snapping at almost any kind of food, from juicy worms to tough seeds.

ABOVE *Ornithomimus* would have stood taller than an adult human, at well over 2 meters (6½ feet) when in this erect posture. For sprinting the head and neck were probably lowered, and the tail raised, so that both were horizontal and level with the body, forming one long, arrow-like shape.

DINO FACTFILE
Ornithomimus

Meaning: Bird mimic, avian pretender

Pronunciation: Or-nith-owe-mim-uss

Period: Late Cretaceous

Main group: Theropoda

Length: 4 meters (13 feet)

Weight: 170 kilograms
(370 pounds)

Diet: Probably omnivorous

Fossils: Western USA

| 0 | 1 | 2 | 3 | 4 | 5 | 6 | 7 |

DROMICEIOMIMUS

Today's second largest bird, after the ostrich, is the emu of Australia (*Dromaius novaehollandiae*), which can be as tall as a large adult human. Since *Struthiomimus* had been named after the ostrich, it seemed logical to give the name of *Dromiceiomimus* to one of the next bird-like dinosaurs to be studied. It was coined by Dale Russell in 1972 for fossils found in Late Cretaceous rocks in Alberta, Canada. The fossils previously, in the 1920s, had been attributed to two species, *Struthiomimus brevitertius* and *Struthiomimus samueli*. In fact, *Struthiomimus brevitertius*, (established in 1928 by William Parks from a specimen from the Red Deer River near Steveville), included the first well-preserved skull known from any ostrich dinosaur.

The skull of *Dromiceiomimus* shows huge eye sockets, which have led to the view that this Late Cretaceous omnivore fed in the twilight of dusk and dawn. Much of its skeleton is similar to that of other ostrich dinosaurs, but its torso is even more condensed and compact, its forelimbs are elongated, and its pelvic (hip) bones are also distinctive. In the proportions of its legs, its shinbones (tibia and fibula) were around one-fifth longer than its thighbone (femur), the latter having an average length of 47 centimeters (18½ inches). This is greater than the already high shin–thigh ratio found in most ostrich dinosaurs, suggesting that *Dromiceiomimus* was an even faster sprinter than its cousins, maybe exceeding 60 kilometers (38 miles) per hour.

DINO FACTFILE
Dromiceiomimus

Meaning: Emu mimic

Pronunciation: Drom-ee-say-owe-mim-uss

Period: Late Cretaceous

Main group: Theropoda

Length: 3.5 meters (11 feet)

Weight: 120 kilograms (265 pounds)

Diet: Omnivore

Fossils: Canada (Alberta)

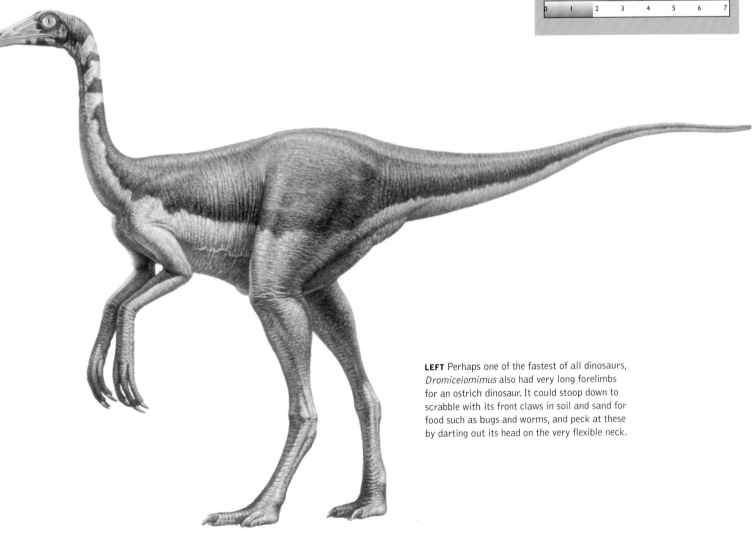

LEFT Perhaps one of the fastest of all dinosaurs, *Dromiceiomimus* also had very long forelimbs for an ostrich dinosaur. It could stoop down to scrabble with its front claws in soil and sand for food such as bugs and worms, and peck at these by darting out its head on the very flexible neck.

GALLIMIMUS

DINO FACTFILE

Gallimimus

Meaning: Chicken mimic, rooster pretender

Pronunciation: Gal-ee-mim-uss

Period: Late Cretaceous

Main group: Theropoda

Length: 8 meters (26 feet)

Weight: 400 kilograms (880 pounds)

Diet: Omnivore

Fossils: Mongolia

In the late 1960s and early 1970s, Polish-Mongolian fossil-finding expeditions to the Gobi desert collected many amazing discoveries. One was the "chicken mimic" *Gallimimus*, with two almost complete skeletons, another missing only its skull, and another skull with various smaller pieces, at the site of Altan Ula, Mongolia. Far from being the size and shape of a hen, this ostrich dinosaur was the largest of the well-known types in its group, at some 8 meters (26 feet) in total length. It dated from 75–70 million years ago. Based on these Gobi remains, Mongolian paleontologist Rinchen Barsbold with Polish colleagues Halszka Osmólska and Ewa Roniewicz named *Gallimimus* in 1972.

Gallimimus was big and long in almost every respect except for its head. Its main torso was relatively elongated compared to those of its relatives – other ostrich dinosaurs

– as were its gangly front limbs, each bearing three digits tipped with small claws. On a long and flexible S-shaped neck, the strikingly small head had a long, toothless beak that seemed suited to any kind of food, animal or vegetable. The front of the lower beak was shaped like a scoop, and there were comb-like flanges inside the mouth, perhaps used for shoveling soil and sifting out food items from mud. Big eyes stared out sideways from their sockets, one on either side of the skull, keeping a watch all around for enemies and other dangers. Rearing up straight, *Gallimimus* could crane its neck to raise its head more than 4 meters (13 feet) above the ground. On the move, its body and neck tilted forward to become more horizontal, balanced over the powerful hips by the long, stiffened tail, placing the head around 2 meters (6½feet) above the ground.

RIGHT The front feet of *Gallimimus* are less hand-like, for grasping, and more spade-like, suited for digging and shoveling. But the huge size of this ostrich dinosaur makes it unlikely that it could survive on a diet of tiny prey items like grubs or worms.

STRUTHIOMIMUS

Standing about as tall as an adult human, *Struthiomimus* was the first ostrich dinosaur to be described from fairly complete remains. Most of a skull and skeleton from Alberta, Canada, were studied and named in 1916–17 by Henry Fairfield Osborn, then curator of the American Museum of Natural History. He noted the great similarity in the reptile's size, shape and proportions to today's flightless birds, such as the ostrich, and so called the new find "ostrich mimic." The whole ostrich dinosaur group was founded on his proposals, and *Struthiomimus* is still one of the best known of its North American members. Further possible finds of *Struthiomimus* remains have been found as far east as New Jersey.

Struthiomimus dates from around 75–73 million years ago. Its long, low skull and toothless beak, 25 centimeters (10 inches) in length and constructed from almost wafer-thin bony plates and struts, are extremely similar in shape and size to the skull of the modern ostrich. As in other members of the ornithomimosaur group, the bones of the upper and lower jaws would have been covered with horny sheaths to form the beak or bill as seen on the outside. The proportions of the rear legs are also amazingly similar to those of ostriches, with bulging muscles around the thigh, leaving the long shin, even longer foot (metatarsal bones), and three clawed digits on the feet extremely light. *Struthiomimus* could probably swing its long legs back and forth with maximum speed and efficiency when running. It probably used its sharp claws to scrape for grubs in soil, gather food such as berries, or perhaps grab and tear up small prey like lizards, while using its beak to peck at anything edible.

ABOVE Like most ostrich dinosaurs, *Struthiomimus* had very thin skull bones, which were probably linked by flexible joints in life. This meant the jaws could twist or "warp" slightly, making the upper and lower beak tilt for lopsided pecking or snapping.

DINO FACTFILE
Struthiomimus

Meaning: Ostrich mimic

Pronunciation: Strew-thee-owe-mim-uss

Period: Late Cretaceous

Main group: Theropoda

Length: 3.5–4 meters (11–13½ feet)

Weight: 140 kilograms (310 pounds)

Diet: Omnivore

Fossils: Canada (Alberta)

0   1   2   3   4   5   6   7

DEINOCHEIRUS

One of the most puzzling, exciting and potentially awe-inspiring fossil finds was a pair of forelimbs from Late Cretaceous rocks in the eastern area of the Nemegt Basin, which is part of the Gobi Desert in southern Mongolia. Even the day of their discovery in 1965, during the joint Mongolian–Polish expeditions of the 1960s and 1970s, was notable – in a place where droughts last years, it was raining. The specimens included bones from the front limbs, some claws and a few associated bits of ribs and backbones. No other parts of the creature have been found. In 1970, Halszka Osmólska and Ewa Roniewicz, Polish members of the expedition, named the find *Deinocheirus*, meaning "terrible hand."

The forelimbs broadly follow the ostrich dinosaur pattern, with all three digits around the same length, although the overall proportions of the limbs are relatively slender. The great shock was their size. Each forelimb was around 2.4 meters (8 feet) long, each digit alone was bigger than a human arm, and the hook-shaped claws are among the largest of any dinosaur, measuring more than 25 centimeters (10 inches) in length. The recovery and description in 2014 of looted remains of more complete specimens show that *Deinocheirus* was a large and unusual ornithomimosaur, up to 12 meters (40 feet) long and weighing several tonnes. However, its hollow bones reduced it's overall weight. The legs were relatively short with blunt toe claws. The backbones had tall neural spines forming a sail-like structure and the tail ended in a short bird-like pygostyle, which might indicate the presence of tail feathers. The meter-long skull had a wide hadrosaur-like bill and deep lower jaw.

BELOW Known mainly from isolated forelimb bones and claws, this reconstruction of *Deinocheirus* – like any other – is extremely speculative. The enormous size of the fossils means that the dinosaur could easily have been as long as *Tyrannosaurus* and able to reach as high into the trees as the modern giraffe.

ELAPHROSAURUS

Elaphrosaurus's combination of features has resulted in it's assignation to several different theropod groups. Most recently it has been grouped with some Asian dinosaurs, such as *Noasaurus*, in the noasaurid abelisauroids. A major problem is that the main skeleton of *Elaphrosaurus* is known only from a specimen found in East Africa, which lacked a skull – and so the usual distinguishing features of skull bones, jaws and teeth, which provide so much information, are missing. The rock layers of the region that contained the skeleton also harbor many small teeth, which could have fitted into the jaws of *Elaphrosaurus* if they were toothed.

The shape and proportions of *Elaphrosaurus* were certainly ostrich-like and ostrich-like, with long slim rear legs; slender forelimbs with three digits each; a lightweight body; long, stiff tail; and long, flexible neck. The single fossil specimen came from quarries at Tendaguru in what was then German East

Africa (later Tanganyika, now the larger portion of Tanzania). The site also yielded many other notable finds, not least *Brachiosaurus*, *Kentrosaurus* and *Dicraeosaurus*, during a four-year expedition begun in 1908 and led by Werner Janensch, the German paleontologist who named *Elaphrosaurus* in 1920.

ABOVE *Elaphrosaurus* has long puzzled experts as to its basic grouping. Recent reviews group it with some Asian dinosaurs in the noasaurid group as a long, slim predator, likely with teeth in its jaws, rather than in the beaked ornithomimosaur (ostrich dinosaur) group.

DINO FACTFILE

Elaphrosaurus

Meaning: Light lizard

Pronunciation: El-aff-row-sore-uss

Period: Late Jurassic

Main group: Theropoda

Length: 6 meters (20 feet)

Weight: 200 kilograms
(440 pounds)

Diet: Uncertain

Fossils: East Africa

0   1   2   3   4   5   6   7

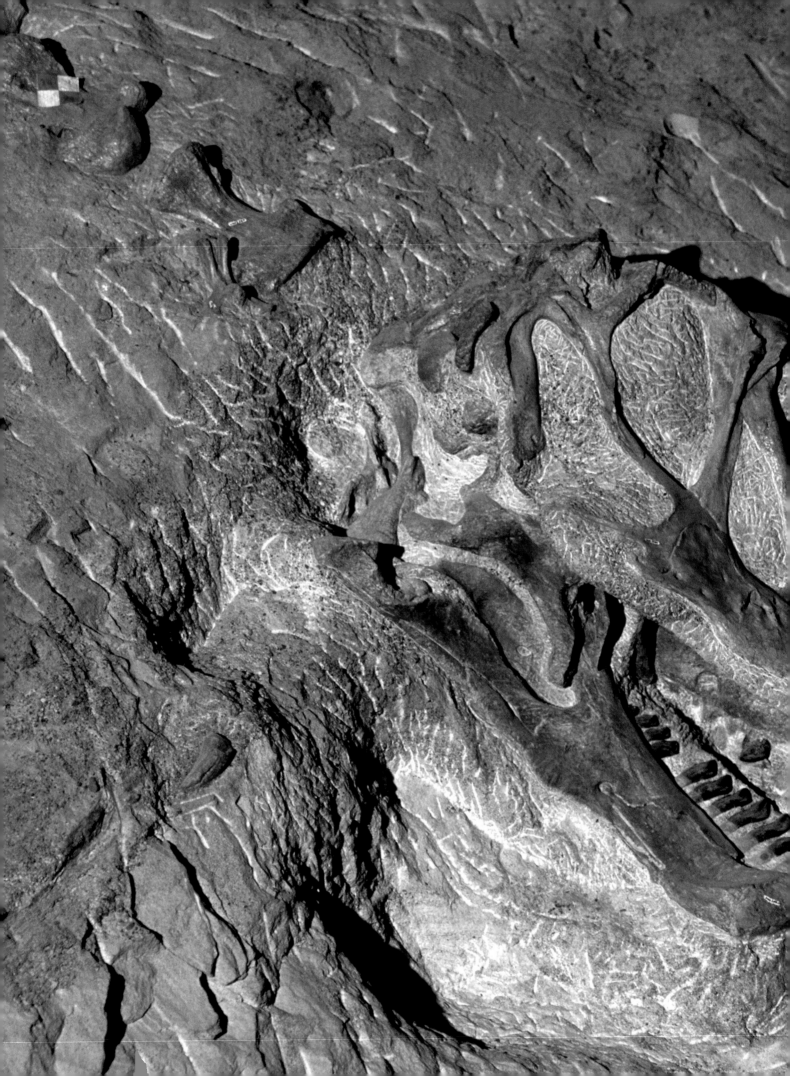

CHAPTER SIX

THE GIANTS

BIG, BIGGER, BIGGEST — IT SEEMS THAT EVERY FEW YEARS A NEW RECORD-HOLDER IS DISCOVERED AMONG THE MOST MASSIVE ANIMALS EVER TO SHAKE THE EARTH WITH THEIR STEPS.

BREAKING RECORDS

THE RIVALRY BETWEEN MAMMALS AND DINOSAURS FOR THE TITLE OF LARGEST ANIMAL EVER TO HAVE LIVED IS MUCH CLOSER THAN IT SEEMED TO BE SEVERAL YEARS AGO. NEW FINDS OF FOSSILS FROM GIANT DINOSAURS OF THE SAUROPOD GROUP, SUCH AS *ARGENTINOSAURUS*, MEAN THAT THESE REPTILES RIVAL TODAY'S GREAT WHALES, SUCH AS THE BLUE WHALE, FOR THE TOP SPOT. THERE WERE SEVERAL MAIN GROUPS OF SAUROPODS THROUGH THE AGE OF DINOSAURS, AND EACH HAD ITS GIANT MEMBERS. THE DIPLODOCIDS WERE EXCEPTIONALLY LONG AND THRIVED DURING THE LATE JURASSIC PERIOD, ESPECIALLY IN NORTH AMERICA. *CAMARASAURUS* AND ITS COUSINS VARIED GREATLY, FROM BIG TO ENORMOUS, AND ALSO LIVED AT THIS TIME, IN NORTH AMERICA AS WELL AS IN EUROPE AND ASIA. THE BRACHIOSAURIDS HAD ESPECIALLY LONG FRONT LEGS, AND THEY ALSO ENJOYED SUCCESS IN THE LATE JURASSIC PERIOD IN NORTH AMERICA, EUROPE AND AFRICA. DURING THE CRETACEOUS PERIOD THAT FOLLOWED, THE TITANOSAURIDS APPEARED ON ALMOST ALL CONTINENTS AND BECAME PARTICULARLY PROMINENT IN SOUTH AMERICA.

ADVANTAGES OF BEING BIG

Why did sauropod dinosaurs grow so huge, reaching more than 10 times the weight of today's largest land animals, the elephants? There are several advantages to increased body size. One is enhanced self-defense. Larger dinosaurs had more weight and power with which to defend themselves against predators. They could wield their long tails like massive whips, or swing their long necks like huge blackjacks, or turn and lean on an enemy to squash its life away. Most predators, even the biggest meat-eating dinosaurs, were less than one-fifth of the weight of the greatest sauropods.

STAYING WARMER LONGER

Another advantage might have been in body temperature regulation. One of the main factors that affects heat loss from a warm object to cooler surroundings is the ratio between the object's surface area and its volume. The greater the surface area compared to the volume, the greater the rate of heat loss. Bigger objects have much less surface area relative to volume than do smaller objects, so heat loss is reduced as size increases. This might have been important for the sauropods if they were "cold-blooded," or, more accurately, ectothermic – gaining body heat from their surroundings. After absorbing the sun's warmth by day, a huge dinosaur would retain much of the heat in the core of its body, for use through the cool night. A warmer dinosaur could remain active and alert as it searched for food or fought enemies.

PROBLEMS OF SIZE

But being very big has its problems. The amount of bone needed to support more weight rises at a rate higher than the actual increase in weight. More powerful muscles are needed to move the bulk, again at a greatly increasing rate. Food requirements become gargantuan, posing difficulties in gathering such a large mass of plant matter with a relatively small head, to keep the vast guts supplied. Also, the environment could have been put under strain as plants were consumed in quantities such that they disappeared, especially if these giant sauropods lived in herds – and much of the fossil evidence suggests that they did. Sauropods had their greatest success in the Late Jurassic, when the warm, moist climate encouraged rapid plant growth. Even so, whole areas would have been stripped bare of suitable vegetation, meaning that the herd had to move on.

PREVIOUS PAGE This skull of *Camarasaurus* is from the Dinosaur National Monument site in Utah. The sauropod had a tall skull with three large openings on each side – the huge nostril at the front then the orbit or eye socket; and the infraorbital fenestra, a gap allowing the jaw muscles to bulge, to the lower rear.

LEFT Sauropods on the move would have been an awesome sight, as they scanned the area for suitable plant growth as new browsing. Many examples of their fossilized footprints show these vast dinosaurs moved in close-knit groups.

ABOVE The skull of *Barosaurus* is not known from fossil remains and so is reconstructed in the manner of cousins such as *Diplodocus*. This sauropod had such a compact body that in proportion to its total length, it was more "neck and tail" than almost any other dinosaur.

DINO FACTFILE

Barosaurus

Meaning: Heavy reptile

Pronunciation: Bar-oh-sore-uss

Period: Late Jurassic

Main group: Sauropoda

Length: 27 meters (89 feet)

Weight: 20 metric tons (20 tons)

Diet: Plants

Fossils: Western USA

0	5	10	15	20	25	30

BAROSAURUS

Barosaurus is one of the many sauropods discovered in North America during the "Wild West Dinosaur Hunts" of the late nineteenth century. Othniel Charles Marsh named it in 1890. The name is also applied to specimens once called *Tornieria*. Starting in 1922, three fairly complete *Barosaurus* skeletons were dug out of Carnegie Quarry, Utah, by a team led by Earl Douglass of the Carnegie Museum. Earlier, he had excavated *Apatosaurus* from the same site and had been involved in the setting up of the Dinosaur National Monument there in 1915. More *Barosaurus* remains were uncovered in South Dakota and, more recently, pieces of skull, limbs and other fragments of a specimen from Tanzania in East Africa have also been assigned to *Barosaurus*.

Barosaurus was a large but fairly typical *Diplodocus*-type sauropod of the Late Jurassic period, around 150 million years ago. In fact,

in many respects *Barosaurus* was very similar to *Diplodocus* itself (see opposite), but with slight differences: much longer backbones or vertebrae, a shorter tail, and a much longer neck. Although its cervical vertebrae (neckbones) numbered 15 in total, just as in *Diplodocus*, some of them were more than 1 meter (39 inches) long. The scoops and hollows in their structure mean that the neck as a whole was relatively light. Probably more than four-fifths of this plant-eater's total length of perhaps 27 meters (89 feet) was neck and tail. Presumably it had a small head, although no specimen of its skull has been recovered. The American Museum of Natural History in New York shows a "mother" *Barosaurus* skeleton rearing on its hind legs to an enormous height, to protect her offspring from a small allosaur. Her head would be level with the fifth story of a building.

LEFT *Diplodocus* is usually shown without spines or plates in its skin, but recent discoveries suggest that it may have had a row of low spikes along its back.

DIPLODOCUS

Dinosaurs known from partial remains recently discovered may have been longer than *Diplodocus* (see pages 138, 140), but this Late Jurassic leviathan is still just about the longest dinosaur known from fairly complete specimens, and it still has one of the longest tails known – 13 meters (43 feet). Sam Williston found partial remains near Canyon City, Colorado, in 1877 and the next year Othniel Charles Marsh gave them their name. Twenty-two years later, a much more complete specimen was recovered from Albany County, Wyoming. The name means "double beam" and is said to refer to the caudal vertebrae (tailbones), of which there were more than 70. In the middle section of the tail, each vertebra had a downward projection that carried a front and rear extension or skid on the base, facing forward and back, like an upside-down T with a very short upright. Toward the rear section, the

vertebrae become simpler in form, so that at the whip-like tail tip they are simple rods.

Diplodocus has lent its name to a whole group of sauropods with similar skulls. The forehead is low and slopes down to a somewhat blunted snout, and the peg-like teeth are around the front of the upper and lower jaws, working like a comb or rake to gather foliage. One recent study, however, indicates that dinosaurs of this type could not lift their heads very high. The nostrils are high on the forehead, almost between the eyes. As in most sauropods, each of the four feet had five digits, but only the first bore a proper claw. Despite the great length of *Diplodocus*, its slim legs and body suggest that it was relatively lightweight, possibly about 10–15 metric tons (10–15 tons). Recent finds of skin impressions that are probably from *Diplodocus* show a row of spines along the back.

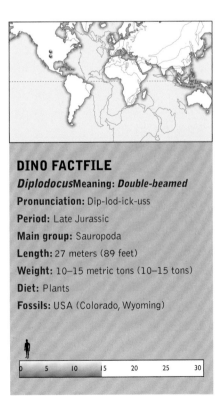

DINO FACTFILE

Diplodocus Meaning: ***Double-beamed***

Pronunciation: Dip-lod-ick-uss

Period: Late Jurassic

Main group: Sauropoda

Length: 27 meters (89 feet)

Weight: 10–15 metric tons (10–15 tons)

Diet: Plants

Fossils: USA (Colorado, Wyoming)

| 0 | 5 | 10 | 15 | 20 | 25 | 30 |

ABOVE One of many giant sauropods known from relatively few outsized fossils, *Supersaurus* is a contender for longest (although not heaviest) dinosaur. It was probably a member of the diplodocid family.

SUPERSAURUS

DINO FACTFILE

Supersaurus

Meaning: Super reptile

Pronunciation: Soo-pur-sore-uss

Period: Late Jurassic

Main group: Sauropoda

Length: Estimated 34 meters (112 feet)

Weight: Estimated 35–40 metric tons (35–40 tons)

Diet: Plants

Fossils: USA (Colorado), Portugal

| 0 | 5 | 10 | 15 | 20 | 25 | 30 |

Supersaurus was a *Diplodocus*-type sauropod in North America in the Late Jurassic period. James Jensen first excavated its fossils in western Colorado in 1972, but it was not named until 1985. Enough of the skeleton has been recovered to show that this was a truly massive beast, probably over 30 meters (98 feet) long but possibly almost 34 meters (112 feet), and as much as 40 metric tons in weight. The shoulder blades alone are far larger than an adult human, at 2.4 meters (8 feet) in length. The ribs measure 3 meters (10 feet), and some of the individual neckbones (caudal vertebrae) are 1.4 meters (4½ feet) long. Unfortunately, the remains are scattered and are nowhere as complete as for other giants, such as *Brachiosaurus*, so the true dimensions of *Supersaurus* remain a matter for speculation.

Supersaurus probably lived like other sauropods, swinging its long neck for hours at a time to gather vast amounts of plant food, which it swallowed without chewing, to fuel its massive bulk. If it could stretch its head upward, it might have been able to eat leaves 15 meters (49 feet) off the ground. This dinosaur is placed in the family Diplodocidae, which is characterized by a long, whip-like tail, and teeth shaped like pegs or pencils. Its cousins included *Amargasaurus*, *Apatosaurus*, *Barosaurus* and the similarly enormous *Seismosaurus*. James Jensen has proposed another giant, *Ultrasauros* (with an "o"), but this is now regarded by many sauropod experts as a misnomer for a chance finding in Colorado of mixed fossils of *Supersaurus* and *Brachiosaurus* (see page 146).

ABOVE The very limited fossils of *Dicraeosaurus* show a curious mix of features from several sauropod groups, including the diplodocids and cetiosaurids. In particular it had few neck and tail bones compared to most sauropods – perhaps only 12 in the neck, making its body look relatively long.

DICRAEOSAURUS

Fossils of this Late Jurassic sauropod, which could be called medium-sized for its group, even though it was far longer than any land animal today, were excavated by German-organized expeditions in 1908–12 to Tendaguru, then in the colony of German East Africa (later Tanganyika and now part of Tanzania). The fossils represent many parts of the skeleton, including a fine skull specimen.

Tendaguru yielded many other now well-known remains, including *Brachiosaurus* and *Kentrosaurus* (the "spiky reptile"), an African cousin of Stegosaurus. The fossils were studied by Werner Janensch, curator of the Natural History Museum of Berlin, and named by him in 1914 (see also page 157).

Dicraeosaurus is now placed with the South American sauropod *Amargasaurus* (see page 144) in the Dicraeosauridae and together with the closely related diplodocids in the larger grouping of diplodocoids. The "two forks" in the name *Dicraeosaurus* refer to the neural spines or upward extensions of the various vertebrae (backbones), which branch or fork into two.

These probably held up a ridge of fleshy skin, or a thinner, low, sail-like structure, which could have had various functions, such as temperature regulation and/or visual display (possible functions for these kinds of sails are discussed on page 45).

The skull shows typical diplodocid features: the eyes are set high up on the top; the nostrils are also set high up, almost between the eyes; the snout is long, low and horse-like; and the teeth are fine and almost pencil-shaped, set in two curved clusters around the fronts of both jaws.

Dicraeosaurus's tail, with its forked, skid-like chevrons beneath some of the vertebrae, was not as long and whippy as the tail of its sauropod relative *Diplodocus*.

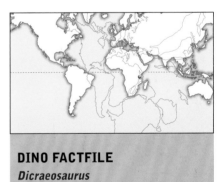

DINO FACTFILE
Dicraeosaurus

Meaning: Two-forked reptile

Pronunciation: Die-kree-owe-sore-uss

Period: Late Jurassic

Main group: Sauropoda

Length: 12 meters (39 feet)

Weight: 3 metric tons (3 tons)

Diet: Plants

Fossils: Tanzania

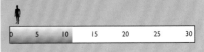

SEISMOSAURUS

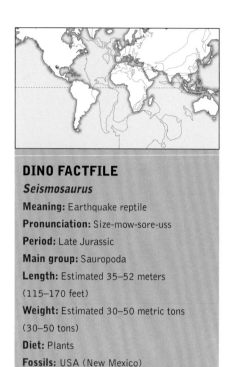

DINO FACTFILE

Seismosaurus

Meaning: Earthquake reptile

Pronunciation: Size-mow-sore-uss

Period: Late Jurassic

Main group: Sauropoda

Length: Estimated 35–52 meters
(115–170 feet)

Weight: Estimated 30–50 metric tons
(30–50 tons)

Diet: Plants

Fossils: USA (New Mexico)

The 1990s saw scientific reports of many newly discovered giant dinosaurs, indeed there was intense competition to find and name the biggest dinosaur. One was *Seismosaurus*, so named because it presumably shook the ground like an earthquake as it moved, perhaps at a trot or even a gallop. The Late Jurassic remains were located in New Mexico and named in 1991 by David Gillette. They included parts of the vertebrae forming the spinal column (backbone), some ribs, pieces of the pelvis (hipbone), and other pieces. The vertebrae are some of the longest ever found, at 1.8 meters (6 feet) each – the same as the height of an adult human. Many smooth, rounded pebbles or gastroliths (stomach stones) were found with the fossils. The dinosaur swallowed these to help it grind up its food (which it gulped without chewing) in its muscular gut.

Features of the vertebrae, including their skid-like chevrons underneath, and other preserved bones identify *Seismosaurus* as a *Diplodocus*-type sauropod from the same time, about 155–144 million years ago. Working from the sparse remains, estimates of the overall length of *Seismosaurus* are as high as 52 meters (170 feet) – almost twice that of *Diplodocus*'s 27 meters (89 feet)– but other calculations suggest a length of 40 or perhaps 35 meters (131 or 115 feet). Weight estimates are similarly varied, from 30 up to 80 metric tons (30–80 tons), although *Seismosaurus*, being a slim, lightweight diplodocid, probably did not have the great bulk of the *Brachiosaurus*-type sauropods.

Recent critical assessment of the fossil remains named as *Seismosaurus* has shown such similarities to the species *Diplodocus hallorum* that they are now regarded as one and the same. Since *Diplodocus* was named first, the name *Seismosaurus* is no longer used.

BELOW Although named *Seismosaurus,* the partial skeleton of this giant diplodocid is now recognised as that of the species *Diplodocus hallorum.*

APATOSAURUS (BRONTOSAURUS)

Brontosaurus is one of the best known of all dinosaurs, yet in scientific terms its name does not exist. It did exist once, at least the name, in 1879, when Othniel Charles Marsh described two massive sauropod skeletons from Como Bluff, Wyoming, and coined the famous name, which means "thunder lizard." Two years earlier, Marsh had described another huge sauropod from remains found by Arthur Lakes in rocks near Morrison, Colorado, and named them *Apatosaurus*. Also included in this early batch of sauropods was *Atlantosaurus*, yet another name coined by Marsh, this one for specimens that he had already described as *Titanosaurus*. But he was to find that the name *Atlantosaurus* was already in use, so that it had to be hurriedly changed. Another sauropod, *Camarasaurus*, was also mixed up in the general confusion. Gradually, however, it became clear that *Apatosaurus*, *Brontosaurus* and *Atlantosaurus* were one and the same – and the first name, being the earliest in the scientific literature,

took precedence. So the title *Brontosaurus* was removed from official lists of valid dinosaur names. Nevertheless, *Brontosaurus* has lived large in the public imagination ever since.

Apatosaurus was a close cousin of *Diplodocus*, from the same Late Jurassic period and in the same area of the North American southwest. But it was shorter and sturdier, however, and probably more than twice as heavy. Around a dozen preserved skeletons have been excavated and studied over many years, yet the shape of its skull was not clear until 1975, when Jack MacIntosh and David Berman sorted out some more of the confusion. A new fossil find of a skull showed that *Apatosaurus* did not possess a long, rounded head like that of *Camarasaurus*, as reconstructions had shown up to that time. Instead, it had a low, short-snouted head with nostrils high up almost between the eyes, and weak, peg-shaped teeth. In all these features it resembled *Diplodocus*.

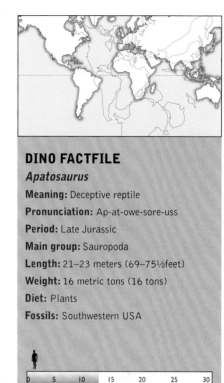

DINO FACTFILE
Apatosaurus
Meaning: Deceptive reptile
Pronunciation: Ap-at-owe-sore-uss
Period: Late Jurassic
Main group: Sauropoda
Length: 21–23 meters (69–75½feet)
Weight: 16 metric tons (16 tons)
Diet: Plants
Fossils: Southwestern USA

0	5	10	15	20	25	30

LEFT Like most of the huge sauropods, *Apatosaurus* must have spent most of its time gathering vegetation. Its pencil- or peg-like teeth continually pulled and raked in plant matter, which was swallowed directly into the huge stomach.

AMARGASAURUS

"La Amarga reptile" is named for the valley in Argentina where fossils of this sauropod were found. Like many Argentine dinosaur remains, they are dated to the Cretaceous period, in this case about 130–125 million years ago. They include a fairly complete skeleton, lacking only the front end of the skull and the tail. They were named in 1991 by Leonardo Salgado and José Bonaparte. The general proportions of *Amargasaurus* are typically sauropodian, with a small head, long neck and, probably, long tail, a bulky, rounded body and four pillar-like legs. But with a total of just 10 meters (33 feet) it is one of the smaller members of the sauropod group, similar in length to a reticulated python, the longest reptile alive today. Its neck was proportionally long, its front legs were shorter than the rear pair, and its feet bore the typical five digits, with the first (the "big toe") clawed, as in most sauropods.

Amargasaurus was a dicraeosaurid and with the diplodocids placed in the larger diplodocid group. It is notable for the row of double spines along much of its vertebral column – neck, back and tail. The role of these spines has been widely discussed. They occur in certain other groups of dinosaurs, including huge theropods (meat-eaters) such as *Spinosaurus*; the plant-eating Iguanodon-like *Ouranosaurus*; fellow sauropod *Dicraeosaurus*; and some non-dinosaur prehistoric reptiles, such as *Dimetrodon* (see page 44). The usual explanation is that they held up a fleshy or skin-like flap or "sail" – or, in the case of *Amargasaurus*, two of them. The flaps may have been for body temperature regulation, visual display, or, perhaps in the case of *Amargasaurus*, intimidation of, and protection from, the massive and powerful predatory dinosaurs that roamed South America during the Cretaceous period.

DINO FACTFILE

Amargasaurus

Meaning: La Amarga reptile

Pronunciation: Ah-mar-gah-sore-uss

Period: Early Cretaceous

Main group: Sauropoda

Length: 10 meters (33 feet)

Weight: 2.6 metric tons (2.6 tons)

Diet: Plants

Fossils: Argentina

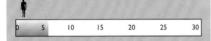

| 0 | 5 | 10 | 15 | 20 | 25 | 30 |

BELOW The extent of the back spines of *Amargasaurus* is debated, with some views that they were on the neck and body only, and others that they extended mainly along the neck. The spines may have been separate structures or coated with a long flap of thin skin, like a sail or fin.

QUAESITOSAURUS / NEMEGTOSAURUS

Fossilized skulls are relatively rare among the sauropods. After all, skulls are among the smallest parts of a sauropod body and consist more of strips and struts of bone than of great slabs or girders. It is perhaps ironic then that these two sauropods, *Quaesitosaurus* and *Nemegtosaurus*, are named solely from remains of skulls. Both were found in the Gobi Desert in Mongolia, both date from the Late Cretaceous period, and both have been compared to the *Diplodocus*-based family of sauropods, and possibly to *Dicraeosaurus* (see page 141). Extrapolating from existing remains, using typical diplodocid proportions, yields an overall length for each of these dinosaurs of around 12–13 meters (39–43 feet), but this is highly speculative. With further finds of other body parts, including perhaps more skulls, both may turn out to be the same type of dinosaur.

Quaesitosaurus (a name variously misspelled as *Qaesitosaurus*, *Questosaurus*, even *Questiosaurus*) was discovered by a Soviet– Mongolian expedition in 1971 and named in 1983. The skull shows that this dinosaur probably had good hearing, since there is a large opening and a chamber in its ear region that would have allowed sounds to resonate there. The overall skull shape is low and broad, with insubstantial, peg-like teeth that appear capable of raking in only soft food, perhaps water plants.

The skull of *Nemegtosaurus* was found during the Polish–Mongolian expeditions of the late 1960s and early 1970s and named in the year that *Quaesitosaurus* was found, 1971. Its name evokes the Nemegt Basin or Valley, a famous fossil site in the Gobi Desert that has yielded the remains of many well-known dinosaurs, although similar fossils have also been found in China. The skull is more complete than that of *Quaesitosaurus*, and also long and low, but not quite as broad across the snout. It has similar peg-like teeth at the front of the jaws only, not in the cheek region like *Quaesitosaurus*.

DINO FACTFILE
Quaesitosaurus / *Nemegtosaurus*
Meaning: Unusual or abnormal reptile / Nemegt reptile

Pronunciation: Kye-sit-owe-sore-uss / Nem-egg-toe-sore-uss

Period: Late Cretaceous

Main group: Sauropoda

Length: Estimated 12–13 meters (39–43 feet)

Weight: Estimated 5–10 metric tons (5–10 tons)

Diet: Plants

Fossils: Mongolia, perhaps China

0	5	10	15	20	25	30

LEFT *Quaesitosaurus* is nearly all guesswork – only parts of its fossil skull have been found. This has a long, horse-like muzzle shape, with weak teeth that must have pulled in fairly soft vegetation.

Brachiosaurus

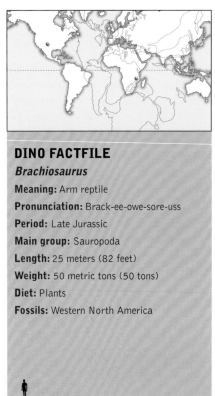

DINO FACTFILE
Brachiosaurus
Meaning: Arm reptile
Pronunciation: Brack-ee-owe-sore-uss
Period: Late Jurassic
Main group: Sauropoda
Length: 25 meters (82 feet)
Weight: 50 metric tons (50 tons)
Diet: Plants
Fossils: Western North America

| 0 | 5 | 10 | 15 | 20 | 25 | 30 |

Monstrous by any standards, *Brachiosaurus* remains the biggest dinosaur well known from complete remains. It has also given its name to a family of sauropods, the Brachiosauridae, that includes many other giants, such as *Sauroposeidon* and *Bothriospondylus*. One of the group's key features is reflected in the meaning of its name, "arm reptile" – the front limbs were much longer than the rear pair, while other families of sauropods, based on *Diplodocus* or *Titanosaurus*, had rear legs longer than the front ones. Great forelimbs gave brachiosaurids a sloping profile from neck down to shoulders, down the back to the hips, and on down the tail, which was relatively short. There are also key features in the brachiosaurid skull. It had a high forehead with nostrils set right on top above the eyes, a kink that angled from the forehead into the low snout, and large spoon- or chisel-shaped teeth, 26 around the front of each jaw.

American paleontologist and fossil hunter Elmer Riggs collected the first specimens of *Brachiosaurus* in 1900 in western Colorado's Grand River Valley. He coined the name in 1903. Expeditions to Tendaguru, then in German East Africa (later Tanganyika, now Tanzania) in 1908 yielded a spectacular skeleton that helped to fill in many details of this great beast. In addition to being one of the biggest dinosaurs, *Brachiosaurus*-like animals were widespread with finds from Portugal and possibly Algeria, but they have not been confirmed as *Brachiosaurus*. Many aspects of its feeding methods and other behavior patterns are discussed on other pages in this chapter.

RIGHT *Brachiosaurus* is usually shown rearing up to reach the tallest vegetation, some 13–14 meters (42–46 feet) above the ground. This is more than twice the height of today's tallest animal, the giraffe. Whether the heart of Brachiosaurus was powerful enough to pump blood to such a great height is much debated.

LEFT Recent reports of the fossil evidence suggest that *Sauroposeidon* and cousins such as *Brachiosaurus* (opposite) may not have been able to raise their heads to full height. Instead the head was swung around more horizontally on its lengthy neck in a great arc, to cover the maximum feeding area while saving the energy of moving the dinosaur's massive bulk.

SAUROPOSEIDON

Brachiosaurus long held the record as the tallest dinosaur, based on its ability to extend its great neck upward rather than forward (see opposite). A recent challenger for the title of "giraffe of the dinosaurs" is *Sauroposeidon*. At full neck stretch on its elongated front limbs, *Brachiosaurus* probably stood around 13–14 meters (43–46 feet) tall, more than twice as tall as today's giraffe. *Sauroposeidon* in the same pose has been estimated at 16 or 18 meters (52½–59 feet). In a modern setting, *Brachiosaurus* could look into a window on the fifth story of a building, but *Sauroposeidon* could perhaps peer into the sixth floor.

A great deal of what is said about *Sauroposeidon*, however, including its overall length and weight, is little more than informed guesswork. Few parts of the huge beast have been identified, mainly neck vertebrae, some nearly 1.5 meters (5 feet) in length, and associated ribs. They were first noticed in 1994 by Bobby Cross, an amateur fossil-spotter who was out walking and

exercising the bloodhounds that he was training for prison and police work in Otaka County, Oklahoma. Huge fossil footprints near Glen Rose, Texas, have also been attributed to Sauroposeidon, which was named in 1999 by American paleontologists Matt Wedel and Richard Cifelli.

In Greek myth, Poseidon was the god of the sea and also of earthquakes; *Sauroposeidon* had a periscope-like neck and probably made the earth tremble as it walked. The great plant-eater lived some 110 million years ago, considerably later than other long-necked types, although *Brachiosaurus* itself may have survived to around the same time. As far as the fossils show, these were among the last of the great longnecks to survive in North America. However sauropods from other families continued for millions of years elsewhere.

DINO FACTFILE

Sauroposeidon

Meaning: Poseidon [earthquake or sea god] reptile

Pronunciation: Sore-owe-pos-eye-don

Period: Early Cretaceous

Main group: Sauropoda

Length: Estimated 34 meters (112 feet)

Weight: Estimated 50–60 metric tons (50–60 tons)

Diet: Plants

Fossils: USA (Oklahoma, Texas, Wyoming)

| 0 | 5 | 10 | 15 | 20 | 25 | 30 |

ULTRASAUROS (ULTRASAURUS)

DINO FACTFILE

Ultrasauros

Meaning: Ultra reptile, beyond reptile

Pronunciation: Ull-trah-sore-oss

Period: Late Jurassic

Main group: Sauropoda

Length: Estimated 25–35 meters
(82–115 feet)

Weight: Estimated 30–100 metric tons
(30–100 tons)

Diet: Plants

Fossils: USA (Colorado)

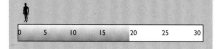

This dinosaur may or may not have existed. It has a checkered history of discovery, identification and naming. Many now view the fossils on which its identity is based as a mixture of specimens from two other giant sauropods, *Brachiosaurus* and *Supersaurus*. Events began with the 1979 discovery of some huge dinosaur remains in the well-known fossil-rich rocks called the Morrison Formation, in western Colorado. James Jensen, a paleontologist who had excavated *Supersaurus* fossils there in the early 1970s, studied the specimens, chiefly a scapula (shoulder blade), some vertebrae (backbones) and part of the pelvis (hipbone or hip girdle), and in 1985 he named this giant *Ultrasaurus*.

But the name "*Ultrasaurus*" had already been given to another, smaller *Brachiosaurus*-like sauropod, from the Cretaceous period. Its fossils had been found in the 1970s, far away from Colorado in South Korea. That find was named *Ultrasaurus* in 1983 by Haang Mook Kim, but, being established from very partial remains, its identity was also dubious. Even so, the confusion could not be allowed to worsen, so in 1991 the American *Ultrasaurus* was renamed by changing one letter, to *Ultrasauros* (species *Ultrasauros macintoshi*). Estimates of its size varied greatly because the remains were so incomplete. The most common maximum estimates were of a length around 30 meters (99 feet) and a weight up to 80 metric tons (80 tons), although one scientist argued for a breathtaking 130 metric tons (130 tons). Any debate will prove to be in vain if it turns out that the shoulder blade is in fact from *Brachiosaurus* and that the vertebrae came from another dinosaur, such as *Supersaurus*.

RIGHT *Ultrasauros* is one of several truly gigantic sauropods named on the basis of slim evidence. Its fossils may turn out to be from two similar dinosaurs, *Brachiosaurus* and perhaps *Supersaurus*.

LEFT *Haplocanthosaurus* has proved difficult to relate to other sauropods and is currently placed on its own as a basal diplodocoid.

HAPLOCANTHOSAURUS

When first discovered in North America, *Haplocanthosaurus* or "single spine reptile" was though to be a cetiosaur-like sauropod, and its scientific history is mixed up with that of England's "whale reptile" (see page 163). In 1901, John Bell Hatcher, an industrious American paleontologist, discovered *Haplocanthosaurus* remains, in fact, parts of the skeletons of two individuals, in Colorado. The site near Canyon City had already yielded numerous sauropod and other remains, such as *Diplodocus* and *Camarasaurus*, many of them described and named by Othniel Charles Marsh or his great rival, Edward Drinker Cope. Hatcher described *Haplocanthosaurus* in 1903, naming it after the neural spines or upward exensions on its vertebrae. From details of the vertebrae, *Haplocanthosaurus* might be a smaller cousin of *Brachiosaurus*; and it was also decided that the *Haplocanthosaurus* genus included dinosaurs previously called *Haplocanthus*.

In the meantime, English fossil experts had been following the study of *Haplocanthosaurus* with great interest. A number of reports noted the growing list of similarities between it and *Cetiosaurus* (see page 163), which had already been named for over 60 years and known as a dinosaur for more than 30. By making detailed comparisons between the two dinosaurs, the fossil experts saw that the two were different enough to have their own genera. They were further thought to belong to the same group of medium- to large-sized sauropods, then referred to as cetiosaurids. However, in 1999, it was thought that *Haplocanthosaurus* differed sufficiently to be placed in its own group, the haplocanthosaurids. More recent analyses have indicated various possible relationships within the sauropods, but none with any certainty. Most recently, it has been seen as a very basal or derived diplodocoid.

DINO FACTFILE
Haplocanthosaurus
Meaning: Single-spine [spike] lizard
Pronunciation: Hap-low-kan-thoe-sore-uss
Period: Late Jurassic
Main group: Sauropoda
Length: 14.8 meters (49 feet)
Weight: Estimated 12.8 metric tons (12.8 tons)
Diet: Plants
Fossils: USA (Colorado, Wyoming)

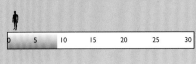

LEFT After many years of obscurity, the titanosaurs are becoming better known due to exciting new finds, mainly in Argentina. However, the original genus *Titanosaurus* itself now appears not to have any distinct features and the name is considered a "dubious name" (*nomen dubium*).

TITANOSAURUS

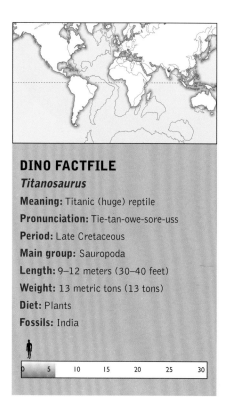

DINO FACTFILE
Titanosaurus

Meaning: Titanic (huge) reptile

Pronunciation: Tie-tan-owe-sore-uss

Period: Late Cretaceous

Main group: Sauropoda

Length: 9–12 meters (30–40 feet)

Weight: 13 metric tons (13 tons)

Diet: Plants

Fossils: India

0	5	10	15	20	25	30

"Titanic reptile" is one of a select group of dinosaurs that is both well known, and yet not well known. Its remains were studied and named as long ago as the 1870s and established a whole dinosaur family, Titanosauridae. Subsequent finds of sauropod fossils were compared with this and other families of giant long-necked, long-tailed, plant-eating dinosaurs, and thereby slotted into place in the lists of classifications. However, the original fossils, from which *Titanosaurus* was named by Richard Lydekker, a British paleontologist, in 1877, and the family in 1885, were a sparse and mixed set from India. Later remains came from Europe, and from South America too. As with the meat-eating dromaeosaurids and the duck-billed hadrosaurids, the family now contains members known much more thoroughly from much more complete fossils than the original member on which the family was based.

The titanosaurid family includes more than 20 genera of sauropods, mainly from Late Jurassic to Late Cretaceous times, and mainly from the southern land masses. They have various features in common. Examples are *Saltasaurus*, *Chubutisaurus*, *Neuquensaurus* and the truly mammoth *Argentinosaurus* of South America; and possibly Janenschia of Africa. *Titanosaurus* itself was thought to have the usual sauropod body, with a total length of up to 18 meters (59 feet). In 1996, Ruben Martinez excavated the first good specimen of a titanosaurid skull. It has a low, longish snout, narrow, well-spaced teeth, and nostrils high on the forehead in front of the eyes. The original *Titanosaurus* fossils included only a few caudal vertebrae (tail backbones) and a slender femur (thighbone), none of which are distinct to characterize the genus *Titanosaurus*.

CAMARASAURUS

Probably the best known of all North American sauropods, from its plentiful fossil remains, *Camarasaurus* has given valuable insight into the herding and breeding patterns of these huge dinosaurs. It once also gave its name to a whole family of long-necked giants, the Camarasauridae. Its four limbs were of roughly equal length, in contrast to *Brachiosaurus*'s longer forelegs, or *Diplodocus*, with its longer hindlegs, so that its back was almost parallel to the ground. Its build was thick-set and compact for a sauropod, with a big body, and a neck and tail that were relatively short for sauropods.

The name *Camarasaurus*, meaning "chambered reptile," is derived from the hollows found in its large vertebrae. These helped to save weight. The skull was short and relatively short-muzzled, with powerful jaws and sturdy, spoon-like, deep-rooted teeth that extended backward almost into the cheeks, unlike the front-only teeth of some sauropod families.

Camarasaurus could probably crop in tougher vegetation than its contemporaries in the Late Jurassic forests of what are now the states of Colorado, Wyoming and Utah.

The history of *Camarasaurus* fossils and naming are mixed up with the histories of several other large Late Jurassic sauropods from the region, including *Diplodocus* and *Apatosaurus* (see page 143). It was named in 1877 by Edward Drinker Cope from the evidence of some vertebrae (backbones) found earlier that year near Canyon City, Colorado. Other remains – which had been given names such as *Uintasaurus*, *Morosaurus*, *Caulodon*, or species of *Apatosaurus* – were reassigned as *Camarasaurus* in 1958 by Theodore White. One of the key finds, in the early 1920s, was of a very complete and well-preserved specimen of a young *Camarasaurus* at the National Dinosaur Monument in Utah. A much newer find, made in Colorado and currently dubbed *Cathetosaurus*, is probably *Camarasaurus*.

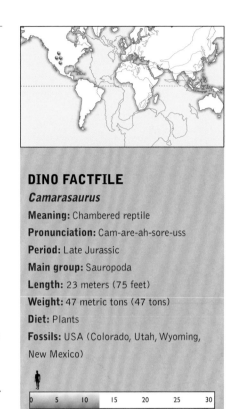

DINO FACTFILE
Camarasaurus
Meaning: Chambered reptile
Pronunciation: Cam-are-ah-sore-uss
Period: Late Jurassic
Main group: Sauropoda
Length: 23 meters (75 feet)
Weight: 47 metric tons (47 tons)
Diet: Plants
Fossils: USA (Colorado, Utah, Wyoming, New Mexico)

| 0 | 5 | 10 | 15 | 20 | 25 | 30 |

RIGHT For a sauropod, *Camarasaurus* was relatively short-necked and short-tailed.

OPISTHOCOELICAUDIA

DINO FACTFILE
Opisthocoelicaudia

Meaning: Tail backbone with cupped rear,
posterior tail cavity, hollow-backed tailbone
(and many other versions)

Pronunciation: Owe-piss-thoe-seel-ee-cawd-ee-ah

Period: Late Cretaceous

Main group: Sauropoda

Length: 10–12 meters (33–39½ feet)

Weight: 15–20 metric tons (15–20 tons)

Diet: Plants

Fossils: Mongolia

Noted for one of the longest and most complex names of any dinosaur, *Opisthocoelicaudia* was a medium-sized titanosaur sauropod with similarities to *Saltasaurus*. It lived some 60–70 million years later, however, during the Late Cretaceous period, and on another continent entirely, Asia. Its fossils were recovered in 1965 by one of a series of Polish–Mongolian expeditions to the Gobi Desert in Mongolia. They were the largest bones to be dug out of the Nemegt Basin there, but they lack the skull and most of the neck. The specimen and some associated fragments were described and named in 1977 by Magdalena Borsuk-Bialynicka, a Polish paleontologist.

Opisthocoelicaudia was probably 10–12 meters (33–39½feet) long and sturdily built so that its body weight may have equaled that of *Diplodocus*, which was twice as long but far

slimmer. In its general structure and behavior, *Opisthocoelicaudia* was most similar to titanosaurids. The complex name refers to the caudal vertebrae (tailbones). The forward-facing surfaces of some of these were domed, or convex, each nestling into the scooped or concave rearward-facing surface of the vertebra in front. This contrasts with the joints between the tailbones in most other sauropods, where both of these surfaces are much flatter. The entire backbone also shows other interesting features, such as well-developed pleurocoels (hollowed-out cavities or openings in the sides), and roughened areas for the attachment of strong muscles and ligaments.

RIGHT Fossils of plants and animals found with those of *Opisthocoelicaudia* suggest that it lived in open lowland forests, and probably consumed 70-80 kilograms (154–176 pounds), the weight of a well-built adult human, of vegetation each day.

SHUNOSAURUS

This long-necked, medium-sized plant-eater from the Middle Jurassic was grouped with the cetiosaurid sauropods, but modern analysis places it with animals such as *Mamenchisaurus* and *Barapasaurus* as a basal eusauropod. *Shunosaurus* is well known from more than 20 varied but essentially similar and relatively complete skeletons, about five with skulls – unusual among sauropod remains. It was named in 1983 after one of its fossil sites in the Shuozhou (Shuo-xian) area of central China, by three productive paleontologists, Dong Zhiming, Zhou Shiwu and Zhang Yihong.

Shunosaurus was similar in overall size, shape, and behavior to *Camarasaurus*. Compared to later sauropods, *Shunosaurus* was more heavily built and had a relatively shorter neck and tail, with fewer vertebrae (backbones) along the spinal column – 12 in the neck, 13 in the main back, four fused together to form the sacrum (part of the hip girdle) and 44 in the tail. The most notable feature was the tail "club." As this was not noticed from the first specimens reconstructed, it is missing in earlier restorations. The lobed club was formed from enlarged tail-tip vertebrae and probably had two (or two pairs) of spikes or spines. The overall shape resembles a scaled-down version of the hammer-like tail of an ankylosaurid armored dinosaur, such as *Euoplocephalus* (see page 229). To date, *Shunosaurus* is the only sauropod with such a feature, presumably used in self-defense.

DINO FACTFILE
Shunosaurus

Meaning: Shuo reptile
(from its discovery site)

Pronunciation: Shoo-noe-sore-uss

Period: Middle Jurassic

Main group: Sauropoda

Length: 9.5 meters (31 feet)

Weight:3 metric tons (3 tons)

Diet: Plants

Fossils: China

| 0 | 5 | 10 | 15 | 20 | 25 | 30 |

LEFT *Shunosaurus* had spoon- or ladle-shaped teeth to crop low-growing leaves and stems. Like many of the larger prosauropods, its estimated lifespan was 100-plus years. Its name "Shuo reptile" is derived from Shu, an ancient name for China's Sichuan region.

"HYPSELOSAURUS" AND AMPELOSAURUS

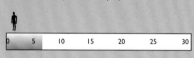

DINO FACTFILE
Ampelosaurus

Meaning: Vineyard reptile

Pronunciation: Am-pell-owe-sore-uss

Period: Late Cretaceous

Main group: Sauropoda

Length: 15 meters (49 feet)

Weight: 10 metric tons (10 tons)

Diet: Plants

Fossils: Europe (France, Spain)

0	5	10	15	20	25	30

"*Hypselosaurus*" was for many years regarded as a smallish dinosaur – for a sauropod. Its total length has been estimated at 8–12 meters (26–39½ feet), and its weight at 5–10 metric tons (5–10 tons). "High ridge reptile" was found in Europe, in France and Spain. It was named early in the scientific history of dinosaurs, in 1869, by Philippe Matheron, who also named the smallish *Iguanodon*-like ornithopod dinosaur, *Rhabdodon*, in the same year. Matheron found some fossil eggs in 1859, which in 1877 were declared by Paul Gervais to be from a dinosaur – although no one took much notice. This remains the earliest report of dinosaur eggs.

However, the mixed preserved bones of "*Hypselosaurus*" are no longer regarded as a safe basis for establishing a dinosaur genus, so the name "*Hypselosaurus*" is now regarded as invalid.

There is an excellent replacement in *Ampelosaurus*, which is as "new" as "*Hypselosaurus*" is "old." Its fossils are about 72 million years old and were found in 2002 at Campagne-sur-Aude, near Espéraza in the southwest of France near the Pyrenees. The specimen is nicknamed "Eva" after its discoverer, geology student Eva Morvan, and is the most complete dinosaur skeleton ever found in France. In life this individual was probably about 15 meters (49 feet) long and 10 metric tons (10 tons) in weight, but it was thought to be a relative youngster at the time of death, since similar bones found in the area are almost twice the size and probably from adults. The fascinating find also includes lumps of body armor. *Ampelosaurus* has many titanosaur features, but its position within this large group of sauropods is uncertain.

RIGHT The fossils of *Hypselosaurus* are no longer regarded as representing one kind of dinosaur, but an ill-defined mixture of types. However the newer discovery of *Ampelosaurus* would be similar in its overall sauropod-like shape, although larger.

BELOW *Cetiosaurus* was the first sauropod to be described for science, but not as a dinosaur. At the time, almost two centuries ago, its remains were thought to be those of a whale. It was not recognized as a dinosaur until 1869, when it found temporary fame as the largest land-living animal discovered to that time.

CETIOSAURUS

Today it may seem difficult to confuse a dinosaur with a whale, but, in the early years of scientific fossil-hunting, matters were very different. The remains of *Cetiosaurus* were first collected in the 1830s, possibly 1809, and later studied by Richard Owen and also William Buckland, the English geologist and naturalist of *Megalosaurus* fame, at Oxford in the 1830s. Buckland's French colleague and rival, Georges Cuvier, then the preeminent authority on fossils and living animals, saw some likeness to whales, especially in size and in associated remains of sea creatures (see page 283). Then British paleontologist Richard Owen discerned similarities to the skeletons of reptiles. In 1841, the year he coined the term Dinosauria for the whole dinosaur group, Owen also named *Cetiosaurus* ("whale reptile"). At this stage, *Cetiosaurus* was still viewed as a non-dinosaur. Only in 1869, after the discovery of a reasonably complete skeleton in Oxfordshire, England,

did Thomas Henry Huxley, close colleague of Charles Darwin and champion of the then-new theory of evolution, finally conclude that *Cetiosaurus* was a dinosaur.

Cetiosaurus was an eusauropod from the Middle Jurassic period, about 16 meters (52½ feet) long and around 11 metric tons (11 tons) in weight. The individual vertebrae (backbones) each had a very large central part, called the vertebral body, with small, flange-like extensions where the spinal muscles were attached. This contrasted greatly to the slim, scooped, large-extensioned vertebrae of later sauropods.

The rear legs were massive and thick-set, and considerably taller than the front limbs, to carry the great body weight. The front limbs of other early sauropods, such as *Patagosaurus*, *Shunosaurus* or *Barapasaurus*, are shorter and weaker in comparison. Cetiosaur fossils have been found in many parts of England.

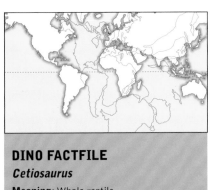

DINO FACTFILE
Cetiosaurus

Meaning: Whale reptile
(Cetaceans = whales and dolphins)

Pronunciation: Set-ee-owe-sore-uss

Period: Middle Jurassic

Main group: Sauropoda

Length: 16 meters (52½ feet)

Weight: 11 metric tons (11 tons)

Diet: Plants

Fossils: England

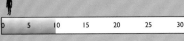

CHAPTER SEVEN

BIRD-FOOT DINOSAURS

THE ORNITHOPODS WERE PERHAPS NOT THE MOST SPECTACULAR OF
DINOSAURS, BUT THEY WERE CERTAINLY AMONG THE MOST NUMEROUS
AND SUCCESSFUL OF ALL DINOSAUR GROUPS.

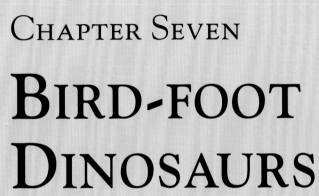

"Bird feet"

Most ornithopod ("bird-foot") dinosaurs had three forward-pointing digits on each of their rear feet. These "toes" were slightly splayed and tipped with curved claws, which were never very sharp. Many kinds also had a fourth digit, which was much smaller and held off the ground, facing to the rear. This structure has many similarities to the feet of numerous birds today, but so did the feet of many other dinosaurs. Ornithopods were named as a group before this more wide-ranging similarity had become apparent.

One group or more?

The ornithopods include a wide variety of dinosaurs, from some that were almost as small as a modern pet cat to others that were larger than a modern elephant. They were all plant-eaters and all belonged to the great ornithischian ("bird-hipped") group, one of the two major dinosaur groups. But, other similarities among the ornithischians are less well-defined. Several types, like *Heterodontosaurus* and *Hypsilophodon*, had specialized teeth not seen in other ornithopods. They seem to have had little defense other than to run – they were probably very fast moving and agile. They were common in certain habitats, especially drier scrublands, and in some regions, particularly Europe and southern Africa. In newer classification schemes some of the smaller, earlier kinds like Lesothosaurus are often included in other groups, leaving those such as *Hypsilophodon*, *Camptosaurus*, *Iguanodon* and its cousins, and the hadrosaurs or duckbills (see next chapter) as "true" ornithopods.

Biggest and best

The largest non-hadrosaur ornithopods, and the best known from fossils, are *Iguanodon* and its cousins. Indeed, they are among the most studied of all dinosaurs. Hundreds and hundreds of preserved ornithopod specimens have been found, not only of bones and teeth but also stomach contents; their droppings, known as coprolites; patches of skin and scales; footprints; and eggs. The iguanodontids appeared in the Jurassic period, perhaps alongside *Dryosaurus* (see page 184). In the period that followed, the Cretaceous, they increased in size and enjoyed enormous success on almost every continent around the world, along with *Camptosaurus*, *Iguanodon* itself, *Altirhinus* and *Muttaburrasaurus*.

Why did Iguanodon and its relatives succeed?

The precise reasons for the success of the iguanodontids are not clear. They may include: the rows of teeth in their powerful jaws, which formed a very efficient chewing mechanism; the beak-like fronts to their mouths, suited for tearing vegetation fronds off their stalks; their adaptable front limbs, which could be used for walking or grasping or fighting (with their "thumb" claws); and their large size, which served as defense against predators. Iguanodon could feed at any level from the ground to 7 or 8 meters (23 or 26 feet) above it. The Cretaceous period was a time of rapidly evolving vegetation, as flowering plants – flowers, bushes, herbs and blossom trees – appeared and spread fast, so perhaps the iguanodontids were suited to this new type of food source. On the behavioral side, these dinosaurs also show patterns of herd-dwelling and migration (see pages 171). But they could not sustain their success, and as the Cretaceous period continued they became less common, possibly giving rise to their great competitors and fellow ornithopods, the "duckbilled" hadrosaurs.

PREVIOUS PAGE Small Australian ornithopods such as *Leaellynasaura* may have been warm-blooded and may have trekked to regular hibernaculum, or winter sleeping quarters. The discovery of the fossils of these *Hypsilophodon*-like dinosaurs, and the environment in which they lived, has changed many ideas about "slow, stupid, cold-blooded" dinosaurs.

LEFT A herd of *Iguanodon* dinosaurs feed on plants in a prehistoric landscape. These herbivorous ornithopod dinosaurs lived during the Early Cretaceous Period in what is now Europe. They reached around 10 metres (33 feet) long.

Dryosaurus

"Oak tree reptile" was named in 1894 by Othniel Charles Marsh. Its fossils have been found at numerous sites in western North America, including Colorado, Wyoming, and Utah, suggesting that it was fairly widespread. It has been included in the family Hypsilophodontidae. However, being Late Jurassic, it would be an early example of this group. It is also larger – with an overall length of over 3 meters (10 feet) – than many other, later members of the group, such as *Hypsilophodon* itself (see page 179). Other views gaining more acceptance are that it represents a separate family of its own, Dryosauridae, which in turn are primitive iguanodonts, which gradually evolved larger size animals during the Cretaceous period.

Dryosaurus was a fast mover on its long back legs, each with three digits (in contrast to *Hypsilophodon*, which had four digits on each of its back feet). The mouth had a horny beak at the front for pecking and nipping off food items, and long, sharp cheek teeth for thorough chewing. Other features include the smaller front legs, with five digits each, and the very long, stiff tail, which tapered gradually. Like other ornithopod herbivores, it must have used speed and agility as its main defense against predators, such as the great *Allosaurus*.

Fossils of a dinosaur very similar in size and structure to *Dryosaurus* were found in Tanzania in East Africa. At first, they were given the name *Dysalotosaurus* ("lost wood reptile"), but further studies have led to this creature being named *Dryosaurus*.

DINO FACTFILE

Dryosaurus

Meaning: Oak tree reptile, tree reptile

Pronunciation: Dry-owe-sore-uss

Period: Late Jurassic

Main group: Ornithopoda

Length: 3–3.5 meters (10–11½feet)

Weight: 50–80 kilograms (110–176 pounds)

Diet: Plants

Fossils: USA (Colorado, Wyoming, Utah)

ABOVE *Dryosaurus* fossils include a fairly complete adult skeleton, parts of a very young individual, various teeth and isolated bones. Along with *Valdosaurus*, it is usually placed in its own family, Dryosauridae, with the iguanodontids as closest relatives.

TENONTOSAURUS

Most members of the ornithopod family Hypsilophodontidae were at the smaller end of the range of dinosaur sizes. *Hypsilophodon* itself was around 2 meters (6½ feet) in length, and others were almost half this size. *Tenontosaurus*, however, was three times longer and many times heavier, perhaps weighing up to 1 metric ton (1 ton). The fossils of *Tenontosaurus* come from several places in the United States, including Montana, Utah, Oklahoma, and perhaps Texas. The dinosaur was named by John Ostrom in 1970.

Tenontosaurus has been regarded as an "aberrant" hypsilophodontid from the Early Cretaceous, placed in this family due to various skeletal features. In particular, the skull and teeth of *Tenontosaurus* resemble those of *Hypsilophodon* (see page 179), although its much greater size and heavier build would mean that its forelimbs were larger and sturdier, in proportion to its body, approaching the size of the rear limbs. But it has also been considered a cousin of *Iguanodon*, due to other similarities in the teeth and in the bones of the forelimbs and hip. Yet another opinion is that it is more closely related to *Dryosaurus* (see opposite).

Reconstructions often show *Tenontosaurus* on all fours, cropping vegetation from ground plants and low shrubs, rather than walking on its hind legs with body horizontal, like *Iguanodon*, or rearing up to reach leaves higher in trees. Similar reconstructions may show *Tenontosaurus* trying to feed but being interrupted by a "pack attack" from the theropod dinosaur *Deinonychus*. At one fossil site the remains of probably three *Deinonychus* were found near those of an adult *Tenontosaurus*, leading to speculation about group behavior in the predator.

DINO FACTFILE
Tenontosaurus

Meaning: Sinew reptile
Pronunciation: Ten-on-toe-sore-uss
Period: Early Cretaceous
Main group: Ornithopoda
Length: Up to 7.5 meters (24 feet)
Weight: Up to 1 metric ton (1 ton)
Diet: Plants
Fossils: USA (see text)

0	1	2	3	4	5	6

LEFT Specimens of *Tenontosaurus* range in length from less than two meters (6½ feet) to more than seven (23 feet). It has a complex combination of features that link it with various ornithopod groups, such as those of *Hypsilophodon*, *Iguanodon* and *Dryosaurus*.

CHAPTER EIGHT

THE
DUCKBILLS

HADROSAURS WERE AMONG THE LAST MAJOR DINOSAUR GROUPS TO EVOLVE, AND HAD MANY NEW FEATURES. THEY MAY HAVE BEEN THE NOISIEST AND MOST COLORFUL OF ALL REPTILES.

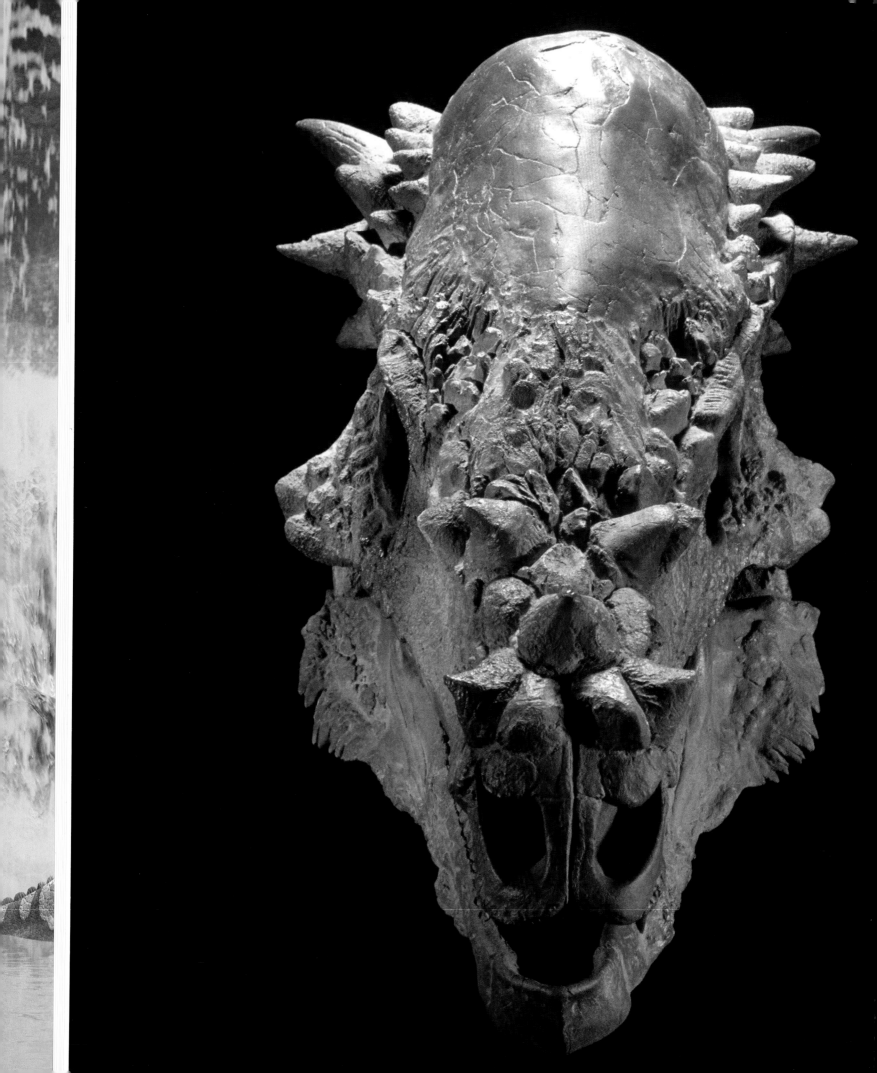

CHAPTER NINE

THE
BONEHEADS

THE PACHYCEPHALOSAURS WERE "BONEHEADS," WITH EXTREMELY
THICK LAYERS OF BONE ON THE TOP OF THEIR SKULLS.

CRASH AND BASH

AT CERTAIN TIMES OF YEAR, HILLY REGIONS AROUND THE WORLD ECHO TO THE THWACKS AND CRACKS OF RUTTING SHEEP AND GOATS. THE MALES LOWER THEIR HEADS AND HURL THEMSELVES AT EACH OTHER, CLASHING THEIR FOREHEADS AND HORNS WITH SO MUCH FORCE THAT THEY ARE SOMETIMES KNOCKED OUT. PACHYCEPHALOSAURS – "THICK-HEADED REPTILES" – MAY HAVE ENGAGED IN SIMILAR HEAD-BUTTING CONTESTS. THESE COULD HAVE TAKEN PLACE BETWEEN RIVALS AT BREEDING TIME, TO DEMONSTRATE THEIR STRENGTH AND FITNESS, AND SO SHOW THEIR SUITABILITY TO BECOME MATES AND PARENTS. PACHYCEPHALOSAURS ARE ALSO NICKNAMED "BONEHEADS," "HELMETHEADS" OR "DOMEHEADS," ALTHOUGH ONLY SOME TYPES HAD SKULL ROOFS WITH ROUNDED OR DOMED SHAPES.

WHY THE THICK SKULL?

Head-bashing is the main suggestion for the greatly thickened top or roof to the skull of pachycephalosaurs. In some types, the bony layer was more than 25 centimeters (10 inches) thick – the span of an adult human hand. This was not the only adaptation to exerting and absorbing great shocks and pressure to the head, while protecting the small brain within the skull. The neck bones were also sturdy and the neck itself was short, to withstand stress. The backbone and rear limbs were also strong, to help resist and also transmit the force of impact down through them to the ground.

LACK OF FINDS

In the rest of the skeleton, pachycephalosaurs seem to have been fairly unremarkable. Their teeth were small and weak, suited to eating soft vegetation. The tail was stiffened by bones and tendons lying alongside the caudal vertebrae (backbones). Toward the end of the tail was an expanded area of bone containing a chamber. The function of this feature is a mystery. An enlarged nerve cord, or muscle supports for tail spikes, have been suggested – but not convincingly – or the chamber may have been a store or repository for high-energy substances such as body fat or glycogen (animal starch), as seen in some birds today. Another problem stems from the extent of the fossil finds. Most pachycephalosaurs are known mainly, or solely, from their preserved skulls, or even just the thickened skull roof. Parts of the rest of the skeleton are rare or absent, with the notable exception of *Stegoceras*, which has been used as a basis or model for reconstructing most of the others.

PROBLEMS WITH HEAD-BANGING

In *Stegoceras* and *Pachycephalosaurus*, the skull roof was curved or domed. This means that, when two heads clashed, unless they did so exactly in line, the domes would easily slip past each other and jerk the animal's necks sideways. Most sheep and goats have flattened foreheads, which help them to avoid such slippage. Perhaps the domeheaded pachycephalosaurs did not butt head to head, but rammed opponents on other parts of the body. Another proposal is that these dinosaurs used their heads to bash predators, in the same way that a bull or ram or rhino lowers its head and charges at an enemy.

SMALL AND LATE

With around a dozen well-known types, the pachycephalosaur group was among the smallest of the main dinosaur groups. They appeared during the Early Cretaceous period, probably in Europe although perhaps in East Asia, but most are known from the Late Cretaceous period, and were spread across all the northern continents. They are placed along with the horned dinosaurs or ceratopsians, such as *Triceratops*, in the larger dinosaur group known as the marginocephalians or "margin heads" (see page 247).

PREVIOUS PAGE In this front-on head view the hugely thickened, smoothed "bone dome" of *Pachycephalosaurus* shines brightly amid the various small spikes, lumps and nodules which decorated the ridge around the upper head.
The whole skull is about as large as a medium-sized suitcase.

LEFT A pair of *Stegoceras* finally come to blows, perhaps after a lengthy period of strutting and posturing. Perhaps they would try to win the contest by visual threats, such as standing tall to emphasize their height and then lowering heads to show their "bone domes," before engaging in the much riskier stage of physical battle.

STEGOCERAS

Stegoceras is the best-known of the pachycephalosaurs or "bonehead" dinosaurs. It had a total length of some 2 meters (6½ feet) and is often likened in size to a goat – the head-butting habit of goats aids the comparison. *Stegoceras* is also one of the boneheads for which fossils other than the skull are known, comprising one partial skeleton and additional fragments. As a result, it is often used as the model for reconstructing other pachycephalosaurs (see page 207). Lawrence Lambe described and named Stegoceras in 1902, from Late Cretaceous remains recovered from the Belly River region of Alberta, Canada. Teeth associated with these skull remains resembled those of *Troodon*, a meat-eating dinosaur named almost 50 years before, so the fossils that we now know as *Stegoceras* were first called *Troodon* too. The link between the teeth and the skull fragments was called into doubt following studies of fossil finds at other sites, however, and in 1924 the find of a skull and part of a skeleton confirmed that *Stegoceras* was distinct from *Troodon*.

Stegoceras had a large skull with the typical bony roof up to 8 centimeters (3 inches) thick, forming a helmet-like dome (its functions are discussed on page 207). Rimming the dome around the rear of the head, and curving around and over each eye, forward to the snout, was a bony edging or "shelf." The teeth were tiny and curved with serrated edges; the brain and eyes were relatively large; the neck was stout; and the front limbs were small and unsuitable for carrying body weight. The rear limbs were larger, and sturdy rather than slim, their proportions suggesting a strong, deliberate mover rather than a fleet-footed sprinter. The tail was long and evenly tapered, and was probably not flexible. The base of the tail had an enlarged or expanded "chamber" (this is discussed on page 207).

LEFT The skull of *Prenocephale* is adorned with various small lumps and nodules of bone, arranged in rows or lines. It is difficult to propose a physical function for these projections, so perhaps they were visual symbols, possibly of sex (male or female) or age (immature or sexually mature).

PRENOCEPHALE

In the 1970s, scientists from Poland and Russia, accompanied by Mongolian experts, mounted several expeditions into the Gobi, which yielded many fascinating fossils, including *Prenocephale*. Perhaps more of an "egghead" than a "bonehead," this pachycephalosaur is known from a fine upper skull described and named in 1974 by Teresa Maryanska and Halszka Osmólska. It was excavated from the finely grained sandstone of the Nemegt Basin, where excellent fossilization conditions preserved parts of the skull's inside, even showing small openings where nerves and blood vessels passed into and out of the brain. Similar fossils have also been identified in North America, in Montana, and in Alberta, Canada. The remains are scarce, however, and even at the original Mongolian site there are very few other parts of the skeleton.

While *Prenocephale*'s head is very similar to that of Stegoceras, there are small

variations, such as the slight angular prominence just above the nasal openings in *Prenocephale*, when seen from the side. There is also evidence of several sets or chain-like rows of small bony lumps. On each side, one runs from the nostril rearward, partway along the side of the snout. There are two more rows above and below the eye, and another to the lower rear of the eye, which merges with a larger series. This stretches around the back of the head, angling upward and then across at the rear. These lumps or studs seem to have been more decorative than functional. The teeth are generally small, with a few slightly larger ones at the front of the upper jaw (which possibly bit down on a horny pad at the tip of the lower jaw) and examples of smaller teeth toward the cheek region. The type specimen of *Prenocephale* (from which it was originally named) is *Prenocephale prenes*, meaning "sloping sloping head." The Canadian representative has been dubbed *Prenocephale edmontonensis*.

DINO FACTFILE
Prenocephale

Meaning: Sloping head

Pronunciation: Pren-owe-seff-ah-lee

Period: Late Cretaceous

Main group: Pachycephalosauria

Length: 2.5 meters (8 feet)

Weight: 130 kilograms (287 pounds)

Diet: Plants

Fossils: Mongolia, possibly USA (Montana), Canada (Alberta)

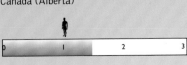

HOMALOCEPHALE AND GOYOCEPHALE

DINO FACTFILE

Homalocephale

Meaning: Level head, even head

Pronunciation: Hom-ah-low-seff-ah-lee

Period: Late Cretaceous

Main group: Pachycephalosauria

Length: 1.5–3 meters (5–10 feet)

Weight: 40–90 kilograms (88–200 pounds)

Diet: Plants

Fossils: Mongolia

Yet another pachycephalosaur or "bonehead" dinosaur, similar to *Stegoceras*, was *Homalocephale*. These dinosaurs had similar overall body proportions: large head on a sturdy neck; shorter front limbs, perhaps with four digits; much larger rear limbs for walking and running, with three weight-bearing digits and one high off the ground on each foot; and a long, evenly tapering, not very flexible tail. Reconstruction is based on fossils of a fine skull and almost complete skeleton from the Nemegt region of Omnogov, Mongolia. *Homalocephale* was named in 1974 by Teresa Maryanska and Halszka Osmólska.

Homalocephale had a thickened bony roof or top to the skull, but this was not quite enough to be called a dome. When seen in profile its skull was noticeably flatter than in similar types, such as *Stegoceras* and *Prenocephale*, and some experts regard *Homalocephale* fossils as juveniles of *Prenocephale*. But like *Prenocephale*, it

had several sets of chainlink-like rows of small bony studs or lumps. These seem to have formed patterns that adorned the head, rather than served a useful, physical purpose. The teeth of *Homalocephale* were small, as in other pachycephalosaurs, and leaf-like. This group of dinosaurs probably ate soft plants, chewing and shredding the foliage before swallowing it. Other parts of the skeleton show that the tail was stiffened by bony rods, and that part of the socket in the hipbone, which was the "bowl" for the "ball" or rounded head of the thighbone, had an unusual flange – different in shape to that of any other dinosaur. A similar dinosaur, *Goyocephale* (meaning "elegant or decorated head"), from the same region, was named in 1982. It also had a flat forehead. Along with other discoveries in the pachycephalosaur group, it suggests that these dinosaurs had two or four curved teeth, almost large enough to be called "tusks," near the front of the mouth.

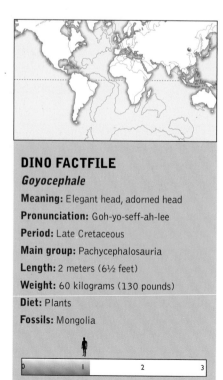

DINO FACTFILE

Goyocephale

Meaning: Elegant head, adorned head

Pronunciation: Goh-yo-seff-ah-lee

Period: Late Cretaceous

Main group: Pachycephalosauria

Length: 2 meters (6½ feet)

Weight: 60 kilograms (130 pounds)

Diet: Plants

Fossils: Mongolia

ABOVE *Homalocephale* had a large head, sturdy neck, and a stiff tail.

BELOW Pachycephalosaurus could probably move on all fours, or on its two rear legs. It may have munched at water plants with its very small, relatively weak teeth.

PACHYCEPHALOSAURUS

Well known as the largest bonehead discovered to date, "thick head reptile" may have reached a total length of 5 meters (16½feet). It was also one of the last members of the group, perhaps surviving up to the great extinction that signaled the end of the dinosaurs, around 66 million years ago. But, like many members of the bonehead group, its body is almost unknown from fossils, and instead is modeled on those of smaller types, such as *Stegoceras*, and then scaled up in the expected dinosaur proportions.

Only one good fossil skull is known for *Pachycephalosaurus*. It was found near Ekalaka, Montana, sometime in 1938–40 by William Winkley as he herded cattle on the family ranch. It differed in various ways from the already-known *Stegoceras*, and was much larger, so in 1943 it was named as a new dinosaur by Barnum Brown and Erich Schlaikjer. (The name *Pachycephalosaurus* had in fact been coined earlier, in 1931, in association with the small meat-eater

Troodon, but that usage was abandoned.) Remains have been located in Wyoming and South Dakota as well as Montana. Despite the lack of complete skulls, there are many parts that show the enormously enlarged roof of *Pachycephalosaurus*'s head, a mass of bone up to 25 centimeters (10 inches) thick. In addition, there are small bony spikes on the snout, and scattered lumps and nodules running around the side of the face, above and below each eye and out to the ridge or "shelf" that curves around the rear of the head. The eyes are relatively large, but the teeth are tiny and almost spiky, probably suited to soft plant food such as leaves and fruit. The main fossil of the skull is some 60 centimeters (24 inches) in length, and some scaled-up estimates of the snout–tail length of *Pachycephalosaurus* have exceeded 8 meters (26 feet), but modern versions are lower. The Pachycephalosauridae were named in 1945 by George Sternberg, when it was agreed these dinosaurs should have their own separate family.

DINO FACTFILE
Pachycephalosaurus

Meaning: Thick-head reptile

Pronunciation: Pack-ee-seff-ah-low-sore-uss

Period: Late Cretaceous

Main group: Pachycephalosauria

Length: 4–5 meters (13–16½ feet)

Weight: 400–500 kilograms (880–1100 pounds)

Diet: Plants

Fossils: Western USA (Wyoming, South Dakota, Montana), possibly Canada

LEFT The extraordinary headgear of *Stygimoloch* was probably for show, rather than for physical battles when the spikes and horns might easily be snapped and broken.

STYGIMOLOCH

DINO FACTFILE

Stygimoloch

Meaning: Demon of the Styx

Pronunciation: Stij-ee-moll-ock

Period: Late Cretaceous

Main group: Pachycephalosauria

Length: 2–3 meters (6½–10 feet)

Weight: 70–90 kilograms (155–200 pounds)

Diet: Plants

Fossils: USA (Montana, Wyoming)

In ancient Greek mythology, the River Styx separated the land of the living from the realm of the dead and demonic – Hades or Hell. With horns, spikes and bumps all over its skull, *Stygimoloch* – "demon of the Styx" – certainly resembles the usual image of a demon. It helps that its fossils were unearthed from the Hell Creek or "River of Hades" region of Montana. Its fossils have also been identified in Wyoming. *Stygimoloch* has been compared to a mixture of pachycephalosaur (bonehead), and ceratopsian (horned dinosaur) – especially the ceratopsian known as *Styracosaurus* (see page 259). Some of the spiky horns of *Stygimoloch* were up to 10 centimeters (4 inches) long. A discovery reported in 1998 shows a much more complete skull of *Stygimoloch*, allowing firmer ideas of the horn pattern around the head. On each side, three or four horns project at a low angle from the squamosal – the bone that forms the "shelf." There are also

many groups of small bumps or nodules along this region. This new evidence supports the view that such bonehead features were used for visual display, rather than head-butting (see page 207).

Stygimoloch was named by Peter Galton, a British paleontologist, and Hans-Dieter Sues, a German fossil expert, in 1983. It was probably a medium-sized pachycephalosaur, up to 3 meters (10 feet) in total length. In the absence of other evidence, it is usually reconstructed with the body shape and proportions of *Stegoceras* and other better-known boneheads. It is dated, like other members of its group, to the Late Cretaceous period, right at the end of the dinosaur age. In recent years, the opinion has grown that *Stygimoloch* remains are those of juvenile *Pachycephalosaurus*.

YAVERLANDIA

Some dinosaurs are named from many complete fossilized specimens. Others are not. *Yaverlandia* takes its name from Yaverland Point, a promontory near Sandown on the Isle of Wight in southern England. Known among fossil-hunters as Dinosaur Island, this small piece of England has produced a wealth of fossils, including dinosaurs such as *Hypsilophodon*, and many Jurassic marine reptiles, such as ichthyosaurs. But only part of a skull of Yaverlandia has been recovered. It resembles the thickened skull roof of other boneheads, but it has two distinctive bulges to the dome. It was found by Frank Abell and has been mentioned in the scientific literature since the 1930s. It was named as a new kind of pachycephalosaur in 1971 by Peter Galton (see also *Stygimoloch*, opposite). Another view, however, is that it may represent part of an armored dinosaur or ankylosaur (see Hylaeosaurus, page 222).

The fossil dates from the Early Cretaceous period, 125–120 million years ago, and so is much earlier in time than other bonehead dinosaurs. It is also from a very different region, since most pachycephalosaur remains are known from North America and East Asia. Also, Yaverlandia is small for a bonehead. From the skull parts, and using Stegoceras and others types as models, it is estimated to have been only about 1 meter (39 inches) long. But the evidence for other small pachycephalosaurs is growing. *Wannanosaurus*, named in 1970 from the Chinese province of Wannan, was perhaps 70 centimeters (27½ inches) long. *Micropachycephalosaurus*, also from China, was named in 1978 and, if it existed as conjectured, it, too, was probably less than 1 meter (39 inches) long, and weighed just 10 kilograms. *Micropachycephalosaurus* is often cited as one of the shortest dinosaurs with the longest of all dinosaur names.

DINO FACTFILE

Yaverlandia

Meaning: Of Yaverland (its discovery site)

Pronunciation: Yav-er-land-ee-ah

Period: Early Cretaceous

Main group: Possibly Pachycephalosauria (see also page 211)

Length: 1 meter (39 inches)

Weight: 20 kilograms (44 pounds)

Diet: Possibly plants

Fossils: Southern England

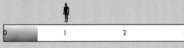

LEFT The "double-dome" head of *Yaverlandia* is shown in this reconstruction. This is the only pachycephalosaur with twin bulges on the roof of the skull, but the fossil evidence is very limited and not accepted by some experts.

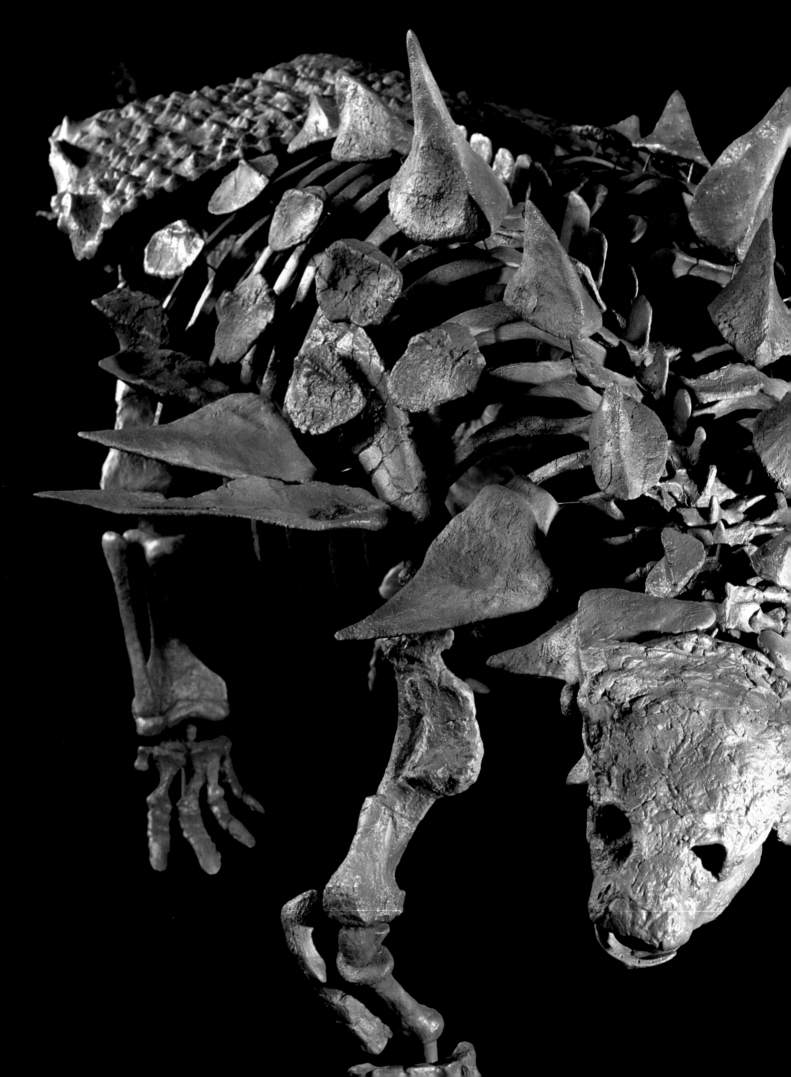

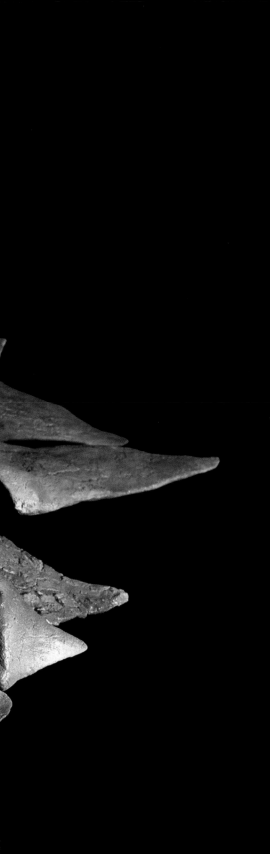

CHAPTER TEN

ARMORED DINOSAURS

NICKNAMES SUCH AS "WALKING TANKS" AND "DINOSAURS IN SUITS OF ARMOR" GIVE SOME IDEA OF THE SIZE, WEIGHT AND BONY PROTECTION OF THE PROBABLY PEACEFUL, PLANT-EATING ANKYLOSAURS.

THICK-SKINNED

ANKYLOSAURS – "FUSED REPTILES" – WERE THE BEST PROTECTED OF ALL DINOSAURS. THE GROUP NAME REFERS TO THE SLABS AND OTHER PIECES OF BONE THAT WERE JOINED OR FUSED OVER THEIR HEADS AND EMBEDDED IN THE SKIN OF THE NECKS, BACKS, FLANKS AND TAILS. ALMOST EVERY IMAGINABLE KIND OF BONY BARRIER – LUMPS, KNOBS, PLATES, SHIELDS, SPIKES, SPINES, SCALES – WAS USED AGAINST THE CLAWS AND TEETH OF MEAT-EATING DINOSAURS AND OTHER LARGE PREDATORS OF THE TIME, SUCH AS CROCODILES. ANKYLOSAURS ARE PLACED IN A LARGER DINOSAUR GROUP, THE THYREOPHORANS OR "SHIELD-BEARERS," ALONG WITH THE STEGOSAURS OR PLATED DINOSAURS.

GROUPS OF ARMORED REPTILES

There were two main subgroups of anyklosaurs. The most obvious distinction between them was that the earlier subgroup, the nodosaurids, lacked the massive lump of bone at the end of the tail that was possessed by members of the other subgroup, the ankylosaurids, and is usually known as the "tail club." Nodosaurids appeared in the Middle Jurassic period and are known from finds on all the northern continents as well as possibly Australia and Antarctica. Some of their kind persisted into the Cretaceous period and became very large: these included *Edmontonia* (see page 222). The ankylosaurids began to spread during the Early Cretaceous period and overlapped in range and time with several nodosaurid cousins. They had complex, folded air passages in their snouts and heads, and they lacked the sharp shoulder spines possessed by most nodosaurids. The ankylosaurids tail-clubbed their way into the very Late Cretaceous, mainly in North America and Asia. They also reached considerable sizes, some being even larger than the nodosaurids. Some classification schemes recognize additional subgroups, such as the polacanthids, based on *Polacanthus* (see page 225).

ARMOR GALORE

Some ankylosaurs had two or three layers of bone over certain parts of the head – overlapping layers of the real skull, and an extra layer on top of that. The bony parts covering their bodies were not, in general, joined to the skeleton beneath. They were dermal ossifications – units of bone that grew in, and were held on very firmly by, their thick, tough, stiff, leathery skins or hides. Some of these bony masses were set entirely within the thickness of the hide, so they were covered by skin too. Others, especially the sharper spines and spikes, had bony centers or cores that, in life, were covered with horn. This made them larger and probably sharper than they appear in the fossils, since the horn

disintegrated before preservation. It is tempting to make a comparison between ankylosaurs and another group of slow, well-protected reptiles, the tortoises, but the nature of the armor in the two groups was very different (see page 35).

SLOW AND PONDEROUS

Such substantial protection made ankylosaurs stiff, heavy, ponderous and slow. Their main defense against large carnivores, like the tyrannosaurs, was probably to crouch down, lowering their squat bodies the short distance to the ground, to protect their more vulnerable undersides. With weights of several tons, they would be extremely difficult for an opponent to topple over. Alternatively, they may have gone on the attack. Nodosaurids might have charged and jabbed with their long, sharp shoulder spines, while ankylosaurids could have swung around to bring their tail clubs into the battle as leg-breaking weapons. For most of the time, however, these dinosaurs roamed woods and forests, probably on their own rather than in herds, searching for soft plant food.

PREVIOUS PAGE *Gastonia* was an early Cretaceous ankylosaur whose fossils come from Grand County, Utah. The image shows the heavily armored body and assorted spikes and spines which gave this dinosaur formidable self-defense. This specimen is a juvenile and its back would be about chest-high to an adult human. *Gastonia* was a cousin of *Polacanthus* and was named in 1998 to honor paleontologist Robert Gaston.

LEFT *Polacanthus* turns to face an enemy, its large neck and shoulder spines providing excellent defense. However the exact positions of the spines, and the angles at which they were attached to the body, are subjects of much discussion.

BELOW *Scelidosaurus* was probably both bipedal and quadrupedal, moving with ease on two or four legs. Its teeth were most similar to those of stegosaurs. However due to finds in 1980 and especially 1985 this dinosaur has become better understood as probably the first true ankylosaur.

SCELIDOSAURUS

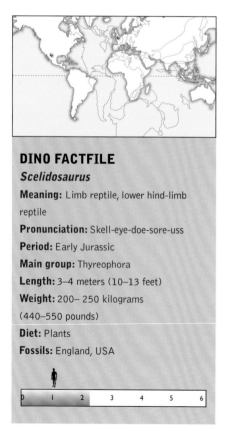

DINO FACTFILE
Scelidosaurus

Meaning: Limb reptile, lower hind-limb reptile

Pronunciation: Skell-eye-doe-sore-uss

Period: Early Jurassic

Main group: Thyreophora

Length: 3–4 meters (10–13 feet)

Weight: 200– 250 kilograms (440–550 pounds)

Diet: Plants

Fossils: England, USA

Scelidosaurus may have had a pivotal place in dinosaur evolution; it certainly presents a problem of grouping. It has been classified as an ornithischian, and, within this huge category, as a thyreophoran or "shield-bearer" and probably ankylosaur – but then the disagreements start. Some experts regard it as an early type of ankylosaur (hence its inclusion in this chapter); others regard it as a stegosaur, or as an ancestor of both groups; still others argue that it is a distinct type with its own family, the Scelidosauridae, perhaps along with *Scutellosaurus* (opposite) and *Emausaurus*, named from fossils found in Germany in 1990.

Scelidosaurus had a small head with a horny, beak-like front to its mouth. Its neck, body, and tail were studded with small pebble-like scales and larger bony plates, some shaped like low cones or slim triangles. It walked on all four limbs, with the rear ones longer and stronger, so that the back sloped up toward the hips. All these features were developed

and exaggerated in the stegosaur group later in the Jurassic period, although *Scelidosaurus* also had a distinctive skull and teeth, which link it more to the ankylosaur group.

Richard Owen, the British paleontologist who established the whole dinosaur group, Dinosauria, in 1841, named *Scelidosaurus* in 1868. Owen had been examining specimens of *Scelidosaurus* since 1859, mainly from Early Jurassic rocks at Charmouth on the south coast of England.

In 1863, a fairly complete skeleton was unearthed. More than a century later, in 1985, also near Charmouth, three amateur fossil-hunters, Simon Barnsley, David Costain and Peter Langham, discovered a specimen, from a juvenile. The tail of *Scelidosaurus* may have been stiff due to tendons that lay alongside the backbones and became ossified with minerals. Current opinion places *Scelidosaurus* as one of the most basal thyreophorans and possibly ancestral to the more advanced thyreophorans – the stegosaurids and ankylosaurians.

SCUTELLOSAURUS

Scutellosaurus was named in 1981 by Edwin "Ned" Colbert, from the bony plates, called scutes, embedded like small, raised shields in its skin. Its main fossils are two partial skeletons, with pieces of skull, from Arizona, plus many detached scutes. This was a small and early dinosaur, dating to 208–200 million years ago, with a mix of primitive and slightly more advanced features. It was once included in the ornithopod group with *Lesothosaurus* (see page 177), but then considered as an early thyreophoran or "shield-bearer". Like *Scelidosaurus* (opposite), it has been touted as

the kind of dinosaur that may have evolved into one of the later, better-known groups of thyreophorans, such as the armored ankylosaurs or the plated stegosaurs; or it could have resembled the common ancestor of both these groups.

Scutellosaurus was small, slim and long, probably weighing not much more than 10 kilograms (22 pounds), despite its light armor of scutes of – triangular wedges, low cones, lopsided limpets and curved "thorns." Hundreds of fossilized scutes have been found, but their exact pattern over the neck, elongated body and even lengthier tail are unknown. The mouth had a narrow, beak-like front and the head was also protected by low, bony plates. *Scutellosaurus* could probably run fairly rapidly on all fours, since its front limbs bear broad and sturdy paws. Perhaps it could rear up to race along on its two larger, longer hind limbs, but the long body and armor probably made it front-heavy. Estimates for the number of individual scutes on one *Scutellosaurus* range from less than 200 to more than 400.

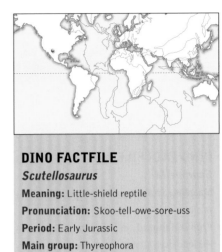

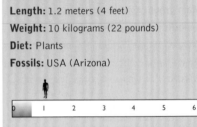

DINO FACTFILE
Scutellosaurus

Meaning: Little-shield reptile
Pronunciation: Skoo-tell-owe-sore-uss
Period: Early Jurassic
Main group: Thyreophora
Length: 1.2 meters (4 feet)
Weight: 10 kilograms (22 pounds)
Diet: Plants
Fossils: USA (Arizona)

| 0 | 1 | 2 | 3 | 4 | 5 | 6 |

LEFT *Scutellosaurus* had small, simple cheek teeth and probably could only eat soft vegetation. In life the body scutes would have been covered or sheathed with horn and perhaps also leathery skin.

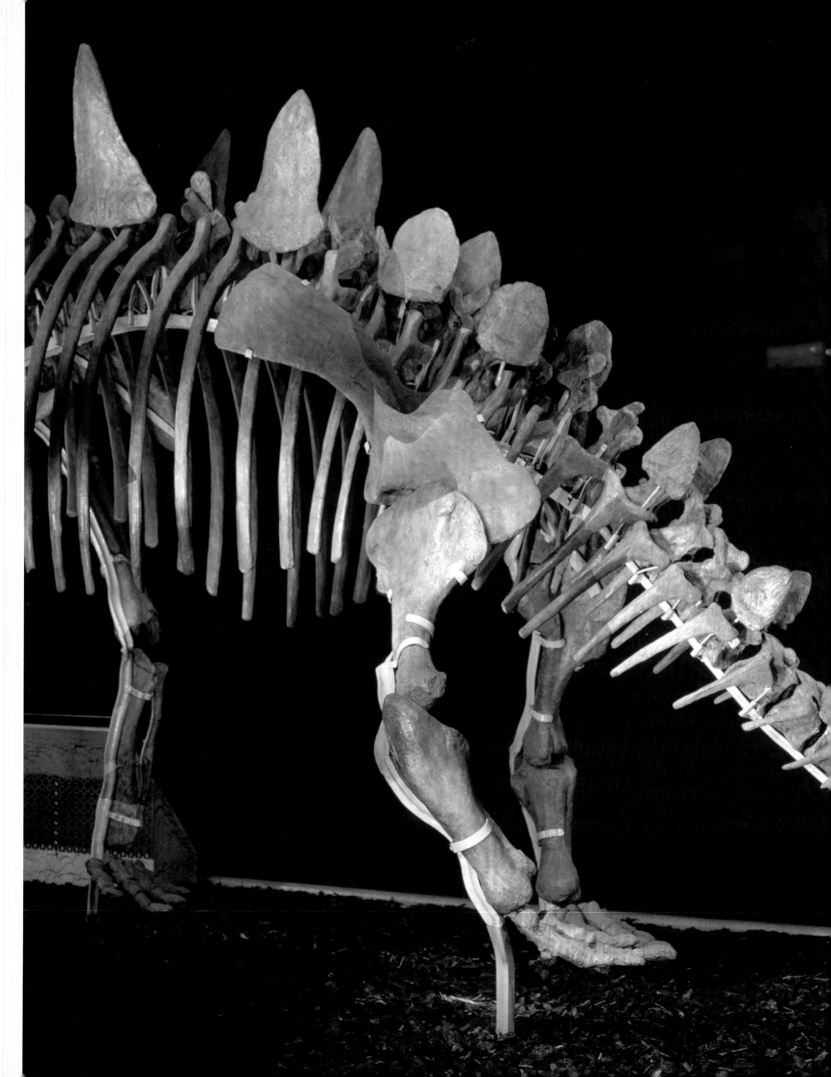

CHAPTER ELEVEN

PLATED DINOSAURS

STEGOSAURS ARE FAMOUS FOR THEIR TINY BRAINS AND SUPPOSED STUPIDITY, YET THEY WERE SUCCESSFUL FOR TENS OF MILLIONS OF YEARS.

PLETHORA OF PLATES

THE TALL PLATES OF BONE ON THE BACKS OF STEGOSAURS HAVE LONG BEEN A PUZZLE TO PALEONTOLOGISTS. *STEGOSAURUS* ITSELF HAD THE HIGHEST AND WIDEST PLATES, EACH ONE THINNER THAN A HUMAN ARM. THEY WERE PROBABLY ARRANGED VERTICALLY IN TWO ROWS, STAGGERED OR OFFSET SO THAT A PLATE ON ONE SIDE OVERLAPPED TWO IN THE ADJACENT ROW. THE PLATES WERE LARGER FROM THE NECK TO THE HIPS, THEN SMALLER AGAIN DOWN TO THE TAIL-TIP. AT LEAST, THIS IS THE PATTERN SHOWN IN MOST RECONSTRUCTIONS. BUT, DESPITE RECENT AND EXCITING FINDS (SEE "SPIKE," PAGE 236) NOT ALL EXPERTS AGREE. THE ARGUMENTS ABOUT PLATE POSITION AND FUNCTION CONTINUE TODAY AS THEY HAVE SINCE THE 1870S.

PLATED PROTECTION

Did the stegosaurs' plates give them physical protection? This is unlikely, since they were not solid but honeycombed with cavities and relatively fragile. Also, they probably stood vertically rather than lying flat to cover the body. Were they principally for camouflage among the trees and general surroundings? Again, this seems unlikely – it seems odd for so large structures to have evolved if their main function is to help an animal become inconspicuous. Camouflage, however, might have been a secondary consideration. Were the plates used for some kind of visual display? They might have been brightly colored and patterned, perhaps differently in males and in females, and in juveniles compared to mature adults, and even in different species that otherwise resembled each other closely in size and form. The colors of certain lizards and other reptiles today change as they grow and mature, and depending on their sex and breeding condition.

TEMPERATURE

The widely accepted theory for how *Stegosaurus* used its plates concerns body temperature control. Stegosaurs and most other dinosaurs were probably "cold-blooded," or, to use a more precise term, ectothermic. They absorbed heat from their surroundings, rather than generating it inside their bodies as "warm-blooded" or endothermic creatures, principally birds and mammals, do today. Warmth was important because as a reptile's body temperature rises, then up to a point the animal can move about faster, feed more efficiently and escape from danger more rapidly. The plates of *Stegosaurus* may have worked as two-way heat-exchangers, in a similar way to the "sails" on the backs of dinosaurs such as *Spinosaurus* and *Ouranosaurus*, and on other reptiles such as *Dimetrodon* (all shown in this book).

WARM AND COOL

At sunrise, after the cool night, *Stegosaurus* may have stood at a right angle to the sun, so that the back plates would receive maximum exposure to the warming rays, heating the blood flowing through their honeycomb cavities and back into the body. In this way, the dinosaur would have warmed up more quickly than it could have without its plates. The staggered arrangement of plates seems to fit this idea, since the gap between two plates in one row would have allowed solar heating to the plate between them in the other row. If *Stegosaurus* became too hot, on the other hand, it might have stood in the shade at a right angle to the breeze, which would carry away body warmth for a maximum cooling effect. The temperature regulation idea of dual heating-cooling functions seems to fit *Stegosaurus*, with its broad, leaf-shaped plates. But, it is much less convincing for other stegosaurs, whose more pointed, spike-like plates had much smaller surface areas (see pages 237 and 240).

PREVIOUS PAGE This reconstructed stegosaurid skeleton shows the tiny size of the skull and how the plates were arranged along the back but not joined to any of the other skeletal bones.

LEFT A stegosaur reacts to an approaching *Allosaurus*-type predator. The back plates of the plant-eater were probably not for protection – in fact, with their lightweight construction, they would be vulnerable to attack.

STEGOSAURUS

DINO FACTFILE

Stegosaurus

Meaning: Roof reptile, tile reptile

Pronunciation: Steg-owe-sore-uss

Period: Late Jurassic

Main group: Stegosauridae

Length: 8–9 meters (26–29¹/₂ feet)

Weight: 2–3 metric tons (2–3 tons)

Diet: Plants

Fossils: Asia, Europe, USA (Colorado)

0   1   2   3   4   5

Stegosaurus has given its name to a distinctive and recognizable major group of dinosaurs with tall plates or spines on their backs. These creatures have also become famous as the "dumbest" dinosaurs, because of the relatively small size of their brains. Such topics are discussed throughout this chapter. *Stegosaurus* was named by Othniel Charles Marsh in 1877, and fossil remains have since been reported from sites in several western states in the USA with close cousins from numerous other sites around the globe. In 1992 a well-preserved and almost complete *Stegosaurus* skeleton, later named "Spike," was discovered near Canyon City, Colorado (in the same state as the very first discovery), showing in more detail the pattern of the 17 plates on its back.

Stegosaurus was the largest known member of the group, being 9 meters (29½ feet) long – equal to today's elephant with its trunk and tail stretched out lengthwise. But, *Stegosaurus* was perhaps slightly lighter than a modern elephant, and had four long tail spikes. *Stegosaurus* lived during the main time-span of its group, the Late Jurassic period, 150–144 million years ago. Its back plates were huge in area: thin triangles more than 75 centimeters (30 inches) at their peaks, jutting up from the back. In the early reconstructions of this dinosaur, the plates were pictured lying flat on the back, like tiles on a roof (hence the group name). Later versions showed the plates projecting from the back in two rows, each pair of plates side by side. More recent reconstructions have the two rows of plates staggered, with one side half a plate in front of the other. At least ten functions have been suggested for the uses of these plates but the front-runner is body temperature control (see page 235).

LEFT Most modern reconstructions show the back plates in two upright rows, one slightly behind the other. The tail spikes would pose a formidable defensive weapon.

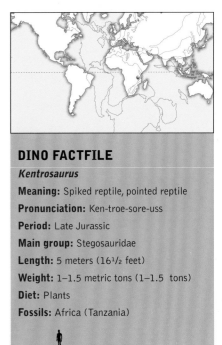

LEFT The tallest spike-like plates on the back of *Kentrosaurus* were 60 centimeters (24 inches) in height. The very large, powerful rear legs of stegosaurs suggest they may have reared up to reach higher-growing plant food.

KENTROSAURUS

Kentrosaurus is often regarded as the African equivalent of North America's *Stegosaurus*, from the same period, the Late Jurassic, around 155–144 million years ago. But, in some respects it is more similar to *Tuojiangosaurus* from East Asia (as shown on page 239). Most *Kentrosaurus* fossils were recovered from the large German-supervised expeditions to the quarries and hills of Tendaguru in the Mtwara region of what was then, in 1908–12, German East Africa (later Tanganyika, now the larger portion of Tanzania). These arduous trips yielded many tremendous discoveries – see, for example, *Brachiosaurus* (page 146). *Kentrosaurus* was named by Edwin Hennig, a German paleontologist, in 1915. Many fossils of *Kentrosaurus* stored in the Humboldt Museum in Berlin might have provided valuable extra knowledge, but some of these were sadly destroyed during bombing raids in World War II. Fortunately, however, other

Kentrosaurus fossils survived and are still located at the Museum.

Kentrosaurus had the typical stegosaurid body shape, with a tiny head containing a minuscule brain, front limbs shorter than its rear limbs, an arching back that curved steeply up and then slightly down to the long rear limbs, and a tapering tail longer than the length of the rest of the creature. The front of the head had a toothless beak for snipping off plants, and the teeth were shaped like their probable food – leaves – but were very small and had vertical ridges. The back plates of *Kentrosaurus* were much narrower than those of *Stegosaurus*, and became progressively more so from the neck along the back, changing shape around halfway along the body to become much narrower spikes, which then continued to the end of the tail. It is difficult to propose that such thin, pointed structures helped with the process of thermoregulation.

DINO FACTFILE

Kentrosaurus

Meaning: Spiked reptile, pointed reptile

Pronunciation: Ken-troe-sore-uss

Period: Late Jurassic

Main group: Stegosauridae

Length: 5 meters (16½ feet)

Weight: 1–1.5 metric tons (1–1.5 tons)

Diet: Plants

Fossils: Africa (Tanzania)

| 0 | 1 | 2 | 3 | 4 | 5 |

WUERHOSAURUS

DINO FACTFILE
Wuerhosaurus

Meaning: Wuerho reptile

Pronunciation: Woo-air-hoe-sore-uss

Period: Early Cretaceous

Main group: Stegosauridae

Length: 5–7 meters (16– feet)

Weight: 2 metric tons (2 tons)

Diet: Plants

Fossils: China, Mongolia

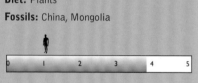

While the heyday of the stegosaurids was the Late Jurassic period, around 160–144 million years ago, some members of the group have been dated to after this time. *Wuerhosaurus* was one of the last, for its fossils were found in Early Cretaceous rocks, around 140–130 million years old. It was almost as large as *Stegosaurus*, but it came from a different region, East Asia rather than North America. The two regions were connected by land bridges at various periods. The main remains of *Wuerhosaurus*, probably of several individuals but sparse in nature, are known from the Wuerho region of China, and the name was provided in 1973 by Dong Zhiming, a leading Chinese fossil expert.

The back plates of *Wuerhosaurus* were probably lower and less pointed or pentagonal than those of *Stegosaurus*. Also, the main body may have been shorter. The great contrast between the front and rear legs was similar, so that the hips were twice as high as the shoulders. This allowed the head to touch the ground easily and naturally, with very little effort compared to other herbivorous dinosaurs, which had to stoop down actively, using their muscle power and balance, to feed on low-growing vegetation. Alternative theories propose that the huge, wide-set hips and back legs allowed *Wuerhosaurus* and other stegosaurids to rear up, lifting the smaller and relatively lighter head and front of the body, perhaps to browse on taller vegetation. The limited flexibility, however, of the various hip, back and neck joints, and the small, weak tooth design do not seem to support this notion.

RIGHT The lower, flatter-topped, almost rectangular back plates of *Wuerhosaurus* are distinctive among the stegosaurs. However as in other members of the group, the plates extend from the neck, enlarge along the body and diminish along the tail. This consistency of design has not clearly been explained.

TUOJIANGOSAURUS

It is probable that the stegosaurid group of dinosaurs first appeared in East Asia, in the Middle Jurassic period (see *Huayangosaurus*, page 241). *Tuojiangosaurus*, from the Late Jurassic, may represent a continuation of this evolutionary path in the same region. It was a sizable stegosaurid, 7 meters (23 feet) in total length, and probably weighed more than 1 metric ton (1 ton). As in many stegosaurids, the large bony plates, which are thought to have projected upward from the neck, back and tail, were embedded in the skin but were not firmly joined to other bones of the skeleton. Remains may yield many such plates, but they have become detached during fossilization, as the skin and flesh rotted, and the fossils became mixed and jumbled. As a result, their original positions, angles and patterns on the body are uncertain.

Tuojiangosaurus has the tiny head, stooped neck, shorter front limbs, arched back and longer rear limbs of other stegosaurids. There were around 15 pairs of back plates. The tail was not quite as lengthy or so substantial as in *Kentrosaurus*, but it was still impressive, with upward projections called neural spines, lower ones known as chevrons, and two pairs of caudal spikes near the tip. Several other stegosaurids also possessed these four tail spikes, so they were presumably an effective feature – probably as weapons for self-defense. The tail was muscular along its length and could be swung with great force. One specimen of *Tuojiangosaurus* was the first nearly complete skeleton of any dinosaur to be discovered in China. It was named in 1977 by Chinese paleontologists, including Zhou Shiwu, Dong Zhiming and Zhang-Yang Li.

DINO FACTFILE
Tuojiangosaurus
Meaning: Tuo River reptile
Pronunciation: Too-oh-jee-ang-oh-sore-uss
Period: Late Jurassic
Main group: Stegosauridae
Length: 7 meters (23 feet)
Weight: 3 metric tons (3 tons)
Diet: Plants
Fossils: China

0	1	2	3	4	5

ABOVE It is unlikely that *Tuojiangosaurus* could lift its head much higher than shown in this reconstruction.

LEXOVISAURUS

DINO FACTFILE

Lexovisaurus

Meaning: Lexovian reptile, reptile of Lexovix

Pronunciation: Lek-soe-vee-sore-uss

Period: Mid–Late Jurassic

Main group: Stegosauridae

Length: 5 meters (16½feet)

Weight: 2 metric tons (2 tons)

Diet: Plants

Fossils: England, France

Several stegosaurids are thought to have possessed shoulder spines, jutting out from the upper rear part of the front limb, below the characteristic twin rows of bony plates along the top of the neck and back. Most are also believed to have sported two pairs of long spikes near the end of the tail, although it is not clear whether these were horizontally opposed (sticking out sideways), or angled upward to form two V shapes (see page 235). A European member of the group, *Lexovisaurus*, has been used as evidence for shoulder spines. This dinosaur was one of the smaller stegosaurids, around 5 meters (16½ feet) long, but its shoulder spines may have been 1 meter (39 inches) or more in length – formidable-looking weapons. If the spines really were one on each shoulder, that is perhaps what they were – formidable in visual display, but not so effective if it came to a

physical battle. Other views place these spines on the hips. In other ways, *Lexovisaurus* was fairly typical of the stegosaurid group, although its back plates were tall and narrow, rather than broad and angular.

Fossils of *Lexovisaurus* have been found at several sites in Europe, chiefly in Northamptonshire in England, and also in northwestern France. The dinosaur was named by Robert Hoffstetter in 1957, and recalls the Lexovix people, one of the ancient Gallic groups from the area around what is now the city of Lyons in France. There are parts of perhaps three individuals, as well as isolated bits of bones, plates and spikes, probably representing both adults and juveniles. Fossilized plates once thought to come from *Lexovisaurus* are now believed to be of the skull of *Leedsichthys*, a giant bony fish (see also *Dravidosaurus*, page 242).

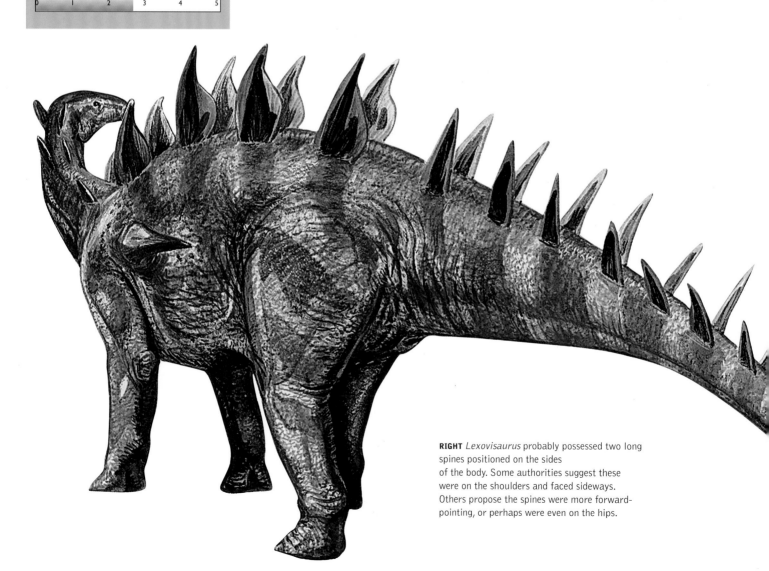

RIGHT *Lexovisaurus* probably possessed two long spines positioned on the sides of the body. Some authorities suggest these were on the shoulders and faced sideways. Others propose the spines were more forward-pointing, or perhaps were even on the hips.

RIGHT *Huayangosaurus* is shown here with a long spike on each shoulder, pointing sideways, although this position is not certain. (See *Lexovisaurus*, opposite.) The back plates of this stegosaur are varied in different specimens, some being leaf-shaped or triangular and others more pointed.

HUAYANGOSAURUS

The general name of "stegosaur" usually covers two subgroups, or families. One is the Stegosauridae, which includes *Stegosaurus* itself and the others shown on previous pages. The second and smaller family is the Huayangosauridae, based on *Huayangosaurus*. Compared to stegosaurids, huayangosaurids tend to have lived earlier, around the Middle Jurassic period, and their remains have been found only in East Asia rather than in several regions. It is possible that the huayangosaurids were the ancestors of the later and more widespread stegosaurids. *Huayangosaurus* was named for the fossil discovery site, in 1982, by Dong Zhiming, a pre-eminent Chinese dinosaur specialist, and colleagues.

Huayangosaurus fossils come from rocks known as the Lower Shaximiao Formation in the Sichuan province of southwestern China. They probably date to 170–160 million years ago and include one almost complete skeleton with skull, another skull, and parts of the

skeletons of several other individuals. They show a fairly small stegosaur-like dinosaur, around 4 meters (13 feet) in length. There were around nine pairs of tall, leaf-shaped bony plates sticking up from the neck and back along the midline. At the hips, these changed shape to become narrower spikes, which continued along the upper surface of the tail. There were probably two pairs of spikes at the tail end, as in the stegosaurids. In contrast to stegosaurids, however, *Huayangosaurus* had a longer head and snout – not so low or flat; small teeth in the front of the upper jaw, rather than an entirely toothless beak; and relatively long front limbs, although these were still shorter than the rear pair. Like other stegosaurs, *Huayangosaurus* was reputed to have a "second brain" in its hip region, but this was just a widened group of nerves connecting to the rear legs and tail, not a brain at all.

DINO FACTFILE
Huayangosaurus

Meaning: Huayang reptile

Pronunciation: Hoo-ah-yang-oh-sore-uss

Period: Middle Jurassic

Main group: Huayangosauridae

Length: 4–4.5 meters (13–15 feet)

Weight: 400–600 kilograms (1100–1320 pounds)

Diet: Plants

Fossils: China

| 0 | 1 | 2 | 3 | 4 | 5 |

CRATEROSAURUS AND DRAVIDOSAURUS

DINO FACTFILE
Craterosaurus

Meaning: Crater or cup (bowl) reptile

Pronunciation: Kray-ter-oh-sore-uss

Period: Early Cretaceous

Main group: Stegosauridae

Length: Estimated 4 meters (13 feet)

Weight: Estimated 500 kilograms
(1100 pounds)

Diet: Plants

Fossils: England

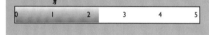

Craterosaurus was possibly a stegosaurid, but it is difficult to tell from its single fossil – one preserved vertebra (backbone) – and even this is not complete. It is probably from the Early Cretaceous period, 140–135 million years ago. At first, this specimen, found in Bedfordshire in southern England, was thought to be from the cranium (braincase) and was named as *Craterosaurus* in 1874 by Harry Seely, who devised the partitioning of the whole dinosaur group into ornithischians or "bird hips" and saurischians or "lizard hips." But the fossil is now thought to be the upper, curved part of the vertebra and has an unusual pitted texture on its upper surface. However, it is not diagnostic for stegosaurids and past descriptions of *Craterosaurus* are little more than guesswork.

Dravidosaurus ("Dravidanadu reptile") was formerly believed to be a stegosaur-type dinosaur from the Indian subcontinent. It was thought to be a late representative of its group, since it lived during the Late Cretaceous period, long after most other stegosaurids had disappeared. It was also held up as an example of how stegosaurids had spread to many regions, since in its time the Indian subcontinent was not joined to southern Asia, but was far to the south, nestling against Antarctica. More recent studies, however, are possibly changing all this, and *Dravidosaurus* fossils, including the narrow head with the pointed beak-like snout and the assorted bony plates, have been reinterpreted. Some experts now propose that they come not from a stegosaurid, or even from a dinosaur, but from a swimming reptile – a type of plesiosaur (see page 279).

RIGHT *Dravidosaurus* is traditionally reconstructed as a typical stegosaur. However, a reappraisal of its fossils has led some experts to suggest that they do not represent a dinosaur at all, but a type of seagoing reptile called a plesiosaur (see page 279).

DINO FACTFILE
Dravidosaurus

Meaning: Dravidanadu (place name) reptile

Pronunciation: Drav-id-oh-sore-uss

Period: Late Cretaceous

Main group: Controversial. Stegosauridae
(dinosaur) or Plesiosauridae (plesiosaur)

Length: 3 meters (10 feet)

Weight: 350 kilograms (770 pounds)

Diet: Soft plants

Fossils: Southern India

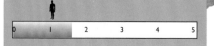

LEFT Apart from the skull shape, reconstructions of *Paranthodon* are based on relatives such as *Kentrosaurus*. The relevance of this stegosaur is its discovery region, South Africa, and that it is reconstructed from the first dinosaur fossils from that area to be formally studied.

PARANTHODON

The only known fossil of *Paranthodon* is part of a skull with some teeth. It was possibly the first dinosaur fossil to be discovered and studied in South Africa. The remains were found in 1845 by Andrew Bain and William Atherstone between Grahamstown and Port Elizabeth, in the Eastern Cape. Bain was a supervisor for military units constructing roads in the area and developed a great knowledge of minerals, rocks and fossils as part of the then new science of geology. Bain and Atherstone recognized a reptilian likeness and proposed that the original animal was a South African version of *Iguanodon*, which four years earlier had been used by Richard Owen to establish the entire group Dinosauria (see page 171). The fossil was sent to London where Owen examined it and named it *Anthodon*, due to its "flower-shaped teeth," in 1876.

Unfortunately, Owen mistakenly included in the description of *Anthodon* some additional remains – more than 100 million years older – of another reptile from the Karoo of South Africa. In 1929, Franz Nopsca recognized the mix-up and saw that the original skull and teeth were from a stegosaur-like dinosaur, to which he gave a new name *Paranthodon*. To add to the confusion, the original *Anthodon* fossils were re-examined and recognized as being from a type of reptile called a pareiasaur, and given yet another name, *Palaeoscincus*. These pareiasaur remains had already been named by Owen as *Anthodon*, however, and so it was finally agreed that the pareiasaur would be called *Anthodon* and the dinosaur *Paranthodon*.

Reconstructions of *Paranthodon* are based on *Kentrosaurus*, a stegosaurid whose fossils come from East Africa (see page 237). The teeth of *Paranthodon* and *Kentrosaurus* share several features, and are more similar to each other than either is to other stegosaurids, such as *Stegosaurus* itself. *Paranthodon* thus remains a fascinating and mysterious find.

DINO FACTFILE
Paranthodon

Meaning: Beside, or in addition to, Anthodon

Pronunciation: Parr-ann-thoe-don

Period: Early Cretaceous

Main group: Stegosauridae

Length: Estimated 5 meters (16½ feet)

Weight: Estimated 0.5–1 metric ton (0.5–1 ton)

Diet: Plants

Fossils: South Africa

CHAPTER TWELVE

HORNED DINOSAURS

FROM THE SIZE OF A SMALL PIG, TO TWICE THE LENGTH AND WEIGHT OF THE LARGEST OF TODAY'S RHINOCEROSES, THE CERATOPSIANS WERE SUCCESSFUL AND DRAMATIC NEWCOMERS AT THE END OF THE DINOSAUR AGE.

THE CERATOPSIAN GROUP

HORNED DINOSAURS ARE KNOWN AS CERATOPSIANS, OR "HORNED FACES." THEY WERE SMALL, THEN MEDIUM-SIZED, THEN LARGE PLANT-EATERS, IN TURN, FROM THE EARLY, MID- AND THEN LATE CRETACEOUS PERIOD. MOST LIVED FROM 80 TO 65 MILLION YEARS AGO, IN ASIA AND THEN IN NORTH AMERICA. THE BIGGEST AND BEST-KNOWN OF THEIR KIND, TRICERATOPS, WAS ONE OF THE VERY LAST DINOSAURS OF THE WHOLE MESOZOIC ERA OR AGE OF DINOSAURS. THE CERATOPSIAN GROUP CAN BE DIVIDED INTO SEVERAL MAIN SUBGROUPS, WHICH IN DIFFERENT CLASSIFICATION SCHEMES ARE CALLED THE PSITTACOSAURS, THE PROTOCERATOPSIDS, AND THE CERATOPSIDS THEMSELVES, WHICH APPEARED LAST.

PARROT-BEAKS

The psittacosaurs were once regarded as types of ornithopod dinosaurs, but further studies, especially of their skulls, showed that these fleet-footed runners were the earliest kinds of horned dinosaurs. There are around ten different types or genera, the best-known being *Psittacosaurus* itself (see next page). This is named for the "parrot beak" at the front of its mouth, which was toothless, and suited to tearing and raking in vegetation. Other types sometimes classified in this group include *Chaoyangsaurus*. All these dinosaurs are known from fossils in Asia, and many well-preserved remains have been found in the Gobi Desert in Mongolia. They did not have the face horns characteristic of later ceratopsians, but, like them, they did show a ridge at each cheekbone, drawn out into a low point.

MARGIN-HEADS

A general feature of all ceratopsians were the shelf-like ridges or expanded areas around the edges of the skull, from the cheek region up to the rear of the top of the head. They are present to differing degrees in all specimens, as occasional lumps or points here and there, or longer ridges, or more complete shelves, or extended frills, over the whole neck and shoulders. These skull-edging or marginal extensions are also known from another plant-eating dinosaur group, the pachycephalosaurs or "boneheads." This has led paleontologists to group ceratopsians and pachycephalosaurs together as cousins to the larger dinosaur group called the marginocephalians ("margin-heads" or "edge-heads").

DEATH IN THE SEMIDESERT

The protoceratopsians are based on another very well-known dinosaur from the Gobi, *Protoceratops*. Extensive finds of adults, juveniles, babies, and nests have allowed scientists to build up a picture of this dinosaur's behavior and breeding patterns. This treasure trove of fossils for just one kind of dinosaur is due in part to the dry, semidesert habitats in which it roamed some 80 million years ago. It seems that windblown sand or toppling dunes covered some specimens in seconds. Protected from the elements and from crunching, or even disturbance by scavengers, these individuals gradually dried out or desiccated within their sandy "tombs," leaving many details of their bones and general anatomy remarkably well preserved.

SMALL HORNS TO BIG

Protoceratopsians had the parrot-like beak at the front of the mouth, and many chewing teeth in the rear of the jaws; they also showed the beginnings of the neck frill and face horn. These head extensions rapidly became larger in the next and last major horn-face group, the ceratopsians. These were all North American, and in turn comprised two subgroups, the centrosaurines and chasmosaurines (see pages 255 and 260).

PREVIOUS PAGE A fine fossil of *Anchiceratops* showing the small eye socket or orbit at the base of each long brow horn, the pointed cheekbone extending out sideways below it, and the gaps or "windows" in the neck frill. This specimen came from Late Cretaceous rocks in Alberta, Canada.

LEFT A charging *Styracosaurus* would intimidate most predators, with its huge frill edged with long spikes, its massive feet pounding the ground and its sharp beak snapping fiercely.

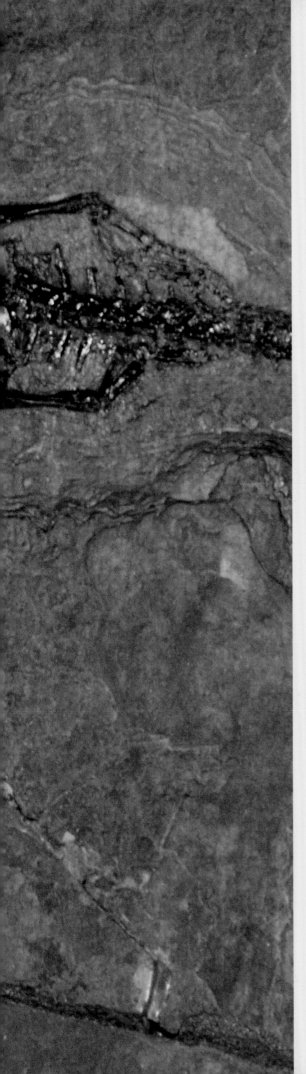

CHAPTER THIRTEEN

OTHER CREATURES OF THE DINOSAUR AGE

DINOSAURS HAD MASTERY OF THE LAND DURING THE MESOZOIC ERA, BUT THEIR NON-DINOSAUR COUSINS SHARED THEIR WORLD BY DOMINATING THE SKIES AND SEAS. THIS REPTILE-DOMINATED EARTH ALSO SAW THE FIRST APPEARANCES OF MAMMALS AND BIRDS.

ANIMALS ALL AROUND

SO OFTEN IS THE MESOZOIC ERA (252–66 MILLION YEARS AGO) CALLED THE AGE OF DINOSAURS THAT THE PRESENCE OF OTHER ANIMALS IS SOMETIMES IGNORED. YET THROUGH THE WHOLE OF THIS GREAT TIME SPAN THERE WERE INNUMERABLE OTHER REPTILES ON LAND, IN THE SEAS AND IN THE SKIES, AS WELL AS OTHER VERTEBRATES SUCH AS FISH AND AMPHIBIANS. EVEN LESS NOTICED WERE THE TEEMING HORDES OF INVERTEBRATE CREATURES IN ALMOST EVERY NOOK AND CRANNY – BUZZING INSECTS, PROWLING SPIDERS, WORMS AND SLUGS IN THE SOIL AND ENDLESS VARIETIES OF CRUSTACEANS, MOLLUSCS, STARFISH, CORALS AND JELLYFISH IN AQUATIC ENVIRONMENTS.

MAMMALS AND BIRDS

Two major absentees at the start of the dinosaur age were mammals and birds. Mammals appeared very quickly, in the Late Triassic, but stayed small and insignificant throughout the era. Birds, such as *Archaeopteryx*, flapped through the air from the Late Jurassic period, about halfway through the Mesozoic. They probably evolved from small meat-eating dinosaurs known as maniraptorans.

EXTRAORDINARY "REPTILES"

Some of the most extraordinary Mesozoic animals were pterosaurs. They are sometimes called pterodactyls, but *Pterodactylus* was only one genus among dozens, and the name pterosaur, meaning "wing reptile," is used for the whole group. It is regarded as an equivalent group to Dinosauria, the dinosaurs, and the crocodiles and alligators, Crocodylia. All three – pterosaurs, dinosaurs and crocodiles – are placed in the supergroup known as the archosaurs or "ruling reptiles." Whatever the exact relationships of the pterosaurs, they had a unique anatomy, the like of which has never been seen before or since.

FURRY FLIERS

Fossils show that some pterosaurs were scaly but others were furry or hairy. Most were able fliers, and the general demands of their aerial lives meant that they were probably warm-blooded. The time span of the pterosaurs mirrors that of the dinosaurs. They evolved in the Triassic period, probably from small ground-dwelling reptiles, and enjoyed great success during the Jurassic and Cretaceous periods, before perishing in the mass extinction. Earlier pterosaurs are known as rhamphorhynchoids. They had long, trailing tails and many had teeth in their beak-like mouths. Later pterosaurs are called pterodactyloids. Most of these were short-tailed, and their beaks lacked teeth. Some pterodactyloids had curious head crests of bone. A few later types reached giant size, becoming the largest flying animals of any age.

FINGER-WINGS

A pterosaur's body was wonderfully adapted to flight, being compact and lightweight, with hollow bones and large chest muscles with which to flap the wings. The strong feet had five clawed digits; some pterosaurs could run or hop, while others may have roosted hanging upside down like bats. The wing structure was quite unlike that of birds, and perhaps superficially more similar to a bat's wing. It was made of a very thin, stretchy flight membrane held out partly by the arm bones, but principally by the hugely elongated bones of the fourth digit. (A bat's wing is held out by four digits, from the second to the fifth.) The first three digits formed short claws on the wing's leading edge. Pterosaurs, however, were neither ancestors nor descendants of birds or bats. Meanwhile, an entirely different route was being taken by other reptile groups of the Mesozoic era: their limbs evolved into flippers as they entered the water and became fully aquatic.

PREVIOUS PAGE Sedimentary rocks were usually laid down in layers or strata, which were gradually compressed by the weight of more strata on top, squashing any animals or other remains "flat," like this marine reptile *Pachypleurosaurus*.

LEFT A pterosaur swoops through the lush lanscape of a Cretaceous forest. Some of these flying animals grew to giant size and had wingspans far greater than any bird today, at 5 meters (16 feet).

NOTHOSAURUS

REPTILE FACTFILE

Nothosaurus

Meaning: False reptile

Pronunciation: Noe-thoe-sore-uss

Period: Triassic

Main group: Nothosauroidea

Length: Up to 4 meters (13 feet)

Weight: Up to 250 kilograms (550 pounds)

Diet: Fish and similar sea animals

Fossils: Europe, Middle East, Asia

The nothosaurids were one of the first groups of sauropterygian reptiles to take up life in the sea. This was during the Triassic period, more than 240 million years ago, before the dinosaurs had appeared. The whole nothosaur group had just about disappeared by the end of the Triassic period, when the dinosaurs were achieving land domination.

Nothosaurs were long and slim, with long, narrow skulls and necks; long sharp fangs mainly in the front of the jaws near the snout tip; slim bodies, with long and flexible tails; and limbs partly modified as flippers. But, nothosaurs also retained some body features from living on land – their limbs were not totally flipper-like, as in the later ichthyosaurs, but each had five digits, which were possibly webbed.

Nothosaurus was a fairly typical genus of the group, with most species at around 1 meter (39 inches) in total length, with one up to 3 meters (10 feet). Various fossils have been found at sites right across Europe, as well as in the Middle East and in Asia. Fossils of a smaller "dwarf" species of *Nothosaurus* have recently been found in Israel. The long teeth and jaws in the arrow-like head suggest a fish-eater that darted and jabbed after prey using its long neck, swimming with its legs, and perhaps swishing its tail for extra propulsion. Once caught by the sharp teeth, which fitted together when the two jaws closed to form a "cage," the prey would have been swallowed whole. The limbs also indicate that *Nothosaurus* might have been able to move on land, if not very rapidly, with a waddling or sprawling gait. Perhaps it behaved like seals today, pursuing food such as fish and squid at sea, and then emerging onto land – "hauling out" – to rest and possibly to breed.

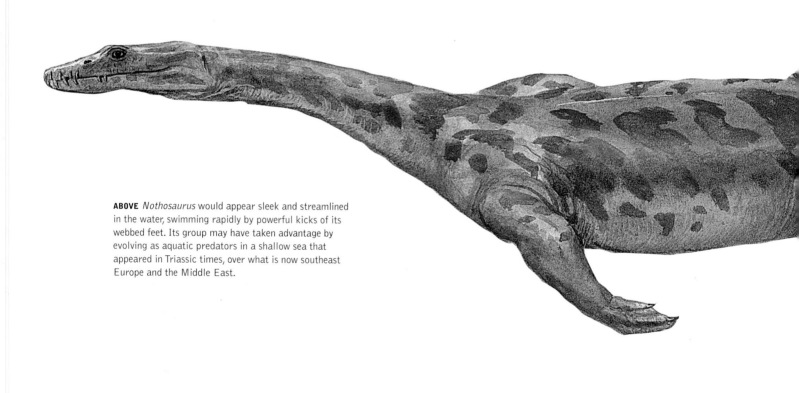

ABOVE *Nothosaurus* would appear sleek and streamlined in the water, swimming rapidly by powerful kicks of its webbed feet. Its group may have taken advantage by evolving as aquatic predators in a shallow sea that appeared in Triassic times, over what is now southeast Europe and the Middle East.

PLACODUS

The placodonts, like the nothosaurs (see opposite), were among the first reptiles to take to the sea. Also like the nothosaurs, they lasted only through the Triassic period. At a glance, *Placodus* resembles a giant newt, some 2 meters (6½ feet) long, or perhaps a crocodile. But placodonts were a distinct group of sauropterygian reptiles. They are named for the flattened teeth in the rear of their upper and lower jaws, which were broad and therefore suited to crushing hard food, probably shellfish. Some sharks today, such as the Port Jackson shark, have similar "table top" teeth. Even the palate (roof of the mouth) had hardened, tooth-like plates. The fronts of the jaws, however, bore teeth shaped more like pegs, and angled forward. These may have been used to lever shellfish off rocks, or scoop them out of mud and seaweed.

Placodus could swim by swishing its long tail from side to side, in the manner of a crocodile. There may have been a low flap or fin along the top of the tail for increased propulsion. *Placodus* may also have kicked with its webbed feet, to steer or for extra speed. It could probably move on land reasonably well, although its legs would have sprawled out sideways, like those of most non-dinosaur reptiles. It has been suggested that *Placodus* lived in shallow coastal lagoons and swamps, where an ability to move on land and water was more helpful than would be a specialized adaptation to just one of these media. There was probably "armor" of knobs and plates over parts of the body. In some later placodonts, such as *Placochelys* and *Henodus*, these plates became much enlarged, resembling the shell of a turtle.

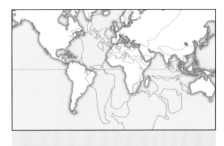

REPTILE FACTFILE
Placodus

Meaning: Flat plate tooth, flattened tooth
Pronunciation: Plack-owe-duss
Period: Middle Triassic
Main group: Placodontia
Length: 2 meters (6½ feet)
Weight: 100 kilograms (220 pounds)
Diet: Shellfish
Fossils: Europe, China

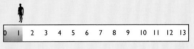

BELOW The entire mouth of *Placodus* was designed for crushing, with flattened teeth covering the upper jaws and mouth roof, and similar slab-like teeth in the lower jaw. The overall body shape suggests a compromise design for swamp-style survival, whether swimming in shallow water or slithering across soft ground.

METRIORHYNCHUS

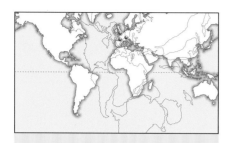

REPTILE FACTFILE
Metriorhynchus

Meaning: Medium snout, moderate nose

Pronunciation: Met-ree-owe-rink-uss

Period: Middle to Late Jurassic

Main group: Thalattosuchia

Length: 3 meters (10 feet)

Weight: 200 kilograms (440 pounds)

Diet: Fish and similar sea animals

Fossils: England, France, Germany

Only one crocodile today habitually ventures into the sea – the estuarine or saltwater crocodile of the Indo-Pacific. It is also the largest living reptile. Crocodilians are one of the smallest reptile groups today, with only 23 species, but they have had a long and varied history, beginning around the same time as the dinosaurs, during the Triassic period more than 200 million years ago. Some lived on dry land, almost like lizards, while others lived in rivers and freshwater swamps, like their descendants today.

Metriorhynchus was one of the dinosaur-age thalattosuchian crocodiles most adapted to the sea. Its fossils have been found as far apart as Chile in South America, and England and France in Europe. It was half the size of the modern saltwater crocodile, but better adapted to swimming and catching fish. The snout was long and slender, with rows of small but very sharp teeth – in these features it resembled one crocodilian alive today, the gharial (or gavial) of the Indian subcontinent. The rear of the skull, bearing the eyes and ears, was broad and boxy, and the neck was short and thick. The front limbs could be used as steering rudders or rise-and-dive hydrofoils. The rear limbs had longer feet and may have assisted with forward power or maneuvering. The tail end was probably expanded into a fin with fleshy upper and lower lobes, the backbone curving down into the lower one – similar to the tails of some sharks. *Metriorhynchus* probably did not have the large, protective bony scales or plates typical of many other crocodilians through the ages, and relied on speed and agility in the water to catch food and avoid enemies.

ABOVE One of the most fully aquatic of all crocodiles through the ages, *Metriorhynchus* lived in the sea when great dinosaurs like *Brachiosaurus* and *Allosaurus* inhabited the land. It has the narrow snout and jaws of a small-fish-eater – crocs with broader or wider jaws usually take larger prey.

SARCOSUCHUS

This monster crocodile was over twice the length and more than five times the weight of any crocodilian (or any other reptile) alive today. Recently its remains have been excavated from the fossil-rich rocks in the Tenere Desert, part of the great Sahara in northern Niger, Africa. These sites have already yielded many exciting discoveries of dinosaur remains, mostly during the 1990s, such as the vast sauropod *Jobaria*; another sauropod, *Nigersaurus*; the sail-backed ornithopod *Ouranosaurus*; and the massive meat-eaters *Carcharodontosaurus* and *Suchomimus* – all described in this book.

Sarcosuchus remains include a fairly complete skull and also parts of a skeleton, dated to 110 million years ago. The skull is almost 2 meters (6½ feet) long and the jaws bear more than 100 very sharp teeth. The upper jaw overbit the lower, and long incisor teeth impaled the victim. There is a bony lump on the top of the snout, as possessed by older males of the crocodile today known as the gharial (or gavial). There were scutes (bony plates) that protected much of the body. The genus *Sarcosuchus* was founded in 1964 with the discovery of fossils by Albert-Félix de Lapparent, a French paleontologist. It was named two years later by France de Broin and Philippe Taquet. The find of a larger specimen in Niger by American dinosaur expert Paul Sereno was announced in 2001. *Sarcosuchus* rivals another huge crocodile, *Deinosuchus* (*Phobosuchus*), from the Late Cretaceous rocks of Texas, as the largest-ever member of the crocodilian group (see page 41). It may have grabbed dinosaurs as they fed along the banks.

REPTILE FACTFILE
Sarcosuchus
Meaning: Flesh crocodile
Pronunciation: Sark-owe-sook-uss
Period: Early Cretaceous
Main group: Crocodylomorpha
Length: 11–12 meters (36–39 feet)
Weight: 8–10 metric tons (8–10 tons)
Diet: Large animals including dinosaurs
Fossils: Niger, Brazil

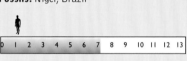

BELOW *Sarcosuchus* remains come from a fossil-rich area known as Gadoufaoua in Niger. About 110 million years ago this was crisscrossed by rivers, and *Sarcosuchus* probably lay in the water, almost unnoticed, or lurked among fringing vegetation.

OPHTHALMOSAURUS

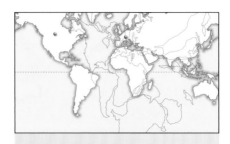

REPTILE FACTFILE

Ophthalmosaurus

Meaning: Eye reptile, sight reptile

Pronunciation: Op-thal-moe-sore-uss

Period: Middle to Late Jurassic

Main group: Ichthyosauria

Length: Up to 6 meters (19 feet)

Weight: 500 kilograms (1,100 pounds)

Diet: Squid, fish

Fossils: North America, Europe

The largest eyes of any animal today, being almost the size of soccer balls, belong to the giant squid. The ichthyosaurs challenge this record for prehistoric creatures, and certainly for the record of largest eyes in any vertebrate (animal with a backbone). The eyeballs of *Ophthalmosaurus* were almost 10 centimeters (3 inches) across – around the size of an adult human fist. (Those of *Temnodontosaurus*, another Jurassic ichthyosaur, were twice as big.) *Ophthalmosaurus* remains are known from several fossil sites, in particular in Argentina, where a range of specimens seem to show how this reptile grew and developed from baby to adult. Fossils of other ichthyosaurs, especially *Ichthyosaurus* itself, show that the babies did not hatch from eggs; they were born, small but fully formed, emerging from the mother. Unlike most other marine reptiles in this chapter, ichthyosaurs seem to have been so fully water-adapted that they could not come ashore to lay eggs.

Ophthalmosaurus probably had huge eyes for the same reason that the giant squid has them – to hunt prey in the dark ocean. The bulging eyeball had a circle of bones around it, called the sclerotic ring, providing support and protection. This skeletal feature is also seen in some dinosaurs. Other fossils found in rocks associated with *Ophthalmosaurus* include fish scales, and also the curly shells of ammonoids and the bullet-like internal shells of belemnoids – both prehistoric cousins of today's squid and octopus.

All of these creatures could have been caught by *Ophthalmosaurus* after a quick pursuit and sudden sideways swipe of its long, narrow, beak-like but tooth-filled snout.

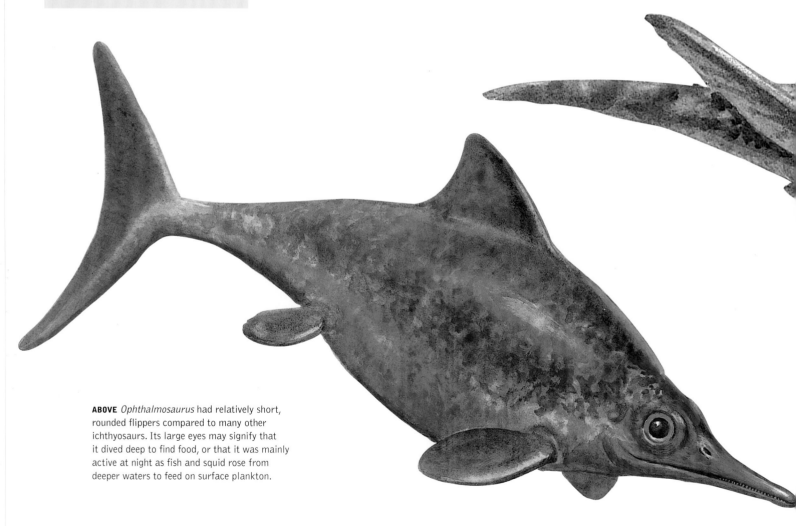

ABOVE *Ophthalmosaurus* had relatively short, rounded flippers compared to many other ichthyosaurs. Its large eyes may signify that it dived deep to find food, or that it was mainly active at night as fish and squid rose from deeper waters to feed on surface plankton.

PLESIOSAURUS

The plesiosaurs were a large and successful group of marine sauropterygian reptiles that lived through most of the Age of Dinosaurs. There were several subgroups, including the short-necked types called pliosaurs, such as *Kronosaurus* and *Liopleurodon* (see pages 281, 282). The group was established on the basis of *Plesiosaurus*, meaning "near reptile," because its skull and backbone were basically reptilian, but it had unusual shoulders, hips and flipper-like limbs. The name dates back to 1821, twenty years before the name "dinosaur" came into being. It was given by Henry de la Beche and William Conybeare to remains from the fossil-rich Jurassic rocks near Lyme Regis in Dorset, on England's south coast. Here the first known professional fossil-collector, Mary Anning, scoured the shore for beautiful and intricate specimens, which she sold to collectors as part of the fashion for natural history.

Plesiosaurus had a smallish head, long neck, tubby body, four limbs shaped like paddles and a short, smoothly tapering tail. The bones of the limb girdles (shoulders and hips), and the chest and abdominal area, were all strongly reinforced and linked by sturdy joints that must have been moved by very powerful muscles. The upper limb bones within the base of each flipper were short and stout, so that the elongated toe bones made up most of each flipper's area. It was once thought that the plesiosaurs rowed with a forward-backward motion of their flippers, like the oars of a rowing boat. It seems more likely however, that they flapped their limbs up and down, using them like a bird's wings to "fly" underwater. Today's sea turtles and penguins move in a very similar manner, flapping rather than rowing.

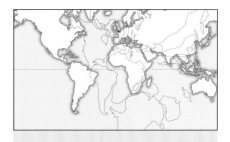

REPTILE FACTFILE
Plesiosaurus

Meaning: Near reptile

Pronunciation: Plee-zee-owe-sore-uss

Period: Early Jurassic

Main group: Plesiosauria (Plesiosauridae)

Length: Up to 3.5 meters (11 feet)

Weight: 150 kilograms (330 pounds)

Diet: Fish and similar marine prey

Fossils: England

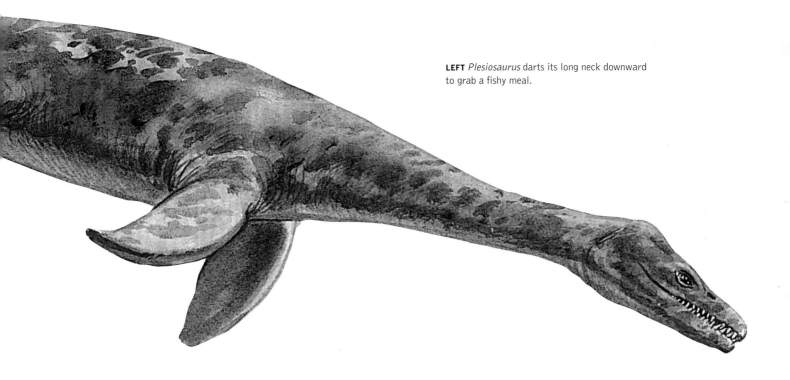

LEFT *Plesiosaurus* darts its long neck downward to grab a fishy meal.

ABOVE *Elasmosaurus* holds the record for the largest number of cervical vertebrae (neckbones) of any animal, at around 72. (Mammals, including human beings, have only seven.)

ELASMOSAURUS

REPTILE FACTFILE

Elasmosaurus

Meaning: Plate reptile

Pronunciation: Ee-laz-moe-sore-uss

Period: Late Cretaceous

Main group: Plesiosauria (Plesiosauridae)

Length: 13–14 meters (43–46 feet)

Weight: 2 metric tons (2 tons)

Diet: Fish and similar animals

Fossils: North America

Fossils of *Elasmosaurus* have been found in North America with close cousins in Japan and elsewhere in East Asia. Toward the end of the dinosaur age, these sites were all parts of the same seabed – or at least the same system of connected seas. *Elasmosaurus* was a long-necked plesiosaur (see *Plesiosaurus*, page 279). In fact, it was the longest-necked of the group, for its neck formed about 6 meters (19½ feet) of its total length of 14 meters (46 feet). *Elasmosaurus* was also one of the last plesiosaurs: the whole group disappeared along with the dinosaurs in the mass extinction at the end of the Cretaceous period.

Elasmosaurus had a tiny head, and quite how it gathered enough food for its bulky body has long been a puzzle. It was once believed that *Elasmosaurus* probably floated or paddled at the sea's surface, its head held several meters above the water, as it peered for fish and other food below the waves. It would have darted its neck down and snatched a victim in its mouth, either jabbing with its long front teeth, or closing its mouth around the item, its teeth coming together like the bars of a cage to prevent the prey escaping. But, since the eyes were on top of the skull of *Elasmosaurus*, looking down into the water from high above would have been awkward, with the snout and jaws in the way. Another theory is that *Elasmosaurus* flapped slowly at fish shoals and darted its neck to grab what it could. Experts are divided on whether the neck was flexible or not. Fossilized gut contents of plesiosaurs in general show they ate a mixture of fish, molluscs such as squid and ammonites, and other small sea creatures.

KRONOSAURUS

This sea reptile was a pliosaur – a member of the plesiosaur group, but in the subgroup Pliosauridae, with the distinctive feature of a much shorter, thicker neck. Pliosaurs were more heavily built, more streamlined, faster and fiercer than other plesiosaurs, and were suited to catching fewer, larger meals with their massive jaws and rows of sharp front teeth up to 25 centimeters (10 inches) long. The huge head, which was mostly mouth, also had large eyes and an offset pair of nostrils that gave it its "water-sniffing" ability, as in other plesiosaurs. A pliosaur swam with all of its four limbs, which had evolved into long, wide, strong flippers, one at each corner of the elongated body. The tail was short and tapering, as in other plesiosaurs, and was perhaps used only for steering. *Kronosaurus* was one of the largest pliosaurs and lived in the Early Cretaceous period. Most of its fossils are known from Australia, where they were first discovered in 1889 in Queensland, which was covered by shallow sea some 120 million years ago. The name was given in 1924 by Heber Longman. For many years, estimates put the total length of *Kronosaurus* at up to 13 meters (43 feet), but recent studies of its fossil skull and other parts, and comparisons with other pliosaurs, suggest that the true length was probably 9–10 meters (29½–33 feet). Other creatures preserved from the time include numerous fish and various molluscs such as squid, ammonites and belemnites. Some of their fossil shells bear tooth marks that could have been made by *Kronosaurus*, whose rear teeth were rounded and suited to crushing hard-cased victims.

REPTILE FACTFILE
Kronosaurus
Meaning: Time reptile
Pronunciation: Kroe-noe-sore-uss
Period: Early Cretaceous
Main group: Plesiosauria (Pliosauridae)
Length: 9–10 meters (29½–33 feet)
Weight: Up to 11 metric tons (12 tons)
Diet: Large sea animals
Fossils: Australia, Colombia

0 1 2 3 4 5 6 7 8 9 10 11 12 13

ABOVE By paddling opposing flippers in opposite directions, *Kronosaurus* could turn on the spot.

LIOPLEURODON

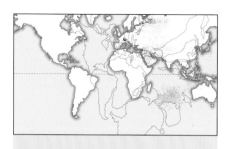

REPTILE FACTFILE

Liopleurodon

Meaning: Smooth-sided tooth

Pronunciation: Lie-owe-plure-owe-don

Period: Middle to Late Jurassic

Main group: Plesiosauria (Pliosauridae)

Length: Up to 10 meters (33 feet)

Weight: 1–1.7 metric tons
(2,200–3,700 pounds)

Diet: Large sea animals

Fossils: Europe

0	1	2	3	4	5	6	7	8	9	10	11	12	13

When we imagine the greatest predators of the dinosaur age, *Tyrannosaurus* and the even larger *Giganotosaurus* usually spring to mind. Yet even they could not compare to Liopleurodon, a reptile like the dinosaurs but a denizen of the open ocean. *Liopleurodon* was a pliosaur, or short-necked plesiosaur, like *Kronosaurus* on the previous page, but probably even huger. Some recent popular accounts have *Liopleurodon* growing to 25 meters (82 feet) long and 100 metric tons (100 tons) in weight. However, this estimate was based on very fragmentary remains. Its true size may have been only around one half of such estimates, however. If so, *Liopleurodon* would have been only slightly smaller than the creature often called the biggest hunter the world has seen, and one that we know for certain exists – the sperm whale of today. This whale can grow to more than 50 metric tons (50 tons) and lives for well over 60 years.

Fossils of *Liopleurodon* have been excavated from various sites in France, Germany, England, eastern Europe and possibly Chile, and include parts of the skull, jaws, teeth and skeletal bones. They have been known for well over a century – *Liopleurodon* was named in 1873 by Henri Sauvage, a French fossil expert – but a discovery in 1991 revealed a much larger specimen with the skull alone being 3 meters (10 feet) long. The mouth and jaws were so huge and powerful that they were probably suited to tackling the occasional single large prey, including other aquatic reptiles like plesiosaurs or ichthyosaurs, rather than gathering a host of smaller victims in the way that great whales and other "filter-feeders" do.

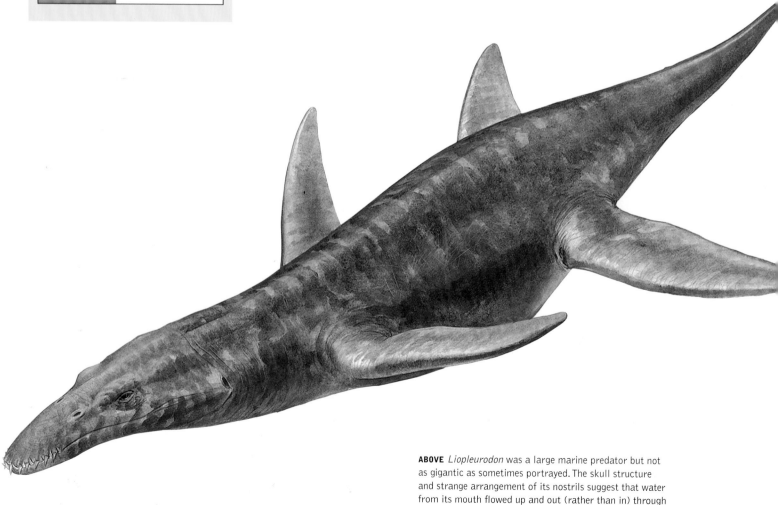

ABOVE *Liopleurodon* was a large marine predator but not as gigantic as sometimes portrayed. The skull structure and strange arrangement of its nostrils suggest that water from its mouth flowed up and out (rather than in) through the nostrils, allowing this pliosaur to detect waterborne scents.

MOSASAURUS

In the 1770s, massive and mysterious fossils of jaws and teeth were dug from a chalk mine near the River Meuse at a site now in the Netherlands in northwestern Europe. Around 30 years later, Georges Cuvier, a French biologist who was then one of the world's leading authorities on animals, noticed their similarity to the jaws and teeth of modern lizards and named them *Mosasaurus*, meaning "Meuse reptile." Cuvier believed that they had been created by God like every other animal, but had perished in a great flood, perhaps the Great Flood recorded in the Bible. This was how most scientists of the time viewed what we now call the fossil record. It was still many years before Richard Owen coined the name Dinosauria or Charles Darwin explained evolution.

Cuvier was right in one respect, however: *Mosasaurus* is believed to have been an ancient but close relative of today's monitor lizards. Mosasaurs were seagoing monsters that appeared in the Late Cretaceous period,

probably evolving from small four-legged predators that lived semiaquatic lives in swamps or along seashores. Mosasaurs became spectacularly huge and fierce, some exceeding 15 meters (49 feet) in length. The head tapered via the neck into the body, which was long and slim like an eel's, with all four limbs being adapted as flippers for control in the water. Most of the pushing power came from the very long, flexible and muscular tail, which was narrow from side to side but fin-like near the end. When the ichthyosaurs faded, mosasaurs vied with pliosaurs like *Kronosaurus* and *Liopleurodon* (see opposite) as the greatest predatory reptiles of the Cretaceous seas. One of the biggest mosasaurs, *Tylosaurus*, is known from fossils found in Kansas. So many mosasaurs have been found in this state that it is famed as the "world center" for this group.

BELOW The massive head of *Mosasaurus* had sharp teeth, not only in the huge jaws but also on the bony palate (roof of the mouth).

REPTILE FACTFILE
Mosasaurus

Meaning: Meuse reptile (from its discovery site)

Pronunciation: Moe-zah-sore-use

Period: Late Cretaceous

Main group: Squamata

Length: 17 meters (57 feet)

Weight: 5 metric tons (5 tons)

Diet: Sea animals

Fossils: USA (Kansas), Europe

MEGAZOSTRODON

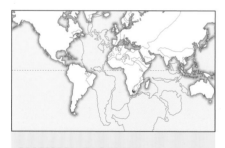

MAMMAL FACTFILE

Megazostrodon

Meaning: Large girdle tooth

Pronunciation: Meg-ah-zos-troe-don

Period: Late Triassic to Early Jurassic

Main group: Mammaliaformes

Length: 10–12 centimeters (4–5 inches)

Weight: 20–30 grams (1 ounce)

Diet: Insects, grubs, worms

Fossils: Southern Africa

0 1 2 3 4 5 6 7 8 9 10 11 12 13

The earliest mammals crop up as fossils in rocks from the Late Triassic period. *Megazostrodon* is one of these. A fairly complete skeleton was excavated from a site in Lesotho in southern Africa, where remains of dinosaurs from around the same time have also been found (see *Lesothosaurus*, page 177). *Megazostrodon* is included in the mammal group for various reasons, especially the detailed structure of its jawbones, some of which had become tiny earbones – one of the mammals' defining features. Its skull, hardly larger than a human thumb, contained sharp teeth that suggest that it was a carnivore – it hunted other creatures, probably small insects, worms and similar soil or leaf-litter animals. *Megazostrodon* had differentiated teeth in various parts of its mouth, unlike most reptiles, including most dinosaurs. *Megazostrodon*'s dentition included straight-edged incisors at the fronts of the jaws, and

pointed canines and molars in the cheek region. The relatively primitive structure of their jaw indicates that they were just outside the true mammals and are referred to as Mammaliaformes.

Megazostrodon had four walking legs and a long snout, and was probably active mainly at night, using its large eyes, acute hearing and sensitive vibrissae (whiskers) to find its way. (Whiskers are modified, extra-long hairs from the mammalian furry coat.) Being nocturnal and warm-blooded would have allowed *Megazostrodon* to move quickly at any time, including the cool of the night. This would have helped it avoid predatory reptiles and other enemies, since such cold-blooded creatures would have been unable to race about at speed in low temperatures.

ABOVE Wide-eyed, with long whiskers, *Megazostrodon* was well adapted for a nocturnal lifestyle.

MORGANUCODON

In many respects, *Morganucodon* resembles *Megazostrodon*, shown opposite – but this is partly because the fossils of each have been used to help reconstruct the other. *Morganucodon* lived during the Early Jurassic period, as the dinosaurs were spreading and diversifying. Like other very early mammals, it was probably nocturnal. It may have emerged from a burrow or crevice at dusk, and then hunted for grubs, bugs and similar small items of food, scratching at the soil or nosing in leaf litter, using its well-developed senses of hearing and smell. Fossils of the cranium (braincase) show that the parts or lobes of the brain that dealt with these senses were particularly well developed. Also, the brain was almost completely encased in bone, as it is in modern mammals. This was not the case in most reptiles or in the mammal-like reptiles called cynodonts that could have given rise to true mammals.

Morganucodon's skull was less than 3 centimeters (1 inch) long. It reveals how the jawbones had changed from the typical reptilian pattern: *Morganucodon*'s lower jaw was made almost entirely of one bone rather than two or three fused together. Other bones had shrunk and become incorporated into the ear, for hearing. It had small incisor teeth in the front of the jaw, two long pointed canines, premolars and long three-cusped molars for chewing its food. *Morganucodon* stood almost upright on its four legs with the erect limb posture shared by dinosaurs, birds and mammals. The fossils of *Morganucodon* were first discovered in caves in South Wales and the name was bestowed in 1941 by F.W. Parrington. More recent finds have been made in China. There is an ongoing controversy over whether *Morganucodon* was a primitive mammaliaform like *Megazostrodon*, or a true mammal.

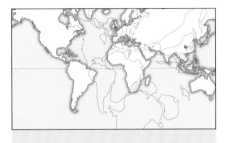

MAMMAL FACTFILE

Morganucodon

Meaning: Morgan's tooth

Pronunciation: More-gan-you-coe-don

Period: Late Triassic to Early Jurassic

Main group: Mammalia

Length: 15 centimeters (6 inches)

Weight: 20 grams (1 ounce)

Diet: Insects and worms

Fossils: China, Britain

| 0 | 1 | 2 | 3 | 4 | 5 | 6 | 7 | 8 | 9 | 10 | 11 | 12 | 13 |

BELOW *Moganucodon* grabs a tasty cockroach in its tiny but sharp teeth. This early mammal probably lived a similar lifestyle to the shrews of today, energetically hunting and ferociously devouring all kinds of small creatures.

ZALAMBDALESTES

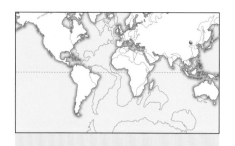

MAMMAL FACTFILE

Zalambdalestes

Meaning: Much-like-lambda robber or stealer

Pronunciation: Zall-amb-dah-less-teez

Period: Late Cretaceous

Main group: Mammalia (Eutheria)

Length: 20 centimeters (8 inches)

Weight: 30–50 grams (1–2 ounces)

Diet: Insects

Fossils: Mongolia

Zalambdalestes lived during the Late Cretaceous period, before the great extinction that wiped out the dinosaurs and many other forms of life. Its fossils come from Mongolia where many and varied dinosaurs thrived at the time, including meat-eaters such as *Velociraptor*, ostrich dinosaurs, and horned plant-eaters like *Protoceratops*. *Zalambdalestes* probably avoided these by hiding in a burrow by day, emerging to feed under cover of darkness. The shape and details of its skull show that it had a long, low snout, presumably with whiskers to feel the way, big eyes to see in the gloom and large ears to detect sounds of danger.

Zalambdalestes had rear limbs that were longer and stronger than the front ones, although all four limbs showed the upright posture typical of mammals. Probably it could leap well, using its rear limbs and very long feet, its calcaneus (rearmost anklebone) in

contact with the ground. Various details in the fossils – such as four premolar and three molar teeth in each side of each jaw, the shape of the molars, and the structure of the shoulder, elbow and ankle – are very similar to those found in today's placental mammals, as opposed to marsupial ones. *Zalambdalestes* is often compared to the elephant shrew in Africa today – an active, busy eater of insects and other small animals, with a long, quivering, trunk-like nose, leaping back legs and long, balancing tail.

BELOW *Zalambdalestes* received its tongue-twisting name from the shape of its teeth. The crushing or working surfaces of some teeth had raised lumps or ridges forming a pattern on each tooth similar in shape to the ancient Greek letter lambda. This dinosaur-age mammal is one of the first known with very long rear feet, probably for leaping.

RIGHT Fossils discovered and studied in the 1990s lend weight to the view that *Deltatheridium* was a type of marsupial mammal, especially from the evidence of how old teeth were replaced by newer ones, and the patterns of grooves and holes in the skull which show the routes of blood vessels and nerves.

DELTATHERIDIUM

This mammal lived at around the same time, 80 million years ago, and in the same region, Mongolia, as *Zalambdalestes* (opposite). It was smaller in size, with a total length, including tail, of some 15 centimeters (6 inches), however, it differed in many respects from *Zalambdalestes*. *Deltatheridium* was one of many mammals from near the end of the Age of Dinosaurs, showing how the mammal group had diversified and spread to various regions over the preceding 130 million years.

Deltatheridium is usually likened in overall appearance to a possum, or perhaps a weasel with slightly longer legs. Its skull was long but the muzzle was relatively tall, giving a large-nosed appearance. The tail was also fairly long. The teeth show the usual mammalian pattern of small, sharp incisors at the front, then one large, pointed, stabbing canine in each side of each jaw and, behind this, lower and wider premolars and molars in the cheeks,

for chewing. The shapes of the molars, when seen from above, that is, in the opposing jaw, are triangular, rather than forming a rounded rectangle. This led to the name of the mammal, "delta" meaning a triangular shape. (Many of these small, early mammals are named after their tooth shapes – see also opposite.) The teeth are arranged so that the upper and lower molars slide past each other and interlock when the jaws close, rather than their topmost surfaces butting together. This gave a powerful shearing and chopping effect, which is also seen in the long-extinct mammal group known as creodonts, which were predators (flesh-eaters). Creodonts are considered to have been placental mammals, but other features of the skull and skeleton are more similar to those of marsupial mammals. *Deltatheridium* probably hunted insects and baby reptiles, and perhaps scavenged using its powerful chewing jaws.

MAMMAL FACTFILE
Deltatheridium

Meaning: Triangle or delta beast

Pronunciation: Del-tah-thurr-id-ee-um

Period: Late Cretaceous

Main group: Mammalia

Length: 15 centimeters (6 inches)

Weight: 80 grams (3 ounces)

Diet: Insects

Fossils: Mongolia

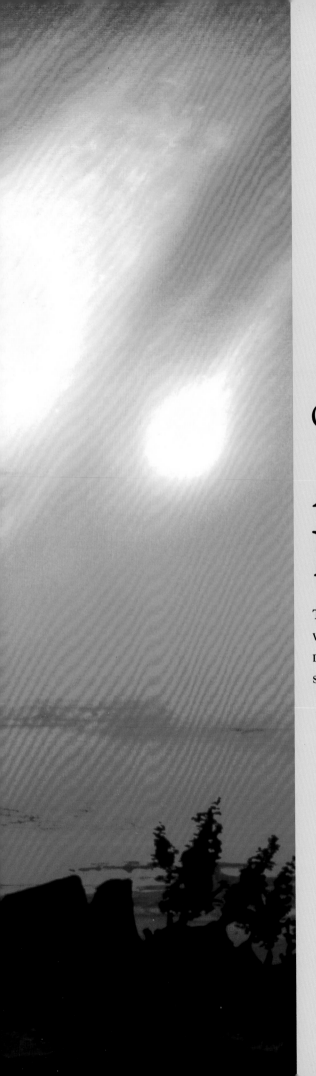

CHAPTER FOURTEEN

AFTER THE DINOSAURS

THE AGE OF DINOSAURS CLOSED ABRUPTLY 66 MILLION YEARS AGO, WITH ONE OF THE GREAT MASS EXTINCTIONS THAT HAVE PERIODICALLY DEVASTATED LIFE ON EARTH. TWO MAJOR ANIMAL GROUPS SURVIVED AND SOON BURGEONED – THE BIRDS AND THE MAMMALS.

MASS EXTINCTIONS

IT MAY SEEM STRANGE, EVEN CONVENIENT, THAT THE TRANSITION FROM THE CRETACEOUS PERIOD TO THE TERTIARY, 66 MILLION YEARS AGO, WAS MARKED BY ONE OF THE MOST CATASTROPHIC EVENTS THE WORLD HAS EVER SEEN. BUT THIS IS SIMPLY THE CUSTOMARY SCIENTIFIC WAY IN WHICH GEOLOGICAL PERIODS ARE DEFINED – BY ABRUPT CHANGES IN THE ROCKS AND THE FOSSILS THEY CONTAIN. THIS PARTICULAR TRANSITION IS KNOWN AS THE CRETACEOUS–TERTIARY, OR K/T, MASS EXTINCTION EVENT. THE "K" STANDS FOR KRETA, THE ANCIENT GREEK WORD FOR "CHALK" THAT IS THE BASIS OF THE TERM "CRETACEOUS," SO NAMED BECAUSE MANY OF THE ROCKS FROM THAT PERIOD ARE CHALKS. MASS EXTINCTIONS WERE NOT NEW, HOWEVER. THERE WERE FIVE MAJOR AND MANY MINOR MASS EXTINCTIONS THROUGH PREHISTORY. THE GREATEST ONE OF ALL MARKED THE END OF THE PERMIAN PERIOD AND THE START OF THE TRIASSIC, 252 MILLION YEARS AGO, AND THEREFORE AROUND 186 MILLION YEARS BEFORE THE K/T EVENT. SURVEYS OF THE FOSSIL EVIDENCE SUGGEST THAT PERHAPS 19 OUT OF 20 LIVING SPECIES DISAPPEARED AT THE END OF THE PERMIAN PERIOD, IN WHAT HAS BEEN DUBBED THE "GREAT DYING." THIS MASSIVE SHOCK TO LIFE SIGNIFIED THE START OF A NEW ERA, THE MESOZOIC ("MIDDLE LIFE"), COMMONLY CALLED THE AGE OF DINOSAURS. THE K/T EVENT CLOSED THAT ERA, AND WITH IT THE DINOSAURS' REIGN. IT MARKED THE START OF THE CENOZOIC (OR CAINOZOIC) ERA OF "RECENT LIFE," THE SUBJECT OF THIS CHAPTER.

WHAT DIED OUT?

Dinosaurs have such a prominent reputation that reports of their demise tend to sideline coverage of all the other living things that disappeared at the same time, which included many reptiles and similar creatures – not only the dinosaurs, but pterosaurs in the air, and mosasaurs, plesiosaurs and others in the sea. Many kinds of marine molluscs and miscellaneous other sea animals also became extinct, as did various plants, especially marine algae or "seaweeds." Larger land animals seem to have suffered most, since after the catastrophe all terrestrial creatures bigger than a modern Labrador dog were gone. Overall, two thirds of all families of living things perished. Curiously, some reptile groups, such as the crocodiles, were only partly affected. Many swamp and freshwater types survived, while marine crocodiles were wiped out. Other reptiles that survived are still with us today, including turtles and tortoises, lizards and snakes.

ON THE WANE?

The K/T event might have taken a few days, several months, or hundreds of years. Looking back so far into the past, it is not possible to discern the timescale precisely. Also, opinions differ on whether the dinosaurs were already on the wane before that event of around 66 million years ago. Some surveys indicate that their overall numbers and diversity had been decreasing for up to 20 million years previously, though these depletions were regional rather than global. In addition, some major dinosaur groups had expanded during this time, such as the "duckbilled" hadrosaurs, the horned dinosaurs or ceratopsians, the great meat-eating tyrannosaurs and the ostrich dinosaurs.

DID DINOSAURS DIE OUT?

Occasional claims are made for dinosaur fossils dating from less than 66 million years ago. In many cases, these turn out to have been misidentified, or are remains of dinosaurs that have been exposed or eroded from older rocks, from before the great extinction, and later incorporated into younger rocks. The overwhelming weight of evidence points to a total mass extinction of the dinosaurs, but the reasons for the event are among the most hotly debated topics in all of paleontology (discussed on the following pages). In one sense, however, dinosaurs may be said to live on, though greatly altered, and with feathers and wings – as birds.

PREVIOUS PAGE There was sudden climate change at the end of the Cretaceous period. The change could have been due to one or several factors, including an asteroid or meteorite strike, massed volcanic eruptions, and altered weather patterns due to continental drift.

LEFT A single volcanic eruption is one of nature's most awesome events. One explanation for the end-of-Cretaceous mass extinction is a whole series of such eruptions, poisoning Earth's atmosphere with choking fumes and blanketing ash.

K/T EXTINCTION THEORIES

The current leading contender for the title of "Dinosaur Killer" is an asteroid (meteorite) impact. A giant "mini-planet" lump of rock, perhaps 10 kilometers (6 miles) across (the size of a large city), came by chance from space and slammed into earth at more than 20,000 kilometers (12,500 miles) per hour. The immense shock at the impact site vaporized everything there – soil, water, animals, plants, even the solid rock under the ground and making up the asteroid itself. This threw massive amounts of debris into the atmosphere, to spread around the globe on the winds. Some of the debris was so hot that as it fell to the ground it sparked wildfires on almost every continent. The resulting haze then blotted out the sun for days, weeks, even years. Plants withered in the cool gloom of the "asteroid winter," and so herbivorous animals starved, followed by the carnivores. Water creatures were afforded some protection from the catastrophe by their aquatic environment.

EVIDENCE

Several lines of evidence support the asteroid theory. In certain rocks formed at the time, there is a thin layer that is unusually rich in the metallic element iridium. This is generally rare on and in Earth, but relatively common in space rocks. Perhaps parts of the asteroid vaporized, floated and settled as the rocks formed. Another clue is a massive bowl-shaped crater, some 200 kilometers (125 miles) across, buried by ooze on the seabed off the Yucatán coast of Mexico. Named the Chicxulub Crater, it may be the impact site. Other events triggered by the collision could have been giant tsunamis, or "tidal waves," which flooded vast areas; a rain of terrifically hot debris that set off wildfires; and shock waves reverberating through the planet's outer, shell-like rocky layer, the crust. These seismic events might have pushed already strained parts of the crust to breaking point, allowing massed volcanic eruptions and self-perpetuating chains of earthquakes. Layers of compressed ash and soot in many areas date back to this time, especially in the Indian region.

CONTINENTS AND CLIMATE

The asteroid theory has many consequences, but some of these could have been concentrated into a relatively short time, without the extraterrestrial stimulus of the asteroid itself. At the end of the Cretaceous, continents were drifting across the globe, mountains were rising in some areas as rift valleys formed in others, and sea levels, as well as patterns of winds and ocean currents, were changing rapidly. Such events may have encouraged unusually fast climate change, combined with a series of widespread volcanic eruptions that poured ash and poisonous gases into the atmosphere. These might have frozen and/or suffocated large land animals, caused a thinning of the atmospheric ozone that protects Earth's surface from harmful solar rays, and formed acid rain that burned and corroded plants. (Two of these events concern us today.) The vast uplands of central India known as the Deccan Plateau were formed by outpourings of runny volcanic lava at around this time. They are cited as evidence of mass volcanic activity, which led to swift climate change.

DISEASE AND COMPETITION

Less refined theories about the demise of the dinosaurs include: epidemics of disease that swept the world, affecting some groups of animals more than others; small mammals beginning to gain success as they ate the eggs of the dinosaurs; "genetic stalemate" or "evolutionary dead ends" for the dinosaurs, as they evolved into highly modified forms that could no longer adapt readily to rapidly changing environmental conditions; and a burst of deadly radiation from outer space, perhaps from the Sun or a nearby exploding star (supernova). However these theories have little serious scientific support.

RIGHT Our planet's surface has long been pockmarked by meteorite collisions, forming craters which are then eroded and eradicated over millennia. This example, Wolf Creek crater from Western Australia, is over a million years old – erosion is very slow in its desert region. It is almost one kilometer (½ mile) across. The end-of-Cretaceous impact could have left a crater 200 times wider, now buried on the seabed.

GASTORNIS (DIATRYMA)

ANIMAL FACTFILE
Gastornis

Meaning: Stomach bird

Pronunciation: Gaz-torn-iss

Period: Paleogene

Main group: Anseriformes
(possibly related to wildfowl group)

Height: 1.8–2 meters (6–6½ feet)

Weight: Up to 140 kilograms (300 pounds)

Diet: Prey of varied sizes, carrion

Fossil sites: USA (Wyoming, New Jersey, New Mexico), Europe (England, Germany, France, Belgium), and possibly China

| 0 | 1 | 2 | 3 | 4 | 5 | 6 | 7 | 8 | 9 | 10 | 11 | 12 | 13 | 14 |

Often referred to by its former name of *Diatryma*, *Gastornis* has no clear equivalent or relation among modern birds. It may have been an offshoot or cousin of the anseriforms or waterfowl group, which today includes ducks, geese and swans, or perhaps the gruiforms, such as cranes, rails or bustards. This massively built creature stood as tall as an adult human being today, and weighed nearly twice as much. Its wings were tiny and useless for flight, but its legs were sturdy and very well muscled, suited to powerful running. On each foot the four long digits, one of them smaller and rear-facing, had huge claws, and *Gastornis* probably could have kicked to death almost any other land animal of the time. The head was as big as a modern horse's, and half of it was the gigantic beak, deep and strongly constructed, which crushed bones as easily as human beings now crunch peanuts. Experts have suggested that in a landscape empty of meat-eating dinosaurs, or any other very large reptiles, rapid evolution of certain bird groups equipped them to take on the role of large land predators before some mammals also adapted to hunting. (For the suggested behavior patterns of *Gastornis*, see *Phorusrhacus* opposite.)

Fossils of *Gastornis* have been found at various sites in New Mexico, Wyoming and New Jersey, and also in Germany, France and Belgium. The oldest remains are from some 55 million years ago, in the Paleocene epoch. The first species was named as *Diatryma gigantea* in 1876 by Edward Drinker Cope, from remains found in New Mexico. More recently, the name *Gastornis* has been accepted.

BELOW The absurdly tiny wings of *Gastornis* are held out of the way as this huge bird lowers its head to attack. The massive beak was ideally suited to shearing gristle and cracking bone. However some experts suggest it was a huge nutcracker too and that *Gastornis* was an omnivore.

RIGHT Most specimens of *Phorusrhacus* were about as tall as an adult human. With useless wings, these birds relied on their massive beaks and feet both to attack prey and for self-defense. Their cousins today may be birds called seriemas, which also live in South America, and which can fly but prefer to run.

PHORUSRHACUS

Phorusrhacids – "terror cranes" – were huge, powerful, flightless birds of the second half of the Tertiary period in South America. This continent was isolated during much of the period, and it did not drift nearer to and join North America until some time in the past few million years. South America's animal and plant life evolved in isolation, and many strange creatures appeared there that had no close relations or equivalents anywhere else. Outwardly, the phorusrhacids resembled other big predatory terrestrial birds that have long been extinct, such as *Gastornis* (see opposite). *Gastornis* lived millions of years earlier, however, and on entirely different continents.

Nevertheless, the behavior patterns of these birds were perhaps similar. They were strong predators, striding or charging across the land on stout, heavily muscled legs. They used their massively powerful, hooked beaks

to catch smaller prey, such as mammals and other birds, or to gash and tear flesh from larger victims, perhaps holding them down with one strong, sharp-clawed foot. They may have sliced lumps from carcasses and probed within to crunch the bones, using their beaks in much the same way that the hyenas of the Old World scavenge today. In South America there were few, if any, large predatory mammals to compete with them.

Phorusrhacus appeared in the Early Miocene epoch, about 25 million years ago, and grew to about 1.8 meters (6 feet) tall. Similar members of the group came and went over following epochs. One of the last and largest was *Titanis*, some 2.5 meters (8 feet) tall, with claws on the two digits of each of its feet. Even larger birds have existed since, including giant moas over 3 meters (10 feet) tall in New Zealand, but these were not fierce predators like the "terror cranes."

ANIMAL FACTFILE
Phorusrhacus
Meaning: Terror crane
Pronunciation: Foe-roos-rak-uss
Period: Neogene
Main group: Cariamiformes
Height: 1.5–2.5 meters (4–8 feet)
Weight: Up to 140 kilograms (310 pounds)
Diet: Prey, carrion
Fossil sites: South America

0 1 2 3 4 5 6 7 8 9 10 11 12 13 14

PLESIADAPIS

The primate group of mammals includes lemurs, bushbabies, monkeys, apes and humans. Whether *Plesiadapis* was one of the earliest primates, or a very close relative of them, is not clear. At a quick glance, it resembled the tree-dwelling lemurs of modern Madagascar. It was about the size of a very large squirrel of today, with four strong, mobile limbs equipped with long, clawed toes for a powerful grip, probably on tree boughs and trunks. It also had a long, flexible tail, which may have been bushy, and may have been useful for balance when *Plesiadapis* was running and leaping through the branches. But *Plesiadapis* had a face and teeth more like those of a modern rodent, such as a mouse or rat. Its snout was slender, and it had long, gnawing incisors at the front of each jaw, then a gap where true primates have canine teeth,

and, in the cheek region, broad molars for chewing and grinding. There are many different opinions about the diet of *Plesiadapis*, ranging from mainly insects and other small animals, to fruits and seeds, to foliage, to sap and grubs found in tree bark, to a mixture of all these items.

Many *Plesiadapis* fossils have been uncovered in northwestern France, and others have been found at sites in Colorado and other areas in and around the Rockies in North America. They mostly date from 60–50 million years ago, although some appear to date from as recently as 35 million years ago. Comparisons are often made between *Plesiadapis* and the modern ring-tailed lemur. Although the lemur is smaller, it, too, spends some time in trees and also frequents the ground, and eats a wide variety of plant foods.

ANIMAL FACTFILE
Plesiadapis

Meaning: Near to Adapis
(another Tertiary mammal)

Pronunciation: Pleez-ee-ah-dap-iss

Period: Paleogene

Main group: Plesiadapiformes

Length: Head and body 80 centimeters
(31 inches), tail 50 centimeters (19½ inches)

Weight: 2 kilograms (4 pounds)

Diet: Unclear (see text)

Fossil sites: France, Rocky Mountains of
North America

0 1 2 3 4 5 6 7 8 9 10 11 12 13 14

ABOVE Strong-toed and bushy-tailed as reconstructed here, *Plesiadapis* seemed well suited to life both in trees and on the ground. Its tail would be useful for precise balance when scampering and leaping through the branches.

ANDREWSARCHUS

The fossil remains of this formidable beast consist of its skull and little else. The skull, which is almost 85 centimeters (33½ inches) long, suggests that *Andrewsarchus* was a huge creature, with a total head-and-body length of more than 6 meters (19½ feet). If so, *Andrewsarchus* would have been the largest meat-eating mammal ever to walk the earth. Its pointed front teeth, especially the canines, were massive, useful for piercing prey and ripping flesh. Its cheek teeth, or molars, were shaped for a combination of cutting and crushing. Despite so many features resembling those of today's carnivores, such as cats, dogs and, perhaps more pertinently, bears and hyenas, *Andrewsarchus* was not a member of the Carnivora group of mammals. In fact, its closer relations were deer, horses and cattle. *Andrewsarchus* was a hoofed mammal, or ungulate: it had nail-like hooves shaped like claws rather than the true claws of a cat or dog. As a result, it was seen as a member of the ungulate subgroup called Mesonychidae (or Acreodi), which were some of the earliest large hunting mammals. However, more recent work has not supported these mesonychid affinities. Instead, *Andrewsarchus* is now placed in the Cetancodontamorpha, which includes whales and hippos and the extinct boar-like enteledonts. *Andrewsarchus* lived in Mid Eocene times (48–41 million years ago).

The limited remains of *Andrewsarchus* were discovered in 1923 during an American-organized fossil-hunting expedition to Mongolia. The venture, which also discovered fossils of many dinosaurs such as *Velociraptor* and *Protoceratops*, was led by Roy Chapman Andrews, then director of the American Museum of Natural History. *Andrewsarchus* was named in his honor.

ANIMAL FACTFILE
Andrewsarchus
Meaning: Andrews's flesh-eater
Pronunciation: And-rue-sark-uss
Period: Paleogene
Main group: Artiodactyla
Length: Head and body possibly up to 4 meters (12 feet)
Weight: 250 kilograms (551 pounds)
Diet: Meat, carrion, perhaps varied animal and plant foods
Fossil site: Mongolia

0 1 2 3 4 5 6 7 8 9 10 11 12 13 14

ABOVE The long, low skull of *Andrewsarchus* gave its muzzle a peculiar shape, unlike the cats and wolves of today. Only the skull of this creature is known with any certainty.

RIGHT At a glance, *Icaronycteris* would be difficult to distinguish from a small insect-eating bat of today. In this picture its mouth is open to emit pulses of very high-pitched sound, ultrasound. Its large ears detect the echoes, which are analyzed to show the location and size of nearby objects.

ICARONYCTERIS

ANIMAL FACTFILE
Icaronycteris

Meaning: Night wing of Icarus (character in Greek myth)

Pronunciation: Ick-ah-roe-nick-tur-iss

Period: Paleogene

Main group: Mammalia (Chiroptera)

Size: Wingspan 38 centimeters (15 inches)

Weight: 30–35 grams (1 ounce)

Diet: Insects, similar small animals

Fossil sites: North America

0	1	2	3	4	5	6	7	8	9	10	11	12	13	14

Bats are among the most specialized of all mammals, and they were also one of the earliest major mammal groups to appear after the death of the dinosaurs. By the Early Eocene epoch, more than 50 million years ago, *Icaronycteris* was flitting through the gloom as it chased small flying insects like moths, almost exactly as bats still do today (or rather, tonight). Its forelimbs were highly evolved as wings made of very thin, stretchy, skin-like flight membranes (patagia), held out by greatly elongated finger bones. Tiny ear bones, preserved as fossils in similar early bats, show that *Icaronycteris* probably used high-pitched squeaks or clicks as a form of echolocation, or sonar, to track and catch prey in midair during the hours of darkness. The sharp-clawed feet had specialized ankle joints that allowed the feet to turn around and face backward, for hanging upside down to rest. Most of these features are shown by other bats from the Eocene epoch (53–33 million years ago) including *Palaeochiropteryx*, *Archaeonycteris* and *Hassianycteris*.

All these features are still found in bats today, but *Icaronycteris* inherited older features from its shrew-like insectivore ancestors. It still had a claw on each second digit: later, bats lost this and they now retain only one claw on each first digit ("thumb"). *Icaronycteris* had more teeth than today's insectivore bats. Its wings were comparatively short, and broad from front to back. The tail was long and "free" – it was not joined to the rearmost part of the wing membrane. The body of a modern bat is compact and rigid, while that of *Icaronycteris* was longer and flexible. Fossils of bats, as for birds, are generally rare due to their thin and fragile nature, but an exciting new discovery is the "Mahenge bat," named after its site in the Singida region of north-central Tanzania, Africa.

BASILOSAURUS

As the dinosaurs became extinct 65 million years ago, so did the large flesh-eating reptiles of the seas, such as the mosasaurs and pliosaurs. Less than 20 million years later, fully aquatic whales with flippers and tail flukes had evolved from their land-living, four-legged ancestors. One of the biggest of these prehistoric whales was *Basilosaurus* of the Late Eocene, 40–36 million years ago, which, in spite of its name, was a mammal, not a reptile. Its fossils have been discovered in rocks formed from ancient, shallow seabeds which are now far inland on several continents, including the Fayum fossil beds (layers) near Cairo, the capital city of Egypt.

The ancestry of whales is hotly debated among prehistoric mammal specialists. Some of the latest fossil and genetic or DNA evidence suggests that hoofed mammals may have been their forebears – perhaps ancient members of the hippopotamus group, or even the flesh-eating mesonychids (see *Andrewsarchus*, page 297).

Basilosaurus rivaled the length of today's great whales, such as the blue, humpback or gray, although it was probably slimmer and more eel-like, and so weighed considerably less. Also, while great whales now filter or sieve small prey from the water, using their mouthfuls of comb-like baleen plates (whalebone), *Basilosaurus* had a mouthful of fearsome teeth for attacking large victims. The front teeth were stout and pointed, like back-curved cones, while those to the rear were like wide-based blades with serrated edges, and were used for slicing. They explain why *Basilosaurus* is sometimes still known by a former name, *Zeuglodon*, meaning "saw-toothed." The front limbs had become flippers, as in modern whales. The rear limbs were still present, but only just – as tiny, three-toed legs that may have projected from the main body. The flukes at the end of the tail had no limb bones.

ANIMAL FACTFILE
Basilosaurus
Meaning: Emperor reptile (it was originally thought to be reptilian)

Pronunciation: Baz-ill-owe-sore-uss

Period: Paleogene

Main group: Archaeoceti

Length: Up to 20 meters (65 feet)

Weight: About 10 metric tons (10 tons)

Diet: Marine prey such as fish, squid

Fossil sites: North America, Middle East

ABOVE *Basilosaurus* had a relatively small head and slim body, and its fossil skull shows that its brain was smaller, in comparison to overall body size, than in today's whales and dolphins. Other fossils associated with its remains show that it probably ate fish, including small sharks, and perhaps smaller whales such as *Dorudon* which was only one-quarter the length of *Basilosaurus*.

RIGHT Despite its rhino-like horns and elephant-style small tusks, *Uintatherium* was not closely related to either of those mammal groups.

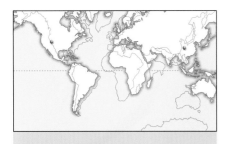

ANIMAL FACTFILE
Uintatherium

Meaning: Uintah beast (see text)

Pronunciation: Ooo-in-tah-theer-ee-um

Period: Paleogene

Main group: Dinocerata

Size: Head and body 3.5–4 meters long (11–13 feet)

Weight: 2 metric tons (2 tons)

Diet: Plants

Fossil sites: North America, China

UINTATHERIUM

With its three sets of paired bony head knobs or "horns," and a pair of large tusks protruding from the upper jaw, *Uintatherium* generally resembles a modern rhinoceros, or perhaps a hippopotamus. Indeed, it was about the size of today's largest rhinoceros species, the white or square-lipped rhinoceros. However, *Uintatherium* belonged to a long-extinct group of huge herbivores known as the dinoceratans, "terrible horns." These appeared about 60 million years ago and peaked around 55–50 million years ago; by 30 million years ago they had all but disappeared. Their place in classification is uncertain. They are often assumed to be ungulates (hoofed mammals), or alternatively the anagalids, a small group of extinct rabbit-like mammals.

Uintatherium was the biggest of the dinoceratans. Its fossils have been found at numerous sites in North America, including several in Utah. The creature was named in 1872 after the Uintah, a Native American

people from that area. The function of the lumpy, bony growths on the head is much debated. They may have been signs of sexual maturity to deter same-sex rivals and attract partners for breeding. Or they could have been weapons to be used in fighting rivals, in the way that male deer use their antlers to battle each other during the rutting season. The tusks, which are enlarged upper canine teeth and are found only in some specimens – probably males – could have also been symbolic, for visual display, or might have been used for physical battles too. The tusks fitted over shelf-like extensions or flanges of the lower jaw, which presumably protected them from snapping if they were knocked while the mouth was closed. The teeth were not especially large or well developed, so *Uintatherium* probably had a soft diet of young shoots and leaves. At some sites, fossils of other animals and plants found with its remains suggest a lakeside habitat.

PARACERATHERIUM

Paraceratherium is the largest land mammal known from any age. It lived mainly during the Oligocene epoch, around 30 million years ago. Fossils of this immense beast have been found at various sites in eastern Europe and in Asia, including China and the Baluchistan region of Pakistan. Remains once known as *Baluchitherium* or *Indricotherium* are now usually included in the genus *Paraceratherium* although the sub-group to which it belongs is usually known as the indricotheres or hyracodontids. Despite its resemblance to a massive horse, and its lack of facial horns, *Paraceratherium* was a member of this extinct group of rhinoceroses. Today the rhinoceroses are among the most restricted and endangered of all mammal families, with just five species,

but in prehistoric times there were many widespread species, including speedy, pony-sized members (see also *Coelodonta*, page 304). The first fossils of *Paraceratherium* were found in 1910 in Baluchistan by an English paleontologist, Clive Forster-Cooper.

It seems that male *Paraceratherium* were larger than females, and they had heavier skulls with more domed foreheads, perhaps used in butting contests at breeding time. A large male *Paraceratherium* had a skull 1.3 meters (52 inches) long, and could stretch its long neck to reach leaves and other plant food 8 meters (26 feet) above the ground. This exceeds the tallest modern animal, the giraffe, by 2 meters (6½ feet). Females were a meter or two (3-6 feet) smaller all around. The front teeth of *Paraceratherium* were unusual: a tusk-like, downward-directed pair in the upper jaw and a forward-pointing pair in the lower jaw. The skull structure around the nasal area suggests that it had very mobile lips, perhaps elongated into a short but flexible trunk like a modern tapir's, for browsing.

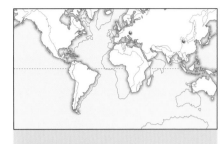

ANIMAL FACTFILE
Paraceratherium

Meaning: Beside horn beast

Pronunciation: Para-seer-ah-theer-ee-um

Period: Paleogene

Main group: Perissodactyla

Size: Head-and-body length up to 7.4 meters (24 feet)

Weight: Up to 20 metric tons (20 tons)

Diet: Foliage, buds, shoots, twigs

Fossil sites: Asia, eastern Europe

0 1 2 3 4 5 6 7 8 9 10 11 12 13 14

LEFT Vast in every dimension, *Paraceratherium* stood as tall at its shoulder as the head height of a giraffe today. It probably belonged to an extinct group of rhinoceroses, called the hyracodontids or "running rhinos."

COELODONTA

ANIMAL FACTFILE
Coelodonta

Meaning: Cavity tooth

Pronunciation: Seel-owe-don-tah

Period: Late Neogene–Quaternary

Main group: Perissodactyla

Size: 3.5 meters (12 feet)

Weight: Up to 2 metric tons (2 tons)

Diet: Grasses and other low-growing plants

Fossil sites: Europe, Asia

| 0 | 1 | 2 | 3 | 4 | 5 | 6 | 7 | 8 | 9 | 10 | 11 | 12 | 13 | 14 |

Commonly called the woolly rhinoceros, *Coelodonta* was indeed a member of the rhinoceros group, and was also extremely furry. It had two long nose horns, humped shoulders, a stocky body, four squat limbs, a short, thin tail and long, dark, shaggy hair. This amount of detail is clear because *Coelodonta* is known, not only from fossilized bones and teeth, but also from whole bodies frozen and preserved in the ice of the far north, in Asia – especially Siberia – as well as in Europe. It can also be recognized in the cave paintings of ancient human beings, dating to less than 30,000 years ago. Some of the art appears to depict woolly rhinoceroses being hunted with spears and other weapons.

Coelodonta was as big as the larger rhinoceroses of today, but with a greater shoulder height of up to 2.2 meters (7 feet). It lived during much of the Pleistocene epoch, from about half a million years ago and probably became extinct during the last major ice age (see previous page), perhaps as recently as 10,000 years ago. The front nose horn was longer than the rear one, and in some individuals – probably older males – it reached almost 2 meters (6½ feet). It differed slightly from a modern rhinoceros's horn in being flattened from side to side, like a thick and curved sword blade, rather than having a more circular cross-section. It has been suggested that *Coelodonta* used its "nose blade" to sweep snow aside and reveal vegetation, and perhaps even slice into semifrozen ground to loosen low-growing plants. In addition, the horn, as in modern rhinoceroses, was a visual symbol of maturity and power, used to deter enemies or attract breeding partners.

RIGHT The fur pattern of the woolly rhinoceros is known from frozen carcasses and ancient human cave art. It was probably dark brown or gray in color. There was also a shoulder hump that varied in size. This was a store of fat that accumulated in well-fed individuals but was then used up by the body in times of food shortage.

DEINOTHERIUM

There are just three living species of elephants, but the elephant group, the proboscideans, has a long and varied prehistory, with numerous subgroups and dozens of species. The earliest kinds of proboscideans, from more than 55 million years ago, were about the size of small pigs, but the trend was soon to a much larger body size, pillar-like legs, and nose and upper lip joined and extended into the characteristic flexible trunk. Some types were tuskless and had shorter legs, and probably lived like modern hippopotamuses. (See also *Mammuthus*, next page.)

The genus *Deinotherium* was one of the largest and longest-lived among the proboscideans. It first appeared in the Miocene epoch, some 20 million years ago, in Africa. Later, it also spread into Europe and Asia, with only minor evolutionary changes.

A typical *Deinotherium* was slightly bigger than the elephants of today, and its trunk was probably stubbier and thicker than that of a modern elephant. Its most distinctive feature was its tusks, which grew, not from the upper jaw as in most other proboscideans, but from the front of the lower jaw. The tusks curved down and back to emerge through the skin of the chin. The way that *Deinotherium* used its curious tusks has been much debated. It may have rooted in soil for underground plant parts, pulled down branches to snap them and reach leaves, or stripped soft bark from tree trunks. *Deinotherium* fossils have been uncovered at several of the African sites where remains of hominids, prehistoric relatives of modern human beings, have also been found.

ANIMAL FACTFILE
Deinotherium
Meaning: Terrible beast
Pronunciation: Day-noh-theer-ee-um
Period: Neogene–Quaternary
Main group: Mammalia (Proboscidea)
Size: Shoulder height up to 4 meters (13 feet), head-and-body length (excluding trunk and tail) 7–8 meters (23–26 feet)
Weight: up to 13 metric tons (13 tons)
Diet: Plant material
Fossil sites: Africa, Europe, Asia

0 1 2 3 4 5 6 7 8 9 10 11 12 13 14

LEFT The biggest individuals of *Deinotherium* rivaled the largest elephants of today, the African savanna species. When its fossils were first studied in the 1820s, experts were so puzzled by the lower-jaw, down-curving tusks that they tried to reconstruct the animal with the jaw attached upside down.

RIGHT *Mammuthus primigenius*, the woolly mammoth, lived in the Ice Age at the same time as people from 500 generations ago.

ANIMAL FACTFILE
Mammuthus

Meaning: First grown mammoth

Pronunciation: Mam-ooo-thuss

Period: Late Neogene–Quaternary

Main group: Mammalia (Proboscidea)

Height: At shoulder 3 meters (10 feet)

Weight: up to 8 metric tons (8 tons)

Diet: Grasses and other plants

Fossil sites: Europe, Asia, North America, Africa

0 1 2 3 4 5 6 7 8 9 10 11 12 13 14

MAMMUTHUS (MAMMOTH)

Mammuthus was a genus of huge proboscideans (members of the elephant group), with as many as eight species. They were mostly large to very large, with long curving tusks. They are known from fossils, subfossils, deep-frozen bodies in the ice of the far north, and from the cave art of ancient human beings. Various anatomical and genetic comparisons – mammoth DNA was obtained and studied in the 1990s – show that mammoths were very close relatives of living elephants, compared to much more distant cousins such as *Deinotherium* (see previous page).

The ice-age woolly mammoth, *Mammuthus primigenius*, was still living less than 10,000 years ago, and some smaller or dwarf forms may have been in existence only 4,000 years ago, on Vrangelya (Wrangel Island) off the coast of the extreme northeast of the Asian continent. The woolly mammoth lived across all the northern continents. It had humped shoulders, a markedly domed top to the head, and a very short tail. It was not the largest mammoth, but it was the hairiest: frozen specimens show that the shaggy strands of the outer furry coat were as long as 90 centimeters (36 inches). These hairs were dark, almost black: earlier reconstructions of "red-haired" mammoths were due to natural chemicals in the soil and rocks seeping into the fur and staining it red.

The steppe mammoth of Europe and Asia, *Mammuthus trogontherii*, had a shorter furry coat and was one of the largest mammoths, probably standing 4.6 meters (15 feet) at the shoulder, and weighing more than 10 metric tons (10 tons). The American or Columbian mammoth, *Mammuthus columbi*, was slightly smaller, lacked fur, and lived only in North America. The ancestor of all these forms may have been the southern mammoth, *Mammuthus meridionalis*.

MEGALOCEROS

Also known as the giant elk or Irish elk, *Megaloceros* was a member of the cervid or deer group, like the living species called the elk (in Europe) or moose (in North America). However, it was more closely related to fallow deer and was not a true elk/moose, although it rivaled the latter in size. Its remains have been found at many sites across Europe and Asia, from Ireland to China. The common name Irish elk comes from many early finds made in Ireland, including parts of up to 100 individuals in a bog near Dublin. The "-ceros" part of the scientific name means "horn," but deer antlers are different from the true horns of mammals such as cattle or antelopes. Unlike true horns, which grow continually in both sexes, antlers are shed and regrown annually, and by males only, except in one living deer species, the reindeer/caribou.

For a male *Megaloceros*, growing new antlers each year must have put a huge strain on its food resources, for it had to gather enough nutrients to build a fresh set of these massive, spreading structures. In some specimens, the antlers spanned more than 3.5 meters (12 feet) and weighed 50 kilograms (110 pounds). *Megaloceros* survived from more than 500,000 to less than 10,000 years ago. Tiny wear marks on antler fossils suggest that they were not solely for show, but were used in battle, as in deer rutting today. A popular notion is that the antlers became so big and heavy as they evolved that *Megaloceros* could no longer hold up its head. It is more likely that predation by humans during the Ice Age, and perhaps climate change, hastened this enormous deer's extinction. Cave paintings portray it as brown with a paler chest.

ANIMAL FACTFILE
Megaloceros (Megaceros)

Meaning: Mega horn [antler], giant horn
Pronunciation: Mega-low-sair-oss
Period: Late Neogene–Quaternary
Main group: Artiodactyla
Size: Head-and-body 2.5 meters (8 feet), height at shoulder 2 meters (6 1/2 feet)
Weight: 400–500 kilograms (880–1,100 pounds)
Diet: Grasses, leaves
Fossil sites: Europe (particularly Ireland), Asia (mainly north)

| 0 | I | 2 | 3 | 4 | 5 | 6 | 7 | 8 | 9 | 10 | II | 12 | 13 | 14 |

RIGHT Remains of mostly antlered rather than non-antlered *Megaloceros* suggest that more of the huge male deer perished, probably during winter, compared to females. Despite the great size of this deer, its general body shape was of a strong, swift runner with plenty of stamina.

URSUS SPELAEUS (CAVE BEAR)

ANIMAL FACTFILE

Ursus spelaeus

Meaning: Cave bear

Pronunciation: Er-suss spell-ay-uss

Period: Quaternary

Main group: Mammalia (Carnivora)

Length: Up to 3 meters (10 feet)

Weight: Up to 500 kilograms (1,100 pounds)

Diet: Mainly plant matter, possibly small prey and carrion

Fossil sites: Europe, Asia

The ursids are bears, and the genus *Ursus* includes half of the eight living bear species: polar, brown/grizzly, and American and Asiatic black bears. *Ursus spelaeus* was the giant cave bear of the ice ages, surviving to just a few thousand years ago. It was similar in size to the modern brown/grizzly bear, but had a longer, more prominent muzzle. Its fur was long and shaggy, its limbs were extremely muscled and powerful, and each foot bore five digits with long, curved claws. It features in the cave art of ancient human beings, and its bones and teeth were used by them, especially Neanderthals, for carvings, in decorative items such as necklaces and in rituals.

The cave bear is so called because many of its remains have been found in caves, especially in the European Alps. These include fossilized bones and teeth, subfossils (materials partway along the process of turning to stone), and mummified scraps of skin and other soft tissue. Other sites known for this species are spread across Europe and Asia, from Britain and Spain east to Russia. In some caves, such as the Drachenhohle (Dragon's Cave) in Austria, there are remains of many thousands of cave bears. Today's bears are solitary, even during winter. Possibly to survive such extreme winters, the ice-age cave bears adapted their social behavior and gathered in groups to sleep deeply in sheltered places, although in the Drachenhohle a flood or similar disaster overtook them. The search for ice-age shelter may well have brought cave bears and human beings into conflict, but the bear was probably mostly herbivorous.

RIGHT The cave bear and ice-age humans perhaps came face to face while searching for shelter from the bitter ice-age winter. Rearing up onto its back legs, this ursid stood more than 3 meters (10 feet) tall, about the same as a large grizzly of today.

BELOW The saber-toothed "tiger" Smilodon was slightly smaller than today's large tigers. For a catlike carnivore its skeleton was relatively robust, that is, of a sturdy and solid build.

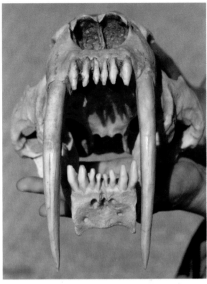

ABOVE "Smiley's" mouth was dominated by the massive canine teeth, each longer than a human hand but slim and blade-like when seen from the front. The equivalent canine teeth in the lower jaw were tiny or non-existent, and the molars or cheek teeth were reduced in number.

SMILODON (SABER-TOOTHED CAT)

Probably the best known of the saber-toothed cats, the largest specimens of *Smilodon* grew to the size of today's lion. They are sometimes called saber-toothed "tigers," but, while they were certainly members of the felid or cat family, tigers are among their more distant cousins. Several species of the genus *Smilodon* are known, including *Smilodon fatalis/ californicus*, with thousands of individuals preserved in the La Brea tar pits of Los Angeles, California. They were trapped in the natural pools of sticky tar along with wolves and other predators that had presumably come to feast on the various mastodonts (ancient elephants) and other large herbivores already floundering there. *Smilodon populator/neogaeus* lived in South America and was slightly larger. It probably evolved there after its predecessors crossed from North America, following the joining of the two continents by the Central American land

bridge a few million years ago. Other types of saber-toothed cats are known from Europe, Asia and Africa.

Smilodon was a powerfully built, heavily muscled cat, especially in its shoulders and front limbs. The "sabers" were upper canine teeth that reached 25 centimeters (10 inches) in length. They were sharp and had serrated rear edges, but they were also narrow from side to side, blade-like, and rather fragile. They would be unlikely to survive a strong bite that hit solid bone. More likely, the cat opened its mouth very wide (120 degrees), and used them to stab, slash and slice the skin and flesh of its victim, perhaps inflicting wounds so that the prey bled to death. Then lumps of meat could be bitten off and swallowed without the risk of damaging the teeth as the prey twisted and struggled. Likely prey included prehistoric forms of bison, camels, horses and giant ground sloths.

ANIMAL FACTFILE
Smilodon

Meaning: Knife tooth

Pronunciation: Smile-owe-don

Period: Quaternary

Main group: Mammalia (Carnivora)

Length: up to 3 meters (10 feet),

Weight: up to 280 kilograms (620 pounds)

Diet: Meat

Fossil sites: North and South America

0 1 2 3 4 5 6 7 8 9 10 11 12 13 14

GLOSSARY

abelisaurids
A group of theropods (meat-eating dinosaurs) from Mid Jurassic to Late Cretaceous, with primitive features, based on the 29-foot-long (9-meter) *Abelisaurus* from South America.

absolute dating
Determining the age of minerals contained in rocks in terms of how many actual years ago they were formed (compare **relative dating**).

acanthodians
One of the first groups of fish with jaws and paired fins, dating from the Early Silurian to the Permian periods. They are sometimes called "spiny sharks" but were not true sharks.

actinistians
Another name for the group of lobe-fin or fleshy-fin (sarcopterygian) fish which includes the coelacanths.

actinopterygians
The group name for ray-finned fish, which are fish with bony skeletons whose fins are supported by spine-like structures called fin rays; they form the great majority of fishes today (compare **sarcopterygians**).

agnathans
"Without jaws," a term usually applied to fish that do not have jaws but mouths like suckers or rasps; the two main types surviving today are lampreys and hagfishes.

alula
A small tuft of feathers part-way along the front or leading edge of a bird's wing, which adjusts the airflow, especially when flying at low speed; also called the bastard wing.

ammonoids
Types of extinct cephalopod molluscs with external spirally coiled shells, large eyes and many tentacles for catching prey; related to octopus and squid.

ankylosaurids
A subgroup of the ankylosaurs (see below) which also possessed large bony lumps at the tail tip (compare **nodosaurids**).

ankylosaurs
Plant-eating armored or plated dinosaurs, well protected by many bony plates, lumps and shields in the skin.

annelids
Segmented worms – a major worm group which includes earthworms – where the body is formed of a long row of many similar ring-like sections or parts, called segments.

anseriforms
The group of birds usually called waterfowl or wildfowl, which today includes ducks, geese and swans.

anthracosaurs
A subgroup of early extinct tetrapod animals which were reptile-like (reptiliomorph) amphibians. They arose in Late Devonian times and died out in Early Triassic times.

anurans
"Without tails," a name usually applied to the tail-less amphibians or lissamphibians, which include frogs, salamanders and caecilians.

apodans
"Without feet," usually applied to the worm-like amphibians or lissamphibians also known as caecilians or gymnophiones.

archosaurimorphs
Diapsid reptiles with a form or body structure resembling that of the archosaurs (see below).

archosaurs
"Ruling reptiles," a large group that arose in the Triassic period and included dinosaurs, pterosaurs, birds and crocodiles.

arthropods
Invertebrate animals with a hard outer body casing and legs with movable joints – a massive group that includes insects, spiders and other arachnids; horseshoe crabs, true crabs and other crustaceans; centipedes, millipedes, also the extinct trilobites and eurypterids.

articulation
A joint or connection, usually between parts of the skeleton or structural framework of an animal, such as between the bones of a dinosaur's skeleton.

axis
The central line or middle band, for example, the middle lobe of the three lobes forming the body of a trilobite.

baleen plates
Long, fringe-edged strips of gristle-like baleen or "whalebone" hanging from the upper jaw of a great whale, used for filter-feeding.

brachiopods
An ancient group of bivalved "shellfish", superficially similar to the molluscan clams but actually belonging to a quite different biological group.

belemnoids
Types of extinct molluscs with internal bullet- or spear-shaped shells, large eyes and many tentacles for catching prey; related to octopus and squid.

blastoids
Extinct sea-dwelling relatives of starfish in the echinoderm group, consisting of a five-rayed, inverted cup-shaped body, held up on a stalk.

boss
A rounded lump or mass, usually of a hard material like bone or horn.

brachiosaurids
Subgroup of sauropod dinosaurs based on *Brachiosaurus* ("arm reptile"), with front legs longer than the rear ones.

caecilians
See apodans.

calyx
Body part shaped like a bowl, cup or trumpet (a term also used to describe the shapes of certain flowers).

camarasaurids
Subgroup of sauropod dinosaurs based on *Camarasaurus* ("chambered reptile"), with weight-saving scoops and hollows in the vertebrae (backbones).

carnosaurs
A general and descriptive name (rather than the name of a specific and well-defined group) for large, predatory, meat-eating or carnivorous dinosaurs, such as *Allosaurus* and *Giganotosaurus*.

caudal vertebrae
Backbones or vertebrae at the rear end of the spinal column, usually forming the animal's tail.

caudatans
See urodelans.

centrosaurines
"Short-frilled" subgroup of ceratopsid or horned dinosaurs based on *Centrosaurus*, where the nose horn was usually longer than the brow horns, and the front of the face was fairly deep and short-snouted (compare **chasmosaurines**).

cephalon
The front or head end, with the mouth and sensory organs like eyes, of certain animals, such as trilobites.

cephalopods
"Head-foot," a group of predatory molluscs with large eyes, big brains and many tentacles, including extinct ammonoids and belemnoids, also octopus, squid, cuttlefish and nautilus.

cephalothorax
The front or head end, with the mouth and sensory organs like eyes, combined with the middle part of the body that bears the limbs, of certain animals such as spiders and other arachnids.

ceratopsians
Horned dinosaurs, a group of beaked plant-eaters, mostly with facial horns and sweeping neck frills or shoulder shields, such as *Triceratops*.

ceratosaurs
A group of theropods (meat-eating dinosaurs), mainly from the first half of the Age of Dinosaurs, which have a common ancestry with *Ceratosaurus*.

cervids
The family name for the hoofed mammals called deer, with antlers rather than horns.

chasmosaurines
"Long-frilled" group of ceratopsid or horned dinosaurs based on *Chasmosaurus*, where the nose horn was usually shorter than the brow horns, and the front of thes face was fairly shallow and long-snouted.

chelicerae
Long, sharp "biting claws" that work like fangs or jaws, in animals such as spiders, scorpions and horseshoe crabs; also the extinct eurypterids.

chelicerates
Arthropods that possess chelicerae (see above).

chelonians
The group name for dome-shelled reptiles commonly known as turtles, terrapins and tortoises.

chilopods
The group name for centipedes, which have strong jabbing **chelicerae** and one pair of legs per body segment.

cnidarians
Group of soft-bodied animals, including jellyfish, anemones, hydras and corals, most of which have stinging tentacles encircling a stalk-like body.

coelurosaurs
General name for small meat-eating and bird-related theropod dinosaurs, that mostly lived toward the beginning of the Age of Dinosaurs, such as *Coelophysis* and *Coelurus*, with hollow, bird-like bones.

collembolans
Small insect-like arthropods also known as springtails, which were some of the very first land animals in the Devonian period.

coracoid
Paired bone in the upper or front shoulder region, especially in a bird, which braces the breastbone and front limb against the vertebral column or backbone; usually an additional bone to the collarbones or clavicles, which together form the V-shaped furcula or "wishbone" of a bird.

creodonts
Flesh-eating mammals, similar in many ways to today's wolves, cats and bears (Carnivora), but which formed a different group and died out by 5–10 million years ago.

crinoids
Animals of the echinoderm group, which includes starfish and seaurchins, that have a flower-like body shape and a very ancient history.

cusps
Raised, pointed or ridged surfaces on a part such as a tooth.

cycads
Plants that resemble palm trees, with a central stalk or trunk and an umbrella-shaped crown of frond-like leaves, which still survive but were much more numerous in the Mesozoic era.

cynodonts
"Dog teeth," creatures with features of both reptiles and mammals, part of the group which used to be called "mammal-like reptiles". They gave rise to the mammals in the Triassic period but themselves became extinct in the Jurassic (see also **dicynodonts**).

decapods
Ten-limbed members of the crustacean arthropods, such as crabs and prawns.

denticles
Small skin scales or projections shaped like cones or teeth, characteristic of the shark group.

diapsids
Major group of reptiles, identified by an opening or window in the skull behind the eye socket, that includes sea reptiles such as ichthyosaurs, snakes and lizards, and the archosaurs such as crocodilians, dinosaurs and pterosaurs.

dicynodonts
Meaning "two dog teeth," creatures belonging to the therapsid group of synapsids with a superficial resemblance to plant-eaters such as hippos. They used to be referred to as "mammal-like reptiles". (see also **cynodonts**).

dimorphism
"Two forms," usually describing the same kind or species which typically has two distinct forms, as when the male is much larger than the female, or vice versa.

dinocephalians
Meaning "terrible heads," a group of large-bodied therapsids, which included both plant and meat-eaters, and many of which are characterised by horns, lumps and projections on their heads, and lived during the Permian period.

dinoceratans
Large plant-eating mammals from early in the Tertiary period, which had features of hoofed (ungulate) mammals and are thought to be related to them. They died out in Late Eocene times.

diplodocids
Subgroup of sauropod dinosaurs based on *Diplodocus* ("double beam"), with very long tails that had twin ski-like chevrons on the underside of each tail bone.

diplopods
The group name for millipedes, which are arthropods with chewing mouthparts and two pairs of legs per body segment.

dorsal fin
A fin or flap on the top or back (dorsal surface) of an animal such as a fish or ichthyosaur.

dromaeosaurs
Medium-sized predatory, meat-eating or carnivorous and feathered dinosaurs, based on *Dromaeosaurus*, including the well-known *Deinonychus* and *Velociraptor* – the group is sometimes known as "raptors."

echinoderms
"Spiny-skins," marine creatures with a five-rayed, wheel-like body design, including starfish, brittlestars, urchins, sea cucumbers, sea lilies and feather stars.

echolocation
Locating objects such as prey in the surroundings, by emitting squeaks, clicks and similar pulses of sound that bounce off or reflect from the objects as echoes, and these are analyzed for the size and distance of the objects.

eurypterids
Medium to large extinct arthropods often called "sea scorpions," with large pincers for attacking prey, included with spiders and scorpions in the chelicerate group.

femur
Familiar name for the thighbone – the main bone in the upper rear limb of four-legged vertebrates.

fenestrae
"Windows," gaps or holes, usually in a plate or slab of a hard substance like bone.

fibula
Familiar name for the calf bone – one of usually two bones in the lower rear limb of four-legged vertebrates (see also **tibia**).

gastroliths
Pebbles or stones swallowed deliberately into the stomach or similar part of the gut of an animal, usually to help mash and grind up food there.

genus (plural, genera)
In the classification of living things, a group of closely related species; many dinosaurs such as *Tyrannosaurus* and *Triceratops* are referred to by their generic (or genus) names (see **species**).

graptolites
Colonial marine organisms, whose flattened fossil remains look like fret-saw blades, whose indentations housed tiny tentacled, filter-feeding zooids. Common in Early Palaeozoic times, their survivors are known as pterobranchs.

gymnophiones
See apodans.

hadrosaurs
Medium to large plant-eating dinosaurs commonly called "duckbills," with wide, beak-like mouths, and many with projections or crests of bone on the head.

hallux
First or innermost digit on the rear limb – often called the "big toe."

heterodontism
Possessing teeth of different shapes and sizes, such as incisors, canines and molars, which are specialized for

group which includes coral creatures, anemones and jellyfish (see **cnidarians**).

hypsilophodontids
Group of plant-eating, bipedal ornithopod dinosaurs based on *Hypsilophodon*, which were mainly small, slim and fast-moving, and and lived during Cretaceous times.

ichthyosaurs
"Fish reptiles," marine reptiles shaped like fish or dolphins, with four limbs modified like paddles, a dorsal (back) fin and a twin-fluked tail.

igneous rocks
Major group of rocks formed when other rocks melt under great heat and pressure, and then cool and harden – like solidified lava from volcanoes.

iguanodontids
Group of plant-eating ornithopod dinosaurs based on *Iguanodon*, which were mostly fairly large and powerful, with three-toed rear feet and thumb spikes, and lived from Mid Jurassic to Late Cretaceous times.

incisors
Teeth with straight, sharp edges like spades or chisels, usually at the front of the jaws, for nibbling, nipping and gnawing.

different purposes, rather than teeth which are all similar in shape and size.

hominids
Members of human-like primate mammals, otherwise known as the great apes, including the orangutan, gorilla, chimp, humans and their extinct relatives from *Proconsul* to *Homo*.

huayangosaurids
Early group of plant-eating stegosaurs or plated dinosaurs based on *Huyangosaurus*, which lived mainly during the Jurassic period.

humerus
The main bone in the upper front limb of four-legged vertebrates.

hydrozoans
Small aquatic animals resembling sea anemones within the larger cnidarian

index fossils
Remains of living things which were widespread, plentiful and readily fossilized, and which survived through relatively short time periods evolving in well-documented ways, so they can be used to compare and date rocks (see **relative dating**).

invertebrates
General name for animals without a backbone (vertebrae or spinal column) – ranging from unicells to sponges, molluscs and arthropods.

labyrinthodonts
An outmoded name for a grouping of extinct amphibian-like animals, mainly from the Devonian to Permian periods.

lambeosaurs
Group of duckbill dinosaurs based on *Lambeosaurus*, with hollow head crests (see **hadrosaurs**).

lepospondyls
Relatively early and diverse group of tetrapods or four-legged vertebrates including newt-shaped, eel-shaped and lizard-shaped animals, that lived mainly from Early Carboniferous to Late Permian times.

lissamphibians
Newer name for members of the group traditionally known as amphibians which survive today – frogs, toads, newts, salamanders and caecilians.

lobe-fins
Fish with fins that have a fleshy, muscular base (see **sarcopterygians**).

maniraptorans
"Grasping hands," large group of theropods (meat-eating dinosaurs) typified by a wrist that can swivel easily, including the dromaeosaurs or raptors.

marker fossils
See **index fossils**.

marsupials
Mammals in which the baby is born at a very early stage of development, and spends time growing in a pocket-like pouch or marsupium on the mother's front (compare **placentals**).

mesonychids
Group of hoofed mammals or ungulates from the early Tertiary period which became adapted as predators for hunting, but which had died out by about 30 million years ago.

mesosaurs
Group of water-dwelling reptiles, broadly resembling small crocodiles, that lived mainly during the Permian period.

metamorphic rocks
Major group of rocks formed when other rocks are changed by great heat and pressure, but do not melt in the process.

metatarsals
Bones between the ankles and toes which usually form the foot of an animal such as a reptile, bird or mammal.

mosasaurs
Group of extinct, large, predatory, sea-dwelling reptiles, probably related to today's monitor lizards, that lived during the Cretaceous period.

muscle scars
Roughened patches on bones, often preserved in fossils, where muscles were attached or anchored to them in life.

mutation
A change in a living thing's genetic make-up or genes, which may cause a visible effect in the living thing itself; mutations can be helpful or positive, harmful or negative, or neutral.

myriapods
Name usually applied to centipedes and millipedes (see **chilopods, diplopodans**).

nautiloids
Predatory marine molluscs of the cephalopod group, related to ammonoids, belemnoids, squid and octopus, with an external coiled shell, large eyes and many tentacles; only a few types survive.

nectrideans
Types of extinct lepospondyl amphibians shaped like newts or salamanders.

nematodes
Major group of worms that live almost everywhere and lack body sections or segments; often called roundworms.

neodiapsids
Major group of diapsid reptiles which originated in Late Permian times with lizard-like forms and subsequently gave rise to the lepidosaurs and archosaurs. (see **diapsids**).

nodosaurids
A subgroup of the ankylosaurs – armored or plated plant-eating dinosaurs – which did not possess large bony lumps at the tail tip (compare **ankylosaurids**).

nothosaurs
Early group of predatory swimming reptiles, that lived mainly during the Triassic period.

onychophorans
Worm-like animals with stubby tentacle-like legs, also called velvet-worms, with a sparse fossil record extending back to Cambrian times and are related to the arthropods.

opisthosoma
Middle section of the body of certain animals, such as the extinct eurypterids ("sea scorpions"), between the head end and the tail.

ornithischians
Meaning "bird-hips," one of the two major groups of dinosaurs, where the lower part of the hipbone called the pubis slanted down and backward; this group includes all plant-eating dinosaurs except the prosauropods and sauropods (compare **saurischians**).

ornithomimosaurs
Group of medium-sized, slim, fast-running theropod dinosaurs with two powerful rear legs and a bird-like beak.

ornithopods
Main group of "bird-foot" plant-eating dinosaurs including including the iguanodonts with *Iguanodon*, its relatives and the hadrosaurs (duckbills).

ornithosuchians
A group of reptiles that includes all archosaurs more closely related to birds than to crocodiles. Mostly walking on their two rear legs and with sharp teeth.

osteoderms
Plates, lumps or pieces of bone that develop within the skin, rather than as part of the main skeleton.

ostracoderms
An informal name for armoured jawless fish which lived between Ordovician and Devonian times.

oviraptorids
Group of theropods (meat-eating dinosaurs) based on *Oviraptor*, with a tall, parrot-like beak.

pachycephalosaurs
"Thick-headed reptiles," a group of plant-eating dinosaurs with exceptionally thickened bone in the top or roof of the skull, variously called "boneheads" or "helmetheads."

paleomagnetism
Magnetism "trapped" in ancient rocks as they formed under the influence of the Earth's natural magnetic field; also the study of these features.

paleontology
Scientific study of fossils and the once-living organisms.

parareptiles
Large grouping of anapsid reptiles, including some of the early land reptiles such as pareiasaurs, also mesosaurs, turtles and tortoises.

pareiasaurs
Group of early, large, squat, plant-eating reptiles mainly from the Permian period (see **parareptiles**).

parietal
One of the paired bones that form the upper rear of the cranium (braincase) or the main skull.

patagia
The thin, lightweight, elastic, sheet-like membrane that forms the main flight surface of a bat's wing.

pectoral fins
Pair of fins usually on the lower side of a fish toward the front of the body, which may have evolved into the front limbs of four-legged animals (compare **pelvic fins**).

pedipalps
Pair of limb-like parts to each side of the head, especially in arachnids – they are modified as leg-like feelers in spiders and large nipping claws in scorpions.

pelvic fins
Pair of fins usually on the lower side of a fish toward the rear of the body, which may have evolved into the rear limbs of four-legged animals (compare **pectoral fins**).

pelycosaurs
Group of large, sprawling-limbed synapsid tetrapods, mainly from Late Carboniferous and Permian times, which were previously called "mammal-like reptiles" and include the well-known "sail-back" *Dimetrodon*.

periods
Spans of time in the entire history of the Earth, which are subdivisions of eras, and which are themselves divided into epochs; most periods cover tens of millions of years.

phorusrhacids
An extinct group of large, powerful and flightless birds of the second half of the Tertiary period, mainly in South America.

phragmocone
Front part of the shell of a belemnoid, an extinct type of mollusc that had the shell embedded within the body (like the squid today).

placentals
Mammals in which the baby is born at a relatively advanced stage of development, having been supplied with nourishment from the mother in her womb via a body part called the placenta (compare **marsupials**).

placoderms
Early group of fish with jaws, true paired fins, and protective bony plates over the head

and front of the body; they originated in the Late Silurian period but went extinct after the Devonian.

placodonts
Early group of water-dwelling reptiles with flattened teeth for crushing hard food, probably shellfish; they lived mainly during the Triassic period.

platyhelminthes
Major group of simple, leaf-shaped worms also called flatworms.

plesiosaurs
Major group of swimming reptiles with tubby bodies, short tails and four legs modified as paddles, that lived through much of the Age of Dinosaurs (see also **pliosaurs**).

pleural lobes
The two side parts of the body of a trilobite, flanking the central part or axis.

pleurocoels
Scoop-shaped hollows or cavities, usually to save weight, such as in the vertebral bones of certain dinosaurs.

pliosaurs
Plesiosaur reptiles with

large heads and short necks (see **plesiosaurs**).

polyplacophorans
Types of molluscs also called chitons or coat-of-mail shells.

poriferans
Group of creatures with the simplest body structure of any animal, lacking nerves, a brain, heart, digestive tract or muscles – often known as sponges.

predators
Animals that hunt and consume other creatures, their prey.

premaxillary
Bone at the front of the upper jaw, found only in certain dinosaurs.

premolars
Broad teeth for chewing and crushing, sited just in front of true molars.

preparator
Person who prepares scientific specimens, for example, extracting and cleaning fossils from their surrounding rock.

primates
Major group of mammals that includes lemurs, bushbabies, monkeys, apes and humans.

proboscideans
Major group of mammals that includes elephants and their many extinct relatives such as mammoths and deinotheres.

prosauropods
A name previously used for a group of medium-to-large plant-eating dinosaurs of the Triassic age, typically with a small head, long neck, bulky body, pillar-like legs and long tail.

prosoma
Front body part of chelicerate animals such as eurypterids and spiders, bearing the eyes, mouthparts and walking limbs.

protoceratopsids
Early group of horned dinosaurs (certopsians) based on *Protoceratops*, where the face horns and neck frills were relatively small.

pterosaurs
Major group of flying vertebrates from the Age of Dinosaurs which is generally considered to have arisen from within the archosaur reptiles and probably the ornithodirans. They were probably warm-blooded and furry.

pygidium
The tail section of a trilobite or similar creature.

pygostyle
The lumpy mass at the tail end of the spinal column of a bird; colloquially called the "parson's nose."

quadrupedal
Walking or running on four legs.

raptors
Variously meaning "thieves," "plunderers" or "hunters," a term that refers to various predatory creatures, such as birds of prey, like eagles and hawks, and among the dinosaurs, the dromaeosaurs such as *Deinonychus* and *Velociraptor*.

rauisuchians
Reptiles resembling crocodiles and closely related to them, which lived mainly during the Triassic period.

ray-fins
See **actinopterygians**.

recombination
In sexual reproduction, when hereditary material or genes come together in various combinations, producing differences among the offspring.

relative dating
Determining the time of formation of certain rock strata compared with older or younger strata usually from their fossil content (compare **absolute dating**).

reptiles
General name for tetrapod animals with scaly skin that lay tough-shelled eggs; in the study of fossils and newer systems of classification, reptiles are defined by particular openings in the skull known as suborbital fenestrae, and the reptile group is sometimes taken to include birds too.

rhipidistians
"Fan-sails," a group of lobe-fin fishes related to coelacanths that were successful in the Devonian period and probably included the ancestors of land-dwelling tetrapods and the lungfish.

rhynchocephalia
A group of mainly Triassic plant-eating reptiles, mostly the size of today's pigs, fairly closely related to the archosaurs or ruling reptiles, that included the rhynchosaurs and leaves one surviving genus, the tuataras of New Zealand.

rostrum
A projecting part from the front of the head, like a beak or nose, in certain animals such as prawns, weevils and some kinds of fish.

sacral vertebrae
Backbones or vertebrae from the hip or pelvic region of the spinal column, usually joined to or forming part of the pelvis or hipbone.

sacrum
Single bony structure formed from several fused sacral vertebrae.

salientians
Name for the frog and toad group – see **anurans**.

sarcopterygians
The group name for lobe-fin or fleshy-fin fish, which are fish with bony skeletons whose fins have fleshy, muscular bases, including lungfish and coelacanths; they form a minority of fish alive today (compare **actinopterygians**).

saurischians
Meaning "lizard- or reptile-hips," one of the two major groups of dinosaurs, where the lower part of the hipbone called the pubis slanted down and forward; this group includes all meat-eating dinosaurs or theropods, and the plant-eating prosauropods and sauropods (compare **ornithischians**).

sauropods
Group of large to extremely large plant-eating, saurischian dinosaurs with a small head, long neck, bulky body, pillar-like legs and long tail, most successful during the Late Jurassic and Cretaceous periods.

scaphopods
Group of molluscs or "shellfish" where the single shell is shaped like a long cone or elephant's tusk, also called tusk-shells.

scapula
A usually broad bone of the shoulder or pectoral region commonly called the shoulder blade.

scutes
Bony plates or bone-reinforced scales in the skin, especially of dinosaurs, crocodiles and similar reptiles, often covered with horn.

sedimentary rocks
Major group of rocks formed when tiny particles of sand, mud or other sediments settle as layers and are compacted and cemented; they are generally the only rocks to contain fossils.

septa
Flaps or cross-walls that divide an animal's shell or other bodily structure into segments.

siphon
In molluscs, a usually cone-shaped funnel in the side of the body, through which water is squirted at high pressure to thrust the animal along by "jet propulsion."

sonar
Sound-based system that works in a similar way to radar, for locating and navigating (see **echolocation**).

species
Group of living things that can breed together to continue their kind, but which cannot breed with members of other species; a group of closely related species forms a genus.

squamates
Group name for the reptiles commonly known as lizards and snakes.

squamosal
Bone forming the lower rear side of the skull, and which in mammals bears the jaw joint with the lower jaw or mandible.

stegosaurids
Later group of plant-eating stegosaurs or plated dinosaurs based on *Stegosaurus*, which lived from the Jurassic to Cretaceous periods.

stegosaurs
Major group of plant-eating dinosaurs, which includes the stegosaurids and other related forms such as *Huayangosaurus*.

sternum
Bone at the front of the thorax (chest), joined to the front ends of the ribs on either side – also called the breastbone.

telson
Tail part of aquatic animals, such as lobsters, prawns and eurypterids, often shaped like a flap or fan.

temnospondyls
Subgroup of the labyrinthodont group of early amphibian-type animals, which appeared in the Early Carboniferous and died out by the Early Jurassic period.

tergites
One of the sections or segments of the rear body part, in animals such as eurypterids and certain insects.

tetanurans
"Stiff-tails," one of the main groups of theropod or meat-eating dinosaurs, that includes the megalosaurs and allosaurs.

tetrapods
Vertebrate animals with four limbs which evolved from the lobe-finned fish in Mid Devonian times and gave rise to all living four-limbed animals. The earliest tetrapods were fully aquatic and only later became adapted for life on land.

thecae
Body part shaped like a cup or socket, for example, the cup-shaped shells of the extinct creatures called graptolites.

thecodonts
"Socket-tooth" reptiles, an old name for a diverse group of archosaurs which evolved in late Permian times.

therapsids
Subgroup of the synapsids, which includes the mammals and their ancestors and evolved during the Permian period, and which included dinocephalians, gorgonopsians, dicynodonts and cynodonts.

therizinosaurs
Major group of theropod dinosaurs with a beak-like mouth, perhaps fiber-like feathers, and huge claws on the forelimbs, that lived mainly in the Cretaceous period.

theropods
Major group of dinosaurs that includes all meat-eating or carnivorous types, from tiny *Compsognathus* to huge *Giganotosaurus*.

thescelosaurids
Group of medium-sized ornithopod dinosaurs based on *Thescelosaurus*, which are related to *Iguanodon* and *Hypsilophodon*.

thoracic vertebrae
Backbones or vertebrae in the chest region of the spinal column, often bearing the rib bones.

thorax
The chest region of animals, such as reptiles, birds and mammals, containing the lungs and heart.

thyreophorans
"Shield-bearers," major group of plant-eating dinosaurs that includes stegosaurs and ankylosaurs.

tibia
Familiar name for the shinbone – one of usually two bones in the lower rear limb of four-legged vertebrates (see also **fibula**).

titanosaurs
Subgroup of sauropod dinosaurs that flourished in the Cretaceous period, including *Saltasaurus* and *Argentinosaurus*.

trace fossils
Preserved signs and traces left by animals, such as fossilized footprints, eggshells and droppings, rather than actual body parts.

trackways
Rows or tracks of footprints.

trilobites
Huge group of arthropods, with a body divided lengthwise into three parts, that lived from the Cambrian to Permian periods.

ungulates
Hoofed mammals, where the digits or toes are capped by hooves rather than ending in nails or claws; the group includes horses, rhinos, deer, antelopes, cattle and many others, both living and extinct.

urodelans
Tailed amphibians or lissamphibians, commonly known as salamanders and newts.

ursids
Members of the bear family of mammals.

vertebrae
The separate bones making up the "backbone" or spinal column of a vertebrate animal.

vertebrates
Animals with vertebrae or backbones – conveniently described as fish, amphibians, reptiles, birds and mammals.

vibrissae
Long, thick, stiff hairs on the snout, used for feeling the way – usually called whiskers.

weigeltisaurs
Group of outwardly lizard-like reptiles (types of diapsids) with extendible skin flaps for gliding, that lived mainly during the Permian period.

INDEX

PICTURE CREDITS

Alamy Images
27, 37, 40, 46, 57, 68, 89, 91, 92, 100, 140, 145, 148, 149, 152, 153, 160, 164, 166–167, 170, 182, 195, 213, 218, 224, 227, 228, 230, 232–233, 238, 239, 241, 242, 263, 269, 284, 285, 302 313, 320.

Ardea.com
9, 52–53, 72–73, 134–135, 186–187, 204–205, 214–215, 244–245, 249, 249.

Richard Burgess
12 and Factfile maps throughout.

Karen Carr
87, 101, 107

Dreamstime.com
2, 8, 11 (tl), 11 (tc), 16, 28, 85 (b), 121, 124–125, 158, 162, 256, 280, 304, 311, 319.

Pamela J.W. Gore
Georgia Perimeter College
26 (t)

iStockphoto.com
10 (tl), 10 (br), 119, 259.

Marshall Cavendish Archive,
136, 206, 208.

Marshall Editions
Steve Kirk 24, 25, 26, 30, 31, 35, 41, 42, 43, 45, 62, 63, 65, 66, 69, 76, 77, 78, 81, 86, 106, 112, 131, 139, 141, 150, 151, 156, 165, 173, 175, 177, 184, 194, 196, 197, 198, 200, 201, 203, 220, 221, 226, 252, 253, 257, 261, 272, 273, 274, 277, 278; *Malcolm Ellis* 295; *Andrew Wheatcroft* 296; *Graham Allen* 297, 298, 299, 300, 303, 308; *Steve Holden* 305; *Andrew Robinson* 307.

Oxford Scientific Films Ltd
82, 93, 94, 98, 110, 130, 155, 180, 219, 223, 229.

Royal Tyrrell Museum
202, 256 (l).

Science Photo Library
16 (bc), 18, 20–21, 22, 38, 39 (tl), 39 (tr), 50, 51, 54, 74, 79, 88, 97, 102–103, 104, 126, 128, 138, 168, 188, 212, 234, 246, 264–265, 266, 283, 287, 288–89, 290, 293, 294, 309.

Shutterstock.com
80, 83, 115, 117, 120, 143, 147, 159, 236, 237, 240, 248, 258.

John Sibbick
6–7, 34, 47, 48, 129, 163, 172, 216, 225, 271, 275

Joe Tucciarone
95, 118, 185, 199, 246, 251

Wildlife Art Ltd
Ken Oliver 157; *Philip Hood* 61, 176; *Myke Taylor* 243; *Wayne Ford* 99.

Wikimedia Commons
60, 132, 154.

ACKNOWLEDGMENTS

Steve Parker would like to acknowledge Jane Parker for research assistance, Dr Paul Barrett of the Natural History Museum in London for valuable additions to and comments on the text, Peter Coates for freshwater reptile information and John Rush for "bringing dinosaurs to life."

The publishers thank Dr Thomas Holtz, Paleontologist and Director of the Earth, Time & Life Program at the University of Maryland, College Park, for his assistance; Sarah Whittley of Wildlife Art Ltd for organizing the production of many wonderful illustrations for this book; and Richard Burgess for all maps.

Further updated information was supplied by Douglas Palmer.